Sarajevo Essays

Sarajevo Essays

Politics, Ideology, and Tradition

Rusmir Mahmutćehajić

State University of New York Press

Published by
State University of New York Press, Albany

For information, address State University of New York Press,
90 State Street, Suite 700, Albany, NY 12207

Production by Judith Block
Marketing by Anne Valentine

Library of Congress Control Number

Mahmutcehajic, Rusmir, 1948–
    [Sarajevski eseji. English]
    Sarajevo essays : politics, ideology, and tradition / by Rusmir Mahmutcehajic.
        p. cm.
    Includes index.
    ISBN 0-7914-5637-4 (alk. paper)—ISBN 0-7914-5638-2 (pbk. : alk. paper)
        1. Yugoslav War, 1991–1995—Bosnia and Hercegovina.   2. Bosnia and Hercegovina—
    Ethnic relations.   3. Bosnia and Hercegovina—Politics and government—1992–
    I. Title.

DR1673 .M334613   2003
949.703—dc21   2002066782

10 9 8 7 6 5 4 3 2 1

*In memory of the elderly ladies from my town who have died in exile
and of the roofs that are no longer there*

Contents

Preface

Sarajevo's experience at the turn of the millennium is what unites the essays in this book. Whether their contents are presented in Vienna, Korčula, Cracow, Budapest, Warsaw, London, Verona, or Sarajevo, the same question always arises: the question of human relationships, of the contrast between confidence and the unknown variable of trust—that is, between the mediating effect of shared belief and the dark dimension of liberty, where shared belief is absent.

Bosnia is not simply a unique phenomenon in the totality of European experience: it also encapsulates the dilemma of the modern heritage of tradition, and its solution. In Bosnia, tradition comes face-to-face with liberalism and secularism, which offer themselves as answers to all future questions. Torn between the two discourses of liberalism and of tradition, Bosnia has become a tragic symbol of the defeat and collapse of Communist ideology, and the triumph of liberalism. However, it did not acquire this status merely by becoming an arena for dialogue about the adjudged relationship between these two sides, two offshoots from the same source. For war was waged against Bosnia. All the tragic and painful experiences Europe has known came together in Bosnia: killings and expulsions, humiliation and destruction, ignorance and deception. The country is covered with the graves of the dead. Of those who survived, most have known bitter experiences, were driven from their homes or incarcerated in concentration camps. And this took place before the eyes of a world that prided itself on having attained the age of democracy and science, of technology and education. In the face of these killings, words and deeds alike were characterized by ignorance and pathos: they could give no answers, even after the first phase of the war was over, and war by other means had begun.

The participants in, and witnesses to the drama are still trapped in the arena of their own experience, which they will pass on to future generations. Tied to the past and, willy-nilly, part of the future, they have no sense of whether the path of history is leading them towards a better or a worse human condition. But they have a choice: to turn away from this ignorance, or to keep following it. Their fear contains, as always, the potential to escape from their present condition or to be engulfed by it. But whatever choice they make, the direction in which they travel will bring either mild passivity or passionate involvement. Their knowledge will never lose its double potential: to differentiate what consciousness reveals, or to unify what it reveals with the inescapable pattern of human existence.

An optimistic view of the world's future may see Bosnia as an exception to the rule. This will allow the majority to forget how they were convinced, by the endless bulletins on their television screens, that Bosnia really did mean something for the development of the world. If such a view prevails, the Bosnian experience will become the province of specialists, of specialists who are cut off from the main flow of discourse and who become ever further removed from real trends as new generations arise. Their books will reside in the ever-growing storehouse of written experience—but the volume of this accumulated knowledge will be so huge as to discourage its potential readers. The Bosnian experience, however, demands a twofold approach: an act of distancing plus an act of commitment; a withdrawal to take stock combined with a respectful advance; a process of careful discrimination combined with a focused summation.

The Bosnian experience may also be seen as the confirmation of a different, less optimistic view of human destiny. In this view, time is running out, no matter how tall and overweening the buildings that are being erected in our city. The hour is at hand, though the majority are not aware of its coming. The world order is about to be turned upside down. While humanity is surrounded by increasing luxury, human life is decreasing in value: campaigns of mass persecution and slaughter are portrayed as courageous, decisive, and even respectable. Meanwhile, the victims are to be protected only if no risk is involved: concern for the lives of the victims' potential defenders actively perpetuates the killing and persecution. Given the fear of death that renders powerless even the wealthy and powerful, any group of thugs, as long as they are willing to run a few risks as they slaughter and expel, are able to do what they will.

This book adds to the corpus of investigations into these issues. Its pages and essays unify the writer's experiences with his continuing efforts to find, at the profoundest levels of individuality and totality, the reasons for the human bent towards evil. The search continues for ways of probing, from within, the dual nature of human potential in order to gain an insight at last into ways of bringing peace to ourselves, or laying the self to rest. Many experts, present and past, have been consulted in the course of this unending quest. But the answer is not to be found, or is intelligible only to the few, while the majority remain in ignorance or unconvinced.

The impact of the Bosnian experience has spawned a wide-ranging body of research into different social structures, structures where fragility appears as an increasing threat to constructs which, together with new social systems and institutions, might otherwise lead us towards a better future. In the essays collected in this book, the investigation has been carried forward into the contrast between liberalism and tradition, ideology and tolerance, ignorance and evil, war and peace, cohesion and disintegration, politics and the world order, collectivism and individualism, atheism, and religion. For all these issues can be encountered in the tragic experience of Bosnia, and in the underlying potential of human nature.

The English version of the book has been translated from the Bosnian original, *Sarajevski Eseji*, published by Durieux (Zagreb, Croatia) in 2000. The author and translator express their acknowledgment to Ms. Milena Marić, Ms. Marina Bowder, Mr. Francis R. Jones, Ms. Colleen London, Ms. Indiana Harper, Ms. Merima Osmankadić, and Ms. Jasmina Husanović, who all contributed significantly to first-draft translations of some chapters.

The poetry of Mak Dizdar that appeared in the Bosnian edition and now in the English translation is from Dizdar's *Kameni spavač/Stone Sleeper*, Sarajevo: DID Publishing Company, 1999.

1

The Question

Ye who are pure shall be scourged all the more and shall by the sword be slain
And loud will they laud the hour of thy flight away into silence and pain
So take up thy buckler and shield and smite with thy
sword that harrying horde
Let death slay death that the one true life might stand
For the time is at hand

Mak Dizdar, *Stone Sleeper*

Introduction: Two Histories

To ask: *Where are we going?* implies two further questions: *Where are we now?*, and *Where have we come from?* The changes taking place in the new millennium coincide with a clearer notion of the potential for an open world. The temporal and spatial boundaries of the world do not exhaust its potential; and the view that the material world is not the only one is the first step to opening up to the multiplicity of levels of being. An open world is both the consequence and the prerequisite for the open human self. As such, the openness of the self and the world to Unicity make it possible for different languages, meanings and symbols to speak of Reality in another manner. Most of the languages of today's world, however, encounter impediments and ignorance at their point of demarcation from others; and these obstacles and ignorance are readily transformed into hatred and eruptions of violence. The entire experience of Bosnia is inseparable from world trends; but it proffers itself in different languages, which shed light on the clash between the human interpretation of Reality and Reality itself. Holistic insights into this are a prerequisite for identifying a clearer response, a response that is closer to reality, on the possible outcomes of this era and of the human condition of the times. The question is then whether these responses on the self, society and the

1

world can offer a different and more encouraging understanding and acceptance of will, knowledge and love in human destiny.

With his self, man defines two things—his being, which includes his desires, and the world, which includes all its forms. In this notion of self, his "now" separates the past and the future, both for himself and for his world. And there are two essentially different outlooks on this duality: in the one, the individual sees future as worse than the past, and in the other, the future as better than the past.

The adoption of the first approach (the future as a time in which suffering will increase and overwhelm us) leads one to become a more concerned and responsible citizen. In this conceptualization of man's movement through time, however, an increasing distancing from principles indicates the darkening and weakening of fundamental human nature. That fundamental nature is perfection; and just as there exist ways of protecting it, so there also exist the means of destroying it. Here, development represents a distancing from that principled center which sees the Holy Scriptures as transcendental over the world of matter, and sees the world as its image. Losing the awareness of that principled dimension of the world's humanity, we as humans enter an ever deepening alienation which René Guénon refers to as the "crisis of the modern world."[1]

This first approach is extremely rare in contemporary society. Indeed, it is distrusted by those who take the second, more current view, that is, of the future as a state in which there will be an accumulation of goodwill and harmony, and in which evil and conflict will disappear. The latter, historical-progress view is a credo in Hegelian and Marxian societies, which are based upon two ideologies: according to one, society is moving toward "the end of history," a time during which liberal democracy will resolve social tensions; in the other, the state will be imbued with the freedom and harmony that flow from a classless society.

The second approach, which foresees a better future, views death and destruction as decreasing in likelihood. Suffering and destruction are features of the past, of a state of underdevelopment. This produces, inevitably, a naiveté towards such matters as Auschwitz, the Gulags, Bosnia, and Kosovo. For those who take this approach, these are aberrations which run counter to laws of history. In the first approach, by contrast, humankind's experience of death and destruction is a consequence of turning away from, and forgetting about, the fundamental human principle spoken of above. The world view here is that all that can be expected in the future is ever-increasing danger.

From these two concepts of humankind and the world, two attitudes arise. The first is a pessimistic wisdom and the second is an optimistic naiveté. In the first, future events are evaluated on the basis of the worst possible scenario, and this can contribute to a change in consciousness and an effort to prevent bloodshed and destruction. The second produces happiness and a variety of ways of finding enjoyment, but at the same time predisposes towards an unwillingness to sacrifice anything for the sake of a better future.

Both approaches to humankind's position in time are attempts to deal with the question of development. Development may be examined in relation to any human "now." Where that "now" is placed—past, present, or imagined future—is irrelevant. What is important is the distancing which change brings us from that "now." If "now" is the original starting point, movement away from "now" may bring decrease or increase of whatever quantity or quality was present in that initial state.

Yet, as human societies become ever more complex, their inevitable fragility carries the danger of increasing bloodshed and destruction. Today's world consists of approximately two hundred states, of which the homogeneous are in the minority. Surprisingly, in less than 5 percent—approximately ten—of these states there exists a single ethnic group constituting at least 75 percent of the population. Moreover, the interrelatedness and interdependence of countries is becoming ever greater. The question of the self-sufficiency of sovereign states has long since lost any sense of meaning: the totality of the world market demands a unified approach, which gives rise to agreements and laws.

Economic laws in this interdependent world impose a principle of dominance, which is seen in terms of occupying the highest place in terms of economic power. This demands the expansion of governance, which in turn perpetuates the supremacy of the leader states. From this there follows not only an accumulation of state power, but also a growing exhaustion of resources. Then the most powerful turn increasingly to the least wealthy, among whom the exhaustion of resources is less extensive. Development leads, therefore, to the inevitable interrelationship of those who are most distant from their starting point with those who are closest to it.

The former find it most appropriate to conceptualize the world in categories such as liberalism, democracy, economic development, free market, human rights, rule of law, and so forth. The latter tend to conceptualize the world according to categories of tradition, in which development means distancing oneself from the notion of principled perfection, forgetting fundamental human values, feeling inadequate regarding one's search for and route towards wisdom and perfection. Yet such a concept of existence, when acknowledged rather than dismissed, establishes a clear relation between the transcendental and the mundane worlds. Such a society has established a doctrine, interpretation, and order which together are designed to resolve the conflict between this and the other world. The impossibility of perfection of the mundane, in such a picture, finds its resolution in the release made possible by transcending this world. Conversely, a "developed" nation's social structure produces disillusionment and alienation among its members. Although at the pinnacle of historical development, such a state does not permit the sense of human fulfillment, which is experienced as responsibility towards oneself and the world, as the achievement of human desire.

Yet, to many members of the "underdeveloped" nations, in which tradition is an integral part of life, the greatest possible development (identified as social well-being and freedom) has become not only the very model to strive for, but also an ideal which is blamed for all forms of "underdevelopment" and the impossibility of eliminating them. Thus, the very development of the modern world becomes a measure of the deprivation of the "undeveloped." Available identities are used to attribute the image of a hostile ideology to the developed state, an ideology which can be understood and overcome only by turning away from it and fighting against it.[2]

Power which reinforces the stereotypes of the world cannot go beyond mere utility. However, greater power leads to considerably greater needs. The discrepancy between human desires and what the world can offer is ever widening. The understanding of the causes and aims of humanity's presence in the world diminishes even as the measure of their power increases. This leads inevitably towards an increase in the distance between "developed" and "undeveloped," and thus, an ever starker confrontation between liberalism and traditionalism, with liberalism on the side of the developed and their power, and traditionalism on the side of the undeveloped and their supposed impotence. However, the borders between states are becoming ever more permeable in accordance with the demands of the flow of people and goods. This imposes a mutual dependence, thus enabling an ever-greater presence of a tradition-based world view.

At the same time, an upsurge in democracy in certain states may produce a weakening both of those institutions of government which make governance possible and of the traditional connections between members of that society. Then traditional intelligence withdraws in the face of modern science, and tradition becomes increasingly a matter of morality and sentimentality— ingredients that cannot compete with the laws of globalization based on economic growth. Left without an organic link between quantity and quality, between means and ends, such states are left vulnerable to ideologies obsessed with autarchy.

The Attempt and Failure of Bosnia

It is difficult to find any text on contemporary world issues published in the last decade of the second Christian millennium that does not discuss the subject of Bosnia.[3] Unfortunately, this is not a consequence of any special interest in the nature of this country and its history, although there has long existed ample justification for this. The interest derives instead from a war in which the world was a witness as this country was laid waste, thereby turning international curiosity into a ritual of shame. And despite an abundance of books about that war, which have been read and interpreted in accordance with various sentimentalist and ideological approaches, both the country and the war that destroyed it remain, for the most part, misunderstood.

Bosnia has long been home to a number of paths and rituals related to Christianity—the Bosnian Church, Catholicism, Eastern Orthodoxy, Islam, and Judaism. It is the only European country that has been based throughout its existence upon a unity of religious diversity—a diversity that was vital for the peace and stability of the world of the past. There is no reason to assume that this new millennium will be any different in its requirements. Such a striving, and the challenges it presents, can be illustrated by some paradigmatic excerpts from its history.

Threats to this diversity have often come from outside her borders. In the year 1203, in the presence of its head of state Ban Kulin, and before the Papal *capellani* and the Papal Ambassador Johannis de Casamaris, Bosnia's religious leaders were forced to deny the content of their Christian faith and ritual because it was not in accordance with the regulations of the Roman Catholic Church. In this process, they were required to change their policy toward the Other, as indicated in the oath given in the document of abjuration: ". . . and further no-one who is known for certain to be Manichean or any other heretic shall be received to live amongst us."[4] This abjuration was forced by external, non-Bosnian authorities, and what was foresworn was the authentic will and way of life of the Bosnian people.

Threats, however, have been balanced by affirmations of Bosnia's unity in diversity. The unity of these different sacred teachings and ways represents the principle of its continuity. Towards the end of the Bosnian kingdom, when the country was riven with discord, in the year 1463, a meeting took place between the friar Anđeo Zvizdović, the custodian of the community of Bosnian Franciscan monks, and Sultan Mehmed el-Fatih, the head of the

Ottoman Empire, which around that time had spread to include parts of Bosnia. This meeting produced a "Letter of Covenant" in which these two leaders recognized one another on the basis of the sacred principles of their paths towards God. This included the statement:

> Let no man hinder or obstruct either the above-mentioned (i.e., Christians) or their churches. Let them live in our dominion. And for those who have fled, let them be free and secure; let them return and live without fear within their monasteries in the lands of our dominion.[5]

In nearly all of Bosnia's towns, over most of the past centuries, there have lived Christians (both Catholic and Orthodox), Muslims, and Jews. The typical panorama of a Bosnian town is defined by its churches, mosques, and synagogues. This has survived in spite of numerous external attempts to destroy it. In the midst of the anti-Fascist struggle in 1943, the Bosnian people replied to the bloodshed and destruction with a renewed avowal of their country. They stressed their wish that their "country, which is neither Serbian, nor Croatian, nor Muslim, but rather inclusively Serbian, Croatian, and Muslim, should be a Bosnia and Herzegovina, which is a free land united in brotherhood, in which there shall be ensured full equality and impartiality for all its citizens, whether Serb, Muslim, or Croat."[6]

These examples from Bosnian history indicate a general desire by the Bosnian people to protect their right to different sacred paths. Though such overt declarations (like changes in the country's legal status) have been associated with the presence of external forces, the essential feature is one of religious diversity. The various religious communities included in a vast empire or gathered together in a single country were connected by a single language and an awareness of their genealogical interrelatedness; but sacred tradition, not citizenship, was the concept which informed these basic rules of faith, trust, confidence, and tolerance. People followed the instructions of tradition to live responsibly and independently but in a country shared by all, in communities conscious of their individuality but nonetheless open towards others, with tolerance and respect toward one another but with a firm sense of their own values.

Moreover, the question of establishing and strengthening political freedom or social cohesion in this country could not be separated from its physical survival. Because Bosnia was, on the whole, a pluralist society, its freedom was equally an expression of confidence within and between its communities. Confidence and trust were a precondition for, as well as a measure of, freedom and the possibility of public good in its civil, political, and social manifestations:

Without confidence, all contracts, promises, and obligations—whether economic, social, or political, public or private—can only be maintained by third-party enforcers. (. . .) Without confidence, the ability to articulate and maintain the very idea of a Public Good (let alone one defined in terms of the interconnection of political liberty and social cohesion) becomes highly suspect.[7]

The recent war against Bosnia was directed to a preordained plan whereby the actions of its neighbors and their allies, plus certain internal elements, were bent on destroying this unity in diversity. It was finally halted through a peace accord imposed by the United States of America and their allies. Included in this negotiation process were the major instigators of the war—above all, Serbia and Croatia—and the peace agreement accepted the partition created by the war. Thus, the country was brought to a crossroads from which one could proceed either towards total disintegration, or towards the reunification of the country—either outcome being equally probable.

The free market, privatization, and the introduction of capitalism were inevitable in either outcome. Communist Bosnia had been destroyed by the war, and needed to be transformed into a democratic and capitalist country. However, there were many reasons to suppose that the free market alone, especially if installed by aggressive Western investors, looking to gain a quick profit, would be offering only crumbs of genuine assistance for the civil institutions and democracy it and they claimed to support.

The question of a civil society is crucial to the renewal and survival of Bosnia, as a means of addressing the mutually conflicting ethno-national programs which insist upon a symbiosis of liberal and traditional arguments for carving boundaries between the various ethnic and religious groupings. Nevertheless, under current conditions, the external enforcers of Bosnia's upkeep cannot achieve their goal of reestablishing confidence if this symbiosis fails to differentiate between the *two* fundamental factors for the establishing and strengthening of confidence—not only the need to build an internally consistent civil society, but also tradition. These two goals are interlinked: any long-term attempt to establish a social order and sustained interaction is possible only on the basis of the development of stable relations of trust among members of that society. It is not simply a matter of predicting and explaining the behavior of participants in a social unity: this, for the most part, can be allowed for within the concept of rules, thus, enabling one to have confidence in normative patterns. Trust is rather the need to allow for the possibilities of behavior on the part of the Other which cannot be fully described or presented.[8] Unfortunately, this essential awareness of the freedom of the Other is equally likely to be expressed in violence and ignorance.

The Manifold Expressions of Truth

Throughout the history of Bosnia, there have thus been two opposite social tendencies. In the one, religious differences are resolved in a shared living space on the basis of confidence in a framework of various sacred paths. In the other, those differences are in conflict with one another.

In earlier centuries, these two fundamental tendencies were connected with the varying religious affiliations of the people of Bosnia. The differences were justified on the basis of individual sacred traditions: indeed, the sense of the sacredness of the Others and their right to be different, which permeated Bosnian society, was the very source of its members' definition of Us. Of course, there existed a clearly defined distinction between religious communities. Each holy doctrine and sacred path, whether Catholic, Orthodox, Muslim, or Jewish, was exclusive to its members. But the very fact that the adoption of one holy doctrine and its sacred path was exclusive to the individual who chose it, that one could not choose two holy doctrines and two paths, meant that human salvation could not be seen as secured for Us but denied to the Other. Since salvation, which is interpreted by all holy doctrines and towards which all sacred paths are directed, is possible only in the Absolute, then likewise every exclusiveness is ultimately a general inclusiveness: thus, there was no denial of the right of the Other to belong to a different doctrine and follow a different path with an equal potential for salvation. There was a parallel here with the general concept of "wrong:"[9] The violation of trust and responsibility towards the Other would represent a sin, a violation of God's instructions that were carried by the spirit in every being and every phenomenon.

In other words, the rightness and completeness of tradition (*din, traditio, religio*) includes particularity of language, symbols, and meanings; yet salvation lies behind it. What lies behind is the Divine unity, of which all the diverse languages, symbols, and meanings speak. Thus, all the diverse forms of that one and only tradition that always lies behind its individual and different forms in space and time make possible its "translation," or transmission. Furthermore, this means the need to hear the Others, regardless of what constitutes their otherness. The word of "tradition" is, therefore, that very fullness of diversity and multiplicity which reveals from hour to hour and everywhere the same, unalterable truth.

This gives us our image of the interwovenness of the various sacred traditions throughout the entire Bosnian territory.[10] Historically speaking, there have been no ethnically or religiously homogeneous parts of Bosnia. Almost all children in this country grew up in an environment containing the call to prayer from the minarets and the ringing of church bells from the steeples. One had to learn to establish one's own identity within a clear multiplicity of sacred ceremonies, and the demand for recognition of these different features presupposed a recognition and respect of the Other. Thus, the Bosnian We is based on the logic of "both *A* and *B*" rather than "either *A* or *B*"—that is, We, as a unit of society, history, and territory, cannot survive unless we first reject the exclusive right of any individual over that entirety. This is the first step towards confirming that the whole society belongs to each individual part of its unity of diversity.

This is not a radical notion. The survival of such a paradigm can be observed throughout the territory of Bosnia over its thousand year history. At the same time, it can be observed that the causes of bloodshed and destruction have been a consequence of either failure to understand this, or its deliberate betrayal. In peripheral areas of this territory, there are places where this paradigm has been demolished. A historical perspective confirms that such changes in this fundamental state are the consequence of external designs on Bosnia and projects undertaken in connection with them.[11] Generally speaking, Bosnian society throughout its history can be seen as an undertaking to establish, in various ways, forms of action through which tensions between the transcendental and mundane orders may be resolved. Jointly and individually, these actions have influenced the development of structures and institutions. This historical effort is described by Shmuel N. Eisenstadt:

> Organizationally the crucial aspect is, of course, the existence of some type of organized church which attempts to monopolize at least the religious sphere and usually also the relations of this sphere to the political powers. But of no lesser importance is the doctrinal aspect—the organization of doctrine, that is, the very stress of the structuring of clear, cognitive, and symbolic boundaries of doctrine.[12]

Inasmuch as Bosnia's entire history is connected with the discussion of Christology and its many interpretations, it is possible not only to speak of the organizational features of each religious community, but also of a doctrinal accord regarding the sacredness of the individual, regardless of his choice of holy doctrine and sacred path. The acceptance of every human individual as a fundamental part of the totality of humanity crosses organizational and doctrinal boundaries: "Whosoever gives life to a soul, shall be as if he had given life to mankind altogether."[13] This truth, which is fundamental to every social order, is also expressed in the words of Emile Durkheim:

Since each of us incarnates something of humanity, each individual consciousness contains something divine and thus finds itself marked with a character which renders it sacred and inviolable to others. Therein lies all individualism, and that is what makes it a necessary doctrine.[14]

This picture of Bosnia's historical multifacetedness was maintained as a constant in a society which was permeated with the sense of the power of the transcendental over the mundane. The position of the individual in each of the holy traditions present in Bosnia represents an image of transcendental order. Salvation is, according to these doctrines, the bridging of the tensions between the one and the other. It is not possible to explain the survival of the multireligious and multiethnic society of Bosnia throughout history without including this premodern connectedness to an awareness of the sense of that which is sacred. In fact, it should be noted that the Bosnian kings accepted the Bosnian Church as a religious organization outside the authority of existing church structures; and that the Ottoman Empire recognized this too, finding a basis within Islam, where religious and ethnic diversity occurs as a sacred feature of the world. Additionally, Bosnia was the place where, for the first time in the history of Europe, Muslims were recognized by the Austro-Hungarian Empire as citizens having equal rights with their Christian counterparts.

The long sought for disintegration of the Ottoman Empire, and then of the Austro-Hungarian Empire, was brought about through a strengthening of the nationalist programs which were established to seek the a priori right of liberty from "foreign rule." These programs involved the creation of "national" elites (i.e., powerful coteries claiming to speak for the "people" as a whole), ideologies, and politico-ethnic organizations. These three essential elements of the nationalist program were rational undertakings which were accomplished within the confined circles of each national elite, but their purpose was the building of the nation-state as a part of the will of "the people." Each individual would enter into the program only within an organized majority of individuals from that society. Therefore, the role of ideology was to convince, to sway, and to strengthen individuals in their alliance with the program of building the nation-state.

This was a completely deliberate, planned undertaking, expressing the nature of the new era of rationalism.[15] And it was in complete contradiction to the generalized understanding of the distinction between right and wrong[16] that both permits and holds together religious diversity within one society. Nationalism is not compatible with the notion of "both *A* and *B*" (as opposed to "either *A* or *B*"). This, as we have seen, exists and functions within the sphere of religious universality, which cannot survive within the reductionism of the nation-state program.

Passivity, Emotion, and Knowledge

Programs for both Serbian and Croatian nation-states were established and developed within the framework of two multinational empires, the former in connection with Serbian Orthodoxy, and the latter with Catholicism. The question of drawing borders or separation from the Other arose within both programs. Both of them, on this basis, attempted to divide and separate.

In Bosnia, both groups represented sectors of population within a presumed ethno-religious whole. Here, however, the groups were intermingled; and with them, the Muslim population. Until modern times, this interweaving exemplified a society within which there existed a consciousness of relatedness, friendship, and confidence. The reasons for tolerance were grounded within the exclusivity and completeness of each individual sacred tradition, where the existence of the Other and the different found their justification in the Divine Unity of God as manifested in each different form of tradition.

But it was precisely these features of social cohesion which were identified as critical barriers to the achievement of nationalist objectives, for an interweaving which involves friendship, confidence, and trust will prevent the demarcation of separate ethno-religious territories. The call for liberation from imperial rule was yoked with the struggle for recognition, and in this struggle the essential Others became those who were closest in terms of ethnoreligious identity, those with whom the differences were very small. Thus, friendship with and confidence towards the Other became a basic obstacle to separation, and therefore their annihilation was calculated into the program.

Any attempt to understand the process of bloodshed and destruction is inseparable from understanding those deepest layers of Self which can remain unshaken even after the borders of social makeup have been changed and the basic rules of social unity demolished. It is at this point that one encounters the question of understanding and belief, two layers of Self established in accordance with the ethno-religious program.[17]

That predominance of "disengaged reason" is the fundamental element of modernity. That is why the weakening and apparent unsustainability of the Bosnian unity in diversity is part of the spread of modern ideologies in the complex region of southeastern Europe. And here modern-day concepts of tolerance—as Adam B. Seligman writes in his introductory text—reach the social scene, while the principled tolerance that derives from the essence of the sacred traditions is repressed.

The world contains forms, and the human Self contains desires. Every tradition is in its own way the denial of the isolation of things in the world, about which various human desires constellate. Those four vital entities—the world, forms, the Self, and desires—determine three essential aspects of human nature: the passional, the emotional, and the intellectual. Although there is only one Truth, these aspects are expressed in various ways in the human being. It could be said that in each tradition, along with the respecting of the Other, there is one Truth to which the doctrines of various traditions correspond. When the material that belongs to the various traditions is submitted to a fundamental examination, the difficulties in explaining the differences can be identified. Distinctions exist primarily in the use of language, though every tradition offers accommodation in the area of its doctrine in order to enable various ways of expressing the Truth. It is left to the holy and wise to see the single reality that lies behind these variously shaped differences. Each tradition, when perceiving the Truth behind this diversity, conveys it in its own particular way. The difference between religions in their exoteric and esoteric content can be confirmed. The question of the transcending of this state requires confirmation of the conditionality or relativity of each form and each expression. In this way, Truth becomes distinguished from individual forms and languages, so that it can be described through each of them. But while the Truth is constantly present, the human Self can be absent, for humans may forget Oneness. The presence of Truth in the Self does not depend upon language or form. Both absence and presence may have various names, but the Truth itself does not depend upon this.

Of course, it is unimaginable that one doctrine could include all this diversity. Nonetheless, a doctrine that does not account for the inexhaustible potential of expressing its very essence cannot be a tradition in the full sense of the word. At the center towards which all traditions lead lies the Full Light. Language as reflection is conditioned by the center, but the center is not conditioned by language. In other words, in the variety of individual traditions, it is always possible to establish two fundamental aspects of content: the doctrine and the way. Further, human nature includes three levels: will, love, and knowledge. Each of these is in turn distinguished in two complementary ways which appear respectively as detachment and action, peace and fervor, discrimination and unification. Knowledge and the way connect them. They are two sides of the same being, and degrees or stations of wisdom: will-love-knowledge or fear-love-knowledge.

Regardless of the abundance of possible ways of expression (which are not repeated in form, although they always remain connected with one and the same reality), it is possible to bring them into an order through which their multiplicity confirms the Oneness of the perennial doctrine. However, the exclusivity of a certain tradition does not require insight into the forms through which the doctrine of another is expressed. For this reason—the limitation in the reading of various forms of tradition—it is not unusual to encounter a different tradition being perceived as "incorrect," with the resulting loss of the view that Oneness can be manifested and confirmed only through its multiplicity. Therefore the parallel presentations of various expressions of the supra-individual and non-individual truth, dependent neither on time nor on language, are essential in order to eliminate the widespread confusion concerning the conditionality of traditions arising out of a multiplicity of expressions.[18]

Faith and intelligence can appear to be opposed. Faith, as a security which originates beyond the state of being, surpasses intelligence. On the other hand, the discernment from which intelligence begins, in order to reach Oneness, surpasses faith. Which of these views is followed is a matter of emotional choice. Much confusion arises precisely from this. It follows, then, that it is possible for there to exist at the same time both exoteric and esoteric languages. Faith in its higher expression is what we call "*religio cordis*"—religion of the heart, that is, inner religion. Corresponding with this is *religio caeli*.[19] This is the expression of eternal Truth in which are manifest signs of enlightenment in the self and in one's horizons. Faith may be satisfied with little—in contrast with intelligence, which requires precision and is never sated in its game of shaping expressions. It constantly crosses from one thought to another, from one sign to another, without dwelling anywhere. The faith of the heart, on the other hand, will find confirmation in the tiniest manifestation. Such an encounter, no matter how small, can offer fulfillment enough for the religion of the heart.

These distinctions and differences between and within traditions are expressed in the relationship of the individual self towards the external forms which make up the totality of the world. The way one feels one's nature or interprets it to the self, one's desires, forms and the world as a whole determine one's passion, emotion, and intelligence. These are facts of human existence. The passional individual accepts the world and the self as the will of totality. Passion rules individuals and submerges them in the world of phenomena. The outcome is to be found in sacred asceticism or sacrifice. For such a person, the signs in the selves and horizons are not a ladder to infinity, and doctrine contains both a threat and a promise. The metaphysical nature of existence is manifested to the individual in the minutest measure. For the intelligent person, the signs in the selves and horizons are visible: they have no limit and they are transparent. Beyond them there is infinity and the Oneness of Truth. This is the separation from forms and desires. Reality is that against which this kind of separation can be achieved. Emotional individuals are caught between these two possibilities: in manifestations they expect either a voice or music. If the passional individual is led by fear and desire, and the intelligent person by knowledge, then the emotional individual can be said to be led by hope and love. Expressions of dedication will permeate their relationships toward forms and toward desires. This is the sensing of life on the basis of predestiny.

The Apprenticeship of Submission and Freedom

"Freedom alone is capable of lifting men's minds above mere mammon worship and the petty personal worries," wrote Alexis-Charles-Henri Clérel de Tocqueville[20]; and as such, it is the most arduous of all apprenticeships. Perhaps this is so. Tradition would, however, take the position that, of all apprenticeships, the most difficult is submission. The most sublime freedom is that which is inexpressible. It is confirmed by pure Being revealing itself in multiplicity and movement. This is the God of all forms of the Semitic expression of Truth, not simply the most supreme/sublime Self, but rather the only true reality. Everything bears witness to Him. In Him every symbol disappears: everything disappears, in fact, except God's face. In Him there is no limitation. Therefore, His face is full of freedom. Submission to Him is the freedom of his creation. The greater that submission, the greater the freedom. If this freedom requires separating from movement for the sake of peace, from the multitude for the sake of Oneness, and from the sign for the sake of that which is signed, then this is submission. Within this submission or freedom all phenomena participate:

> Hast thou not seen how to God prostrate themselves all who are in the heavens and all who are in the earth, the sun and the moon, the stars and the mountains, the trees and the beasts, and many of mankind?[21]

The way or the connectedness between all things leads from God, because He is present everywhere. But there is no single thing through which a path leads to God, because each thing is absent from Him. This is similar to the relationship of the infinite towards any finite thing. Such a relationship neither diminishes nor increases infinite. According to the Holy Revelation, "There is no creature that crawls, but He takes it by the forelock"[22] and "to each of them He offers the rope of salvation".[23] A different relationship is not possible. Even the language of that connectedness, which finds its complete expression in the doctrine of the Covenant, points toward the connection between people on the basis of their belief in God or without it: "Only men possessed of minds remember, who fulfil God's covenant, and break not the compact, who join what God has commanded shall be joined."[24] (Here mention should be made of the etymological content of the concept of *religio*, which means "renewed connection.") From this there is a possible understanding of the explanation in the Holy Revelation:

> We offered the trust to the heavens and the earth and the mountains, but they refused to carry it and were afraid of it, and man carried it. Surely he is sinful and very foolish.[25]

The important word here is "offered." Trust can be accepted or rejected. The heavens, the Earth, and the mountains reject it. This does not mean a necessarily negative characteristic. Their submission is complete: they have completely submitted their will to God's will. Their existence is completely in accordance with God's will. But from the fact that humans accept trust, one can conclude that they are transgressors and ignorant. Between humans and all other things in the totality of creation, there exists this difference: only humans have the freedom to choose submission or nonsubmission to God. Out of such a choice arises the chasm between their being and their knowing. In view of the conditionality of human individuality, the chasm corresponds to a conditional freedom. But that would not be possible if it did not contain violence and ignorance. The presence of violence and ignorance are a "measure" of trust. The traditional path towards freedom lies in its denial for the sake of confirming the one true Self. Humankind is always with and facing the Other. This is a relationship of movement and assessment, which means evaluation.

No perfect truth can possibly derive from the relationship between these two relativities. Confidence (*confidentio*) means the establishment of a relationship between individuals with a responsibility to God, for the face of the other manifests the face of God. The connection is maintained by the awareness that "our God and your God is ever One." The betrayal of responsibility of man-to-man is a violation of what is owed to God. Confidence therefore maintains the recollection of God. It collapses into violence whenever individuals forget that God sees all that humankind is and does. A relationship between people mediated by their relationship with God is reduced to "trust" in the modern world, where the self decrees the postulates of its autonomy as a sufficient source of moral decision.

The concept of "trust" cannot, therefore, represent either "faith" as the relationship between God and individual, or "confidence" as a relationship between individuals derived from the belief in God. Trust denotes a relationship between individuals unmediated by a shared faith in the Supreme Being (such a relationship in this essay is referred to as "trusting,")[26] but not as a perfection which derives from the Absolute, the Creator. Since it is a relationship of creatures, that is, of created beings whose existence is conditional, its inevitable nature is imperfection, which is manifested in "violence and ignorance."

The resolution of the tension between the earthly order (and participation in it) and the heavenly, in which salvation promises freedom from limitations and death, includes this relationship between God and the individual, in the form of an invitation from the former and a response from the latter. Inasmuch as the invitation and the response take place in the finite world, they are, strictly speaking, a connection of each individual with the same God. It is possible to say, therefore, that there are as many different religions as there are different human beings. Acceptance of the Revealed Way means inclusion in one of the historically multifaceted religious communities. Genuine religion includes the distinction of the real from the unreal, which is a capacity found in every individual. But, likewise, there must be an attachment to reality as defined, which requires knowledge of and connection with the appropriate humanly perfected mediation. This forms the basis for the various languages and rituals. Within and between individuals the possibility of confidence exists, because between each individual "Me" and the group "We," relations are established through the supreme and only true "I." This requires agreement that here is a single perennial relevance at the heart of the various holy traditions.

Bosnian premodern society, as a totality of different religious communities, was founded precisely upon confidence within those communities and between them. Each of those communities established its own organization. Each of them developed and maintained its version of the doctrine and the way, but also the awareness of the meeting of that way with all the others in infinity and eternity, in the God who cannot be only "ours" or "theirs," thus maintaining a responsibility towards all the other communities and their members. This is summed up in the statement: "Our God and your God is One and the Same, and to Him we have surrendered."[27] The particular features of holy ritual and its symbols are transcended in each of these communities by the connection between God and each of its members. Otherwise, the rituals and symbols would be mere idols. And this is the source of Bosnian tolerance: its reasons are based neither on *Realpolitik*, nor on indifference towards the Other and the different, nor on notions of universal freedom of choice. It is a different choice, rooted in the single sacred that can and must manifest itself in diverse ways in time and space.

Recent changes in Bosnian society have included secularization. Relations between individuals are increasingly founded upon trust rather than confidence. Individuals cease to understand themselves as a creation "in God's image." Because they view themselves as the highest level of being, all else is beneath them. Thus, they assume the position of the one who "upholds" or "chooses to hold" themselves and every other being "by the forelock," and both ends of the rope of their salvation are held in human hands. The individual's position as a creature has become that of creator. They express their limitations and the unconditionality of their self in relationship with others (and others with them) in violence and ignorance; holy tradition, with its multiplicity of forms, is replaced by secular ideologies.

Among these, the most significant position is taken by the ideology of the nation-state. Every religious community is allowed its own organization and traditional language, but without God as the complete freedom and source of individual salvation. The power of salvation has instead been shifted to the relationship with those people who inherit the religious communities and their legacies. In the ethno-national program, this inheritance becomes transferred to the political elite, ideology, and organization. Holy rituals, their symbols and everything connected with them no longer act as bridges, across which each individual is carried to "the other side," towards God. Instead, they become a part of the conglomerate of means which determine relations in a closed world. The establishing of a political elite requires a coalition with the religious elite, whereby the latter is in a subordinate position. Ideology necessitates a reshaped understanding of religion, which is transferred onto an ideological reading of history.[28] "One nation—one state" is, in this perspective, a false god. Its destructive effect is demonstrated in the ontotopological drive to equate ethno-national identity with territory. And this means that those factors that represent a threat to the desired homogeneity must be eliminated from the ideologically postulated territory. Elites, ideology, and structures become the mediators of trust between individuals. They assume an absolutized role in sustaining society, but do not ensure the satisfaction of the desires and needs of the individual. To countermand this would require a deeper understanding of human needs and the fragility of social structures, both of which are sacrificed when the inner contents of a society's history are lost.

Human deliverance or liberation requires a doctrine and a path. This doctrine cannot come from the individual. It is both non-individual and supra-individual. As such, it is appropriate for every individual. It is ever-present; it is only man who can be absent. To submit, or to be free, means to find the source of the Self.[29]

To grow into our mature better selves, we need the help of our nascent better selves, which is what common standards, authoritative education, and a sense of the public good can offer. Consumption takes us as it finds us, the more impulsive and greedy, the better. Education challenges our impulses and informs our greediness with lessons drawn from our mutuality and the higher good we share in our communities of hope. Government, federal and local, with responsibility for public education once took it upon itself (back when "itself" was "us") to even up the market and lend a hand to our better selves. Now via vouchers the market threatens to get even with public education. This sorry state of affairs is not the work of villains or boors. It arises all too naturally out of the culture of McWorld in a transnational era where governments no longer act to conceive or defend the common good.[30]

In such a picture of the human position, the general perspective on man's original perfection has been lost. Now he can lower himself to the lowest of levels. But even there, in that possibility of greatest humiliation, the possibility of perfection remains as a result of his being created. Not even there is he without consciousness of the *cube*, the symbol of building, which in itself includes the polarity of the simultaneous humiliation and exaltation of every being: "We indeed created Man in the fairest stature, then We restored him as the lowest of the low."[31]

A Lower Freedom

Submission to absolute freedom, in which individual phenomena exist as archetypes, both as source and eternal potential, becomes transformed in this forgotten world of submission into a freedom "beneath the level of reason." Traditionally, reason is a reflection of intellect in the world of multiplicity and movement. Reason is attracted by all phenomena, but none of them can give it peace. The Absolute cannot belong to it, but humans seek after the Absolute. If reason is the highest level of being, there is nothing above it. The world permits its reshaping according to human content beneath the level of reason. This is McWorld, "a theme park, a Marketland where everything is for sale, someone else is always responsible, and there is no common good or public interest. Here everyone is equal as long as they can afford the price of admission and are content to watch and to consume. McWorld as Marketland is, however, not a natural entity engineered by some benevolent deity. It is fabricated and it is owned, and how it is owned tells us a great deal about its nature."[32] This world is not concerned with the fulfillment of humankind's creation, nor with the capacity for perfection. In its transcending of the boundaries of individuality by liberal embodiment in the state, the market, the culture, and suchlike, the supra-individual and the non-individual sources of unity are forgotten and abandoned. Unification is imposed upon the world. Neither its acceptance nor its rejection is a question of place or time, but their expression must be sought in the human self—which may incite to evil, which may reproach, or which may be at peace.[33]

Although the modern individual's Self is largely included in this economy—which at the level of society is not only expressed as a rationalization of selfish interests in the acquisition of wealth, but also as the arena of the human struggle for recognition—contemporary economic theory remains, for the most part, powerless to account for the totality of human behavior. This was pointed out by Adam Smith, when he showed that economic life was deeply rooted in social life, and that it cannot be separated from the customs, habits, and social behavior in which that life is functioning. Therefore, it cannot be separated from culture.[34] It is possible to see economic and cultural life as the simultaneity and opposition of two processes in a single reality: one which tries to unite people in the ideological world, and one in which they attempt to find themselves in the fullness of their Self. These processes contrast, and have different names and interpretations. When feeling oppressed by the first, humans turn towards the second. This may result in the discovery of the faith of one's ancestors—but most often as dead symbols which strengthen sentimentality and morality without any substantiating intellectual doctrine. Such a "finding of the self" in a "struggle for recognition" mostly consists of a blind resistance to McWorld and a repression of "development" (in the modern sense), in which the consciousness of the fundamental principle becomes ever weaker.

Here we should point out the obsession with the determination of civilization(s) on the basis of phenomena and their external connections, whereby the meeting place (i.e., the center or the highest essence) of a civilization, as confirmed by the sum of perceived phenomena, may become neglected or negated. This corresponds to a concern with the peripheral, as a result of which the center is ignored or denied. It may also come about as a result of an obsession with quantity, and the relation of numbers of things to each other, coupled with the ignoring of the fundamental nature of unity. In this way, civilizations become irreconcilable entities, material systems among which the decisive factor is quantity. From this misunderstanding of multiplicity arises the theory of a "clash of civilizations." This is the logical consequence of the excision of all that is beyond human reason. The center which, in a mysterious way, is both present and absent in every phenomenon, ceases to be the means through which even civilizations may be seen only as various manifestations of a nonindividual, supra-individual truth.[35] There is no such thing as a society without, or without the potential for, a transcendental center. Through that center the symbolic meaning of all its forms is maintained. Without it, this meaning begins to disappear, as well as all the phenomena associated with civilization; and even civilizations themselves begin to take on the nature of condensed forms which reason cannot transcend. They become, therefore, material systems which are in irreconcilable opposition.

The dynamic of the contradiction between forms of civilization which have lost the awareness of their transcendental center is indicated in Bernard Barber's concluding remarks:

> What becomes apparent is that the confrontation of Jihad and McWorld has as its first arena neither the city nor the countryside, neither pressured inner cities nor thriving exurbia, but the conflicted soul of the new generation. Nations may be under assault, but the target audience is youth.[36]

Yet the concepts adopted to determine the contrast between Jihad and McWorld do not correspond to the nature of the conflict described. No individual or joint reading of holy doctrine, as delivered in a certain language and ritual, can claim that it must also be sacred for others. There is only the right and the possibility for each individual, in his/her reading, to overcome his/her own ignorance and inclination toward violence—to meet these needs by being rooted within his/her own Self, and then to establish him-/herself in the fullness of peace, that is, in that center without which no civilization is possible. In the original Arabic, this striving was named *jihad*, but—because of its religious content—it has since been subjected to misreading and misapplication. Widespread acceptance of this misreading has set the seal on the refusal to accept its underlying meaning.

The struggle for recognition leads to the discovery or strengthening of ethnic or religious identities. What does this mean for the young post-Communist world? Or for its colleagues in this "most developed" continent? After such ideological collapses, frequently accompanied by the destruction of entire social structures by massacre and by exile, confusion and disorientation face the survivors and bystanders. In the place of the defeated ideology, ethnicized religions, liturgies and symbols, and ethno-national programs are erected. The religious organizations become structures which not only separate and limit people, but also do not offer an escape from the confusion. The blame or guilt of others is intensified, as is also the need for a reading of history which might "explain" the cause of the increased tensions.

This process, which significantly increases the fragility of the social order, has come to be called the "conflict of tradition and modernism," or "religion and secularism." These concepts, however, are nebulous and for the most part trivialized. When the advocates of modernism speak of tradition, they attribute to it the negative contents of their own world view. The same is true of the traditionalists' view of liberalism. And so the gap between the two discourses widens. Alongside this, religious discourse and organizations extend into the secular world where they become reshaped. This is also the case with the discourse of modernism, which is increasingly present in religious organizations. Such phenomena make it difficult for a dialogue where the question of trust and confidence might be examined within the context of discussing the common good. Both sides take over the language of the other, completely misconstruing its substance, resulting in mutually irreconcilable negation. This conflict, which exists in all modern societies, could be termed the "trivialization of religion in the secular world."[37]

The Ideology of Nation

We have said that the Self stands between past and future. Its only absolute certainties are death and the present moment. It can determine nothing except this double certainty. Its underlying essence, which could also be called the "human principle," is unchangeable. What is changeable, however, is its method of manifesting itself—and none of its manifestations ever repeat themselves. They may reveal themselves in chaos or order, development or decline, but all manifestations of the deepest nature of the Self are inseparable from the readings of the past and future inscribed within the Self.

As past and future are uncertain, they are both accompanied by speculation and, as a result, by endless illusion. The Self's yearning for the future in terms of "human progress" is ultimately denied by the certainty of death. Thus, this yearning incorporates the desire to escape or forget death: it predicts "the end of history," divorced from the certainty which is the deepest element of the Self. It produces the need for ideology as a replacement for tradition. "Liberty" is the name most frequently given to this choice: neither the present nor death are seen any longer as obligatory. Confirmation is found in externalization—the state of human affairs which the Prophet Muhammad described as "competing to build huge buildings." An even greater weakness of externalization is the resulting lack of awareness of inner values, in accordance with the law of inversion: the greater the outward display, the smaller the core of principle.

Esoteric doctrine describes the workings of this law through the symbolic relationship between circumferences and center. Any circumference is a peripheral manifestation of, or testament to, the center. Neither a single circumference nor all circumferences together—even though there is a limitless number of possible circumferences around a single center—can contribute to, or detract from the center. A circumference cannot exist without its center, but the reverse is not true. Similarly, the deepest and most central principles of humanity may have a limitless number of manifestations in time and space, but these neither contribute to nor detract from the center itself.

According to a libertarian and secular world view, human history is no more than an increasing number of manifestations, linked by ever more quickly forming relationships. In this context, it is possible to speak of unending change and development. The history of humanity is, according to this concept, a progression from the depths towards ever loftier heights. But the traditional picture of humanity's presence in time is exactly the reverse: individuals were originally perfect but, over time, have fallen away from their original purity. Individuals are seduced ever more by externalities in the shape of luxury and worldly glory. They are undergoing an endless test, an unending choice between the values of God and the riches of the world.

Tradition sees the test as ending decisively in favor of the goodness of God. We see this in the dialogue between Satan and Jesus:

> Again the devil took Him up on an exceedingly high mountain, and showed Him all the kingdoms of the world and their glory. And he said to Him, "All these things I will give You if You will fall down and worship me." Then Jesus said to him, "Away with you, Satan! For it is written, 'You shall worship the Lord your God, and Him only you shall serve.'"[38]

The Prophet reiterates the same message in several ways. An example is the saying:

> God gave one of His slaves the choice of what he wanted: to have the glory and luxury of life in this world, or to have goodness with God. And he chose goodness with God.[39]

Worldly riches correspond to multiplicity and motion: the opposite is unity and peace. Multiplicity and motion demand libertarianism, since none of their states can ever be complete. Libertarianism is the measure of their illusory tendency to growth and speed. It is paradoxical to expect that full and final harmony can be reached by way of this rapid multiplication and increase.

However, unity and peace require submission. This means turning away from multiplicity and motion towards the inner depths, and forming a bond with the heart—the *religio cordis*. Taking the opposite direction leads to alienation from the heart, and a fading of the self in multiplicity and increase. But this path is not without boundaries. Its certain end is the hour implicit in the competition "to build great buildings."[40]

Tradition is an eternal movement of principle, unity and peace. It crosses borders which are closed to multiplicity and motion. The deepest elements of humanity, such as they are, form its goal. It is therefore in tradition, and through tradition, that trust becomes possible in the community, and between communities. If the world of multiplicity and motion is grasped as the only possible arena for humanity, the inevitable result is separation and division. When efforts are put into establishing and maintaining a diversity of forms, the result is an all-embracing structure of ideology, propped up by sentiment and morals. The customary title for this all-embracing form is "civilization." Its most basic characteristic is the desire to increase its own power and scope, but the inevitable accompanying tendency is towards internal division and restriction.

The Chasm of the Future

The ideology of a nation is only one form of ideology. It establishes a joint "self" which calls itself a nation on the basis of its difference from others. It is presented as essential by the elite who embody that supposed joint self. There is a need for it to be organized, which can be satisfied only in the form of state sovereignty. Others can be accepted only if they have no power, if their only rights are those granted to them by the indisputable sovereign power of the nation. When national multiplicity is portrayed in the picture of the past, then hatred and conflict between the different groups is the desirable and predominant representation. Such a picture confirms McWorld: it is presented as the supreme development, moving from chaos towards the peace and harmony of order. McWorld, according to its own description, is established as the decisive development, made possible by the innovations in technology and communications which have arisen at the end of the twentieth century. This is, in a way, the supreme achievement of modernization, which some refer to as Westernization. This development began with the birth of modern science just after the Renaissance, with its paradigm of knowledge as power. Barber sums it up as follows:

> There is little in McWorld that was not philosophically adumbrated by, if not the Renaissance, the Enlightenment, its trust in reason, its passion for liberty, and (not unrelated to that passion), its fascination with control, its image of the human mind as a *tabula rasa* to be written on and thus encoded by governing

technical and educational elites, its confidence in the market, its skepticism about faith and habit, and its cosmopolitan disdain for parochial culture.[41]

Such a McWorld-based understanding accords with a negative attitude towards history—which is, according to Voltaire, little more than a list of human mistakes and stupidity—while educational psychology posits a single universal human nature rooted in correct reason and established in the greater harmony of the chain of Being. Tradition is its opposite, as an order which maintains a nonindividual and supra-individual truth. Thus, arises the opposition between McWorld and tradition, in which both sides see each other, in the context of social reality, as their own negative image. Such a reductionist perspective gives rise to nationalism: McWorld perceives tradition as a retrogressive and unfortunate offshoot of the past, and tradition treats McWorld as a modern, antitraditional degeneration.

The tragic Bosnian experience at the end of the second Christian millennium was marked by massacre, enforced exile, the destruction and burning of villages and cities, and increased distrust and confusion. The rest of the world was incapable of being a positive third force, a means of helping to maintain and strengthen Bosnian society in such a way as to enable its peaceful survival. It seems reasonable to ask: does the dominant liberalist world view have the power to find a purpose within traditional oppositions? And does the traditional world view have the ability to recognize in liberalism the expression of that same human perfection in which it sees its own roots? If these two discourses express two different truths, then their speakers will be in irreconcilable hostility. The resolution of this duality is something upon which the future depends, for all of us, individually and jointly.

Unless this question is addressed, two possible future scenarios may be predicted. The first might manifest itself in the supreme development of social and economic structures containing weakened humans who are susceptible to ever more probable bloodshed and expulsion. Widespread destruction is likely to arise from the increasing gulf between violence and ignorance on the one hand, and the inner self on the other. In the other scenario, a few rare individuals, convinced of their own invincible ideals, will pit themselves in resistance against an overcrowded but empty world. The position of these rare individuals and their relationship towards such a world is reflected in the words of the poet Mak Dizdar:[42]

> *(How often must I tell you that you know*
> *Nothing about me—*
> *Nothing about my arrow and bow*

Nothing about my sword and shield
That you have no idea how sharp is my steel
That you know nothing about my poor
Body or
The bright flame
That burns
Inside)

I'm waiting for you
Because I know you
You'll come back one day

(This you've vowed
By chalice and cross and blade of sword
Drunk with chants of damnation and incense smoke)

So,
Come on then

I've long grown used to your ravages
As if to the throes
Of a disease from far away

As to the icy waters swept savagely along
By this night river of darkness that grows
Ever more swift
And strong.

(Mak Dizdar, Message)

Tolerance, Ideology, and Tradition

Introduction: An Unexpected Movement

The last few decades of the second Christian millennium have seen a widespread trend towards a heightened affirmation of religion in those areas of life, at both the individual and the social level, from which it seemed to have become detached in the West. This development, which has now become quite marked, must be seen in the context of long-term patterns of cause and effect. To interpret it, one must grasp the individual and social developments in the period that is seen as the beginning of our current reality.

The second half of the nineteenth century and the first half of the twentieth were characterized by the promotion of ideological models for the future, accompanied by a further evolution of the process that began with the Renaissance, in which the proposition "God vis-à-vis Man" is transformed into "Man vis-à-vis everything else." This has been succeeded, in the second half of the twentieth century, by a decline in ideological fervor, the collapse of several of the great ideology-inspired movements, and an increasing trend towards religious approaches to this world of disillusion and despair. This has unfolded in the form of a widespread collision between two languages, the language of religion and the language of ideology, resulting in a development more complex than anything previously known: ideological language and secular experience embraced by religious organizations, and religious language and content again pushed to the social margins.

By their own exclusive nature, ideological totalitarianisms have created generalized models in which the languages of tradition are almost completely ignored. Closely related theories and concepts have thus sprung up, which subjugate tradition to their own exclusive models. Where the language of tradition is silenced, or contradicts the language of ideology, tradition is simply, crudely denied. Even for experienced observers this paradox is hard to recognize, but only once the content of "the crisis of the times and its indicators" is distinguished is it even possible to raise numerous vital questions.

The attempt to identify responses to the universal essence of human language in the coming era demands that the multiple forms of contemporary knowledge be examined from the perspectives of ideology, modernity, and tradition alike. The example of tolerance reflects the complexity of this task.[1]

Tolerating the Other

The contemporary notion of tolerance may be linked, simplistically at least, with modern Christian disunity. (This is a tentative connection, and its treatment in this essay is not meant to be taken as a generalization, but as a means of drawing conclusions that are applicable to the world as a whole to be reached.) In the Christian world, exclusivity towards movements generally defined as heretical, such as gnosticism, has as a rule ended in the annihilation of those who lacked the power to oppose "the generally accepted and established Church." Individuals are therefore deprived of the right to a direct relationship with the source of the tradition that they belong to, guided by their own conscience and selfhood, unless this relationship wholly confirms the axiomatic rights of the established Church. From this perspective, Others are the exception, and their survival in the long term cannot be guaranteed in such an environment, since their rights are not encoded in the ruling interpretation of tradition.

The Great Schism altered nothing in this model. To put it simply, it was formed as a balance of power, in which even the history of marginal encounters and conflicts is evidence of the fundamental equilibrium of the model. The issue of the Other was further exacerbated by Europe's religious wars and the later schisms within Christian unity. Their presence on "both sides" made it imperative to identify reasons for tolerance. But the public good, in the main, was reduced to an exclusive interpretation of tradition, and in every marriage of political power and ideology based on tradition, the desire to exclude the Other was encoded.

The reverse process has its foundation in the contradictions of differing interpretations of tradition, derived, in various languages and ideologies, from tradition, or *traditio perennis,* and the desire to establish the right of individuals to moderation and sincerity in the relationship towards themselves, the world, and God as their own potential allowed. The comprehensiveness and exclusivity of individual traditions are seen as obstacles to individual rights. Ethnic collectivism demands the repression of that exclusivity and the promotion of a national ideology as the context within which "rights" can be safeguarded. Diversity is interpreted as freedom, and its highest principle becomes the tolerance of others.

The modern era is therefore founded both on totalitarian, exclusive traditions, in which tolerance of the Other is as a rule unlawful, and on liberalism, which views all men as created "in His image."[2] The source of moral discernment and judgment becomes, in this view, wholly internalized within the self of the free individual. The development of ruling ideologies has at the same time meant the presence of a "second class"—usually denoted as cohabitation on the basis of a concordat on the apportionment of social influence. This means that tolerance derives from a consensus on loyalty to the ruling system. Depending on the extent to which tolerance is related to the totalitarianism and exclusivity of ideology, in a pluralist society the Other is more or less tolerated. Disregard for traditional or ideological elements has even become an important identifying mark of tolerance.[3] But plurality of tradition, when it means differences of language and form, is a less attractive proposition. Only in opposition to the ruling system can different traditions show some level of tactical consensus on the issue, although it is rare for them to find a common language to define their stance on the proposition of "goodwill to all men."

Ideological Diversity

If a given group of ideas are shaped by ideology into a system intended to cover all aspects of existence, and which proffers and promotes itself on the basis of a logical model as a progressive trend of thought and action in which human capacities are limitless, a fixed order is established from the initial totalitarianism of ideology towards a peak; an order to which everything else is seen as subordinate. Tolerance is acceptance, whether voluntary or under compulsion, of everyone else as a priori subjugated to the ideological model. Everything that attempts opposition is blocked by relentless persecution and is ultimately destroyed or rendered helpless. In this model, tolerance is the measure of viability of those elements of the ideological whole that do not threaten to block or destroy the ideological system itself.

In a system of this kind, diversity is defined according to ideological values fixed in advance. Unexpressed conflicts with the subjugated holistic perceptions and concepts of the world are a constant presence in such relations. Every tradition is holistic by definition, and, as such, will be at risk in an ideological system of being detached from its holistic perception and reduced to fragmentariness. This most frequently results in the divorce of tradition from transcendental mystery, and its transformation into traditional ideology. This is the prevalent situation in every major contemporary religious establishment.

Ideology always has a person as its starting point: the individual is the result of development from the bottom upwards, whereas values and qualities are "second-order" features. Its theories and practices fail to acknowledge either nonindividuality or supra-individuality. That which cannot be measured does not exist. Thus, the intellect, as the nonindividual and supra-individual source of knowledge, and reason, as its expression in human individuality, are leveled to the same status.[4] Reason is seen as the highest human quality. There is nothing above it, and its relationship to everything else is "top down." The balance between individual as primary principle and the individuality of humankind and the totality of existence is defined by focusing on "rights" rather than on what is morally "right," as is the case with tradition as a manifestation of "tradition," or with religion as a manifestation of "religion."

Tradition without God becomes mere ideology. (This claim may appear contestable if made outside the world of the Abrahamic faiths. It is possible, however, to appeal to convincing interpretations of Hinduism and Buddhism, and also Daoism, in which only the diversity of language is at issue, which, transcended, might lead to One and the same being.)[5] If the name of God were to be replaced by that of one of His attributes, for example, Unity, Uniqueness, Eternity—the claim would be more accessible to ordinary logic, which can thus approach the issue more closely, if not explore it fully.

Both versions of ideology—the secular, in which neither language nor meaning are necessarily connected with tradition, and the traditional, in which forms and meanings are exoteric displays of tradition, although they have lost their esoteric roots—measure tolerance according to their obsession with rights. This assertion can also be expressed as follows: tolerance is the measure of acceptance of differences of form and meaning within the limits of the ideological system. It is, in other words, a disregard for those elements that do not obstruct the postulated ideological unity.

The Missing Link

The age in which we live can justifiably be called the "age of ideology." It probably represents a climax in the development of the projects that define humankind's relationship towards itself and the world on the basis of the proposition that individuals are sufficient unto themselves, and that the Earth is capable of providing all that can be imagined as humanly necessary. On this foundation, the modern era has seen two very similar concepts develop. The first could be described as a program of liberty, from which liberal democracy and the liberal economy have sprung. The second is known as Communism. As to content and as to organization, both are ideological, which means that they view all elements that are beyond the world of reason, and thus beyond the measurable world, as residual or marginal.

In the final century of the second millennium, then, this duality manifested itself in two specific forms: (1) the liberal, and (2) the Communist world. The duality has taken the form of opposing military systems, ideological warfare, and the endless, painstaking search for ways in which one side can prevail over the other. The symbol of division was the Berlin Wall. The confrontation came to an end, with illusory suddenness, with the fall of Communism and the spread of the values of the liberal world into the realm of the "Communist Empire." The theory of a universal, coherent history, valid for both sides, seems to have found confirmation in these events, and in the feeling that they are the natural outcome of the superiority of liberal democracy and its course towards the "end of history." This end is perceived as involving the disappearance of the internal tensions from which conflicts, and obstacles to full respect for human freedoms, arise. This certain progress and the accumulation of scientific knowledge are taken as fundamental proof of the accuracy of this vision of the future. (The persistence of the Communist side in scientific achievement, however, in which it does not differ from the liberal world, does not fit this interpretation.)

Only in conditions of general recognition, characteristic of liberal democracy, can all human needs of the human be satisfied—the needs of desire, reason, and *thymos*. The first two, which manifest themselves as the constant expansion of human needs and continual advances in the means of satisfying them, can be explained by economic theory. With the fall of the Communist world, a higher facet of the human self became evident, one that cannot find fulfillment in the satisfaction of desire and reason only. The will for freedom, embodied in the liberal state, springs from the aspect called "*thymos*."[6] The renewed promotion of the model of "universal history," therefore, emphasizes this very fact: liberal democracy makes possible the satisfaction of *thymos*, which socialism ignores, prompting its own downfall in so doing. It is in *the desire for acknowledgement* that *thymos* expresses itself. Humans want to be recognized as beings with value and dignity. This wish takes precedence over needs that can be met economically. The lack of general acknowledgement of this human desire manifests itself in the course of history as the opposition between master and servant classes.[7] Liberal democracy comes closer to abolishing this relationship and establishing the principle of national sovereignty and the rule of law: every citizen recognizes the value and dignity of every other. In the model of universal history, the "desire for recognition" forms the missing link between liberal economy and liberal policy.

From the Top Down

What is termed "tradition" represents the totality of relationships of every individuality within the world of diversity with the unity that is revealed and corroborated by that very diversity. This is not the simple sum of the "paths" between beings and Being. It is the essence of the mutual relationship: that through which the individual elements of the totality of existence discover themselves within reality. From the viewpoint of tradition, no individual enters existence without a purpose. Goodness is their primary cause and goal. Expressed in the form it takes in Islam, this is encapsulated in the Prophet's message of the word of God: "My mercy takes precedence over My wrath!"[8] In its link with both final cause and final consequence in its religion, every manifestation is "mercy," and determined by mercy. Using the same logic, we can say that it is "goodness," and determined by goodness. Being aware of the differentiation between the unreal and the real within every manifestation is to confirm goodness as both its motive and its purpose: the sequence of the degrees of being in multiplicity is from the top downwards, from higher to lower, which means that quality and value are of a higher ontological level than mere matter.

Whether Judaism, Christianity, and Islam are considered as three sacred traditions or three manifestations of tradition, their very diversity would confirm that they are part of one transcendental tradition, connected with unity as cause and purpose. The diversity of tongues in which they present one and the same essence can reveal the universal and recognizable measure of the common good in the religious plurality of the world.

Indeed, without this understanding, tolerance, as the sufferance of others from disregard or out of necessity, is constantly at risk in the ideological reductionism of tradition of developing into a desire for affirmation of the absolutized *I*, whether individual or collective, at the expense of the total denial of the Other. But this is a self that identifies itself in relation to a conditional or contingent Other. As the experience of the twentieth century shows, the state of mind in which one relies on oneself as a sufficient moral judge, one who by his own decision needs no heteronomous transcendental moral authority, all too easily degrades into the denial of Others, which is then transformed into their annihilation.

As a result, the existing traditions, whose heightened and strengthened presence marks the turn of the millennium, are faced with—or perhaps one should say lie within—the tasks that the philosophy of liberalism has reached when asking questions concerning the Self. Is a constant strengthening of trust, as a prerequisite of social virtues and the building of progress, possible without also incorporating into the concept of the world as a whole the consensus on Goodness framed in a language derived from religious plurality?[9]

Ideological Reductionism

Every tradition can be reduced to ideology. It thereby becomes subjugated to measures totally contrary to those that originally shaped it when it possessed both an external and an inward significance. In this process, the tradition retains only its external form and is consequently subject to ideological exploitation. There are many examples of such reductionism. Whenever tradition promotes an individual as privileged on the basis of any individuality—racial, ethnic, linguistic, confessional—it loses its inner quality and becomes merely a reading of history in the service of some strategy. The loss of inwardness from the horizons of tradition manifests itself in a heightened need for magnitude, visibility, homogeneity: power becomes the means of a person's realization. The will to power both animates and shapes every calculation and unremittingly raises the stakes. Where inner meaning and absorption with good as the cause and purpose of every individuality are absent, one finds great temples and religious gatherings that appear more like sporting events or political rallies, and the deafening exploitation of sacred discourse originally intended for the subtler medium of contemplation and solitude, so that the language of morality is substituted for the language of power.

Even if ideology has the ability to touch the question of discerning the real from the unreal, by denying the existence of the nonindividual and supra-individual, it disables itself from focusing on the real, since the model it opts for is not one that is the simple choice of any individual. Genuine tradition, however, has a lasting model, chosen from the nonindividual and supra-individual, for individual focus—in the persons of Moses, Christ, and Muhammad, for example. But this focus on a chosen example is never mediated: it is always the relationship of the individual, in full freedom to listen to the voice of one's own conscience and to interpret and draw conclusions during contemplation of the model. Thus, true tradition is both one and all-encompassing, reflecting the deepest internal experience that is corroborated at the level of living and sharing in society, as in the saying of Christ: "Love thy neighbour as thyself."[10]

The case of the partition of Bosnia, for example, offers important evidence in support of this thesis. It is not possible to derive from tradition the reasons comprised in ethno-national projects claiming that others are devoid of all that is good and valid. To deny the other, either through a rejection of dialogue, or through genocide in the fullest sense of the word, negates goodness as a principle of tradition.[11] This ideological reductionism turns tradition into an empty shell, to be used as building material in the ideology of political projects.

Transcendent Unity

As is apparent from earlier remarks, current circumstances call for an explanation of the concepts of tradition and "tradition."[12] Without this it will not be possible even to raise the issue of a transformation of the understanding of tolerance with the aim of creating a language for building and reinforcing trust. Taking as a basis the three sacred traditions of Judaism, Catholicism, and Islam, it can be affirmed that they are holy, because they have one and the same perennial nucleus: the differentiation of the unreal from the "real." According to this differentiation, every manifestation in the totality of ontological diversity is and is not God. Behind and before diversity is unity—in diversity lies the affirmation of unity. Every individuality implies its own path towards unity, and the way that path is traveled. To be directed towards unity means to confirm and simultaneously to contradict the unity in every individuality, for diversity merely reveals and confirms unity. In principle it can be stated, therefore, that the roads from individuality to unity are limitless in number. Each is tradition, and its essence—both as potential and as ultimate essence—is "tradition." Only a free and responsible self is capable of moral judgment. But absolute otherness, transcendent and unique, as the source of the stable identity of an individual self, is sacred: subjugation to it is voluntary and unconditional.

However, in the temporal dimension this universal distinction is not present only as innate human potential. It is only the first and most universal element of tradition. It also manifests itself in diversity, in multiplicity of form. In the light of this distinction, the way from "is not" towards "is" or, to put it differently, from individual towards God, requires realization in its reverse form—from God towards individual. This is seen in prophethood, as the second important component of tradition. God reveals this path through His prophets, who are, in the temporal dimension, the source of knowledge for humans or, to use secular language, the founders of religions. They are not so if one uses the language of tradition. Their position is like that of a bridge between two shores: one shore is time, diversity, and movement; the other eternity, unity, and peace. This other side is the one and the same for every tradition, and without it each one of them is denied. All traditions derived from "tradition" have their own sacred language and customary rites, through which is established, or reconnected, the link between humans and unity. This, indeed, is the original meaning of the word *religion*.[13] Whatever the differences in that which is perceived to flow from Moses, Christ, and Muhammad towards humans—and these are perceived as traditions—what is "behind" Moses, Christ, and Muhammad is Being, eternal and unchanging, one and only, harmonious and indivisible. Against sensory perception and reason, as the only sources of knowledge in modernity, tradition also postulates the necessity of intuitive intelligence as the primal human attunement for experiencing the planes of being beyond the "measurable" world.

The diversity of sacred languages, teachings, and customs is, without doubt, evidence of this unity. Whenever a tradition is divorced from this unity, it becomes an ideology disguised by language, learning, and the forms that were borrowed from the original connection with "unity." Thus, religious rituals become hypocrisy, since they have lost the memory of unity, and the relationship with unity, from which submission to "goodness" derives.

In summary, it is possible to show that the underlying concept present in the different traditions is that of an individual "created in God's image." This concerns humans irrespective of time, space, and language—the one and only person who is revealed in unique, unrepeatable forms in the world of diversity. In each of these individualities is reflected this original perfection and its final reality. Knowledge, will, and disposition are transformed, in learning, ritual, and holiness, into this original nature. Thus, they are a way of achieving the purpose, not the purpose itself. The realization of the original nature is identification of the external with the internal. Through humankind's "Fall" an artificial division was created between the inner self, which came to seem mysterious, and the outer world, which seemed plainer to individual's vision. This inner existence belongs to the realm of the heart—to use the language of tradition—and the external to the realm of the brain. The realm of the heart is not accessible through the approaches of the external world. "Faith is knowledge in the heart,"[14] says the Prophet. To those who seek to put this to the test he sends word: "Have you opened the heart and looked into it?"[15] Since such internal life is beyond the judgment of reason, it is not subject to measurement. To put it differently, it is not possible to impose faith from without, as is summed up in the following: "*No compulsion is there in religion; rectitude has become clear from error.*"[16] Rectitude, the "right path," is the connection between truth and each individuality. But there are as many paths as there are individuals. Every center of individuality—or every human heart, to use the language of tradition—is formed for perfection.

By contrast, the picture of the perfection of the external world is measurable and requires dialogue and agreement on the nature of goodness and duty. In his Letter on Tolerance, John Locke emphasizes that "nobody is born the member of some Church,"[17] which is very much in harmony with the statement of the Prophet: "Every child is born according to *fitrah*. Then its parents make it a Christian, a Jew, or a Zoroastrian."[18] The Revelation, too, so directs: "So set thy face to the religion, a man of pure faith—God's original upon which He originated mankind."[19] This tells us that the inner human nature is identical to submission, which is, ultimately, the same as complete human freedom. Humans come into the world in a full relationship with unity, but this is then distorted in their growth and relationship with their environment. If humans want to return to their original nature, they must again reestablish themselves within unity.

Between Two Certainties

This primordial identity, however, takes on different manifestations in the dynamic of civilization. This dynamic can be determined by the position of the self, authority, and transcendence within it. Humans know of only two certainties: the present moment in which they find themselves, and the moment of their death. Though only these are certain, humans focus more on the more or less probable events and phenomena between them. Humans cannot choose what is certain; they can merely either resist it or submit to it. Any choice based on freedom also implies abandoning or turning away from what has been assessed as bad or less good. Individuals tend to choose what is good. This offers them not only the authority of their autonomous self, but also security—which may assume the form of the sacred—imposed from without. The tensions in the multiplicity of the world cannot be solved. They are perceived as the projection of a higher order. This transcendent or heavenly order of phenomena is the perfect side of the polarization of existence into its heavenly and earthly poles. What is nowadays understood as the world of tradition has always been marked by this axial polarization between the earthly and the heavenly, described in the languages of different traditions.

Modernity, however, has significantly changed the prevailing course of this axial polarization. The main feature of modernity is the appeal to the autonomous self as the sufficient source of human fulfillment on the earthly plane. The order *self—authority—transcendence*, which, in the traditional perspective, is the two-way flow of being, is more or less reduced to the autonomy of the self; this results in an "internalization" of the transcendent authority, which is linked to Paul's insistence on the precedence of faith over the law. As a result, authority and transcendence disappear from the rationalist perspective as crucial components of the totality of being. Only in the conflict of goods and the expansion of moral and cognitive relativism is it established again that the autonomy of the self is an essential element of existence. However, when reduced to autonomy, its identity is insufficient, and therefore subject to a repudiation of the original human nature. This could explain the unexpected change in the liberal reality of the Western world in the 1960s. The secular and liberal identity all of a sudden began to feel insecure in its imaginary world of freedom and self-sufficiency, which resulted in its turning back to traditional aspects of the question for the original human nature.

Tolerance: With and Without a Principled Foundation

The prevailing perception of tradition in modern thought is based on the premises of the liberal and secular public sphere. In this perception, tolerance can theoretically be linked with *Realpolitik*: others are tolerated because there is no way to eliminate them. This kind of tolerance is not of a principled nature; it is a necessity arising from circumstances, and can be called "instrumental." A theoretical foundation of tolerance may also be found in the liberal premise of the nature of man and society. In this context, tolerance is conditioned either by indifference towards the beliefs and behavior of others, which are considered to be a private matter—society being organized around rights rather than around duties towards the common welfare—or by the liberal idea of the autonomous self as the judge of what is good, where tolerance is not founded either on *Realpolitik* or on indifference, but rather on the principled role of individual rights.[20]

In the light of these views of tolerance, typical of the modern world, it can be readily concluded that neither of them complies with the internal demands of the teachings of the revealed religions. Every form of tradition has a clear idea of the supreme good, of which transcendent unity is both the source and the corroboration. New elements springing from the contemporary encounter of different cultures and civilizations call for an examination of this perspective. The forgotten language of tolerance, demanded and shaped by every tradition, needs to be revived. This task will be fully realized only if the existing idea of tolerance, according to which Others should be tolerated, although their knowledge and way of life are more or less erroneous and flawed, can be transformed into a harmonious acceptance of the different human paths leading to goodness. Tradition seems to have an answer to the question of its own many different forms. It is, however, quite implacable when it comes to the project of modernity, which is for tradition but a fatal mistake. The exclusion of tradition in its entirety, as the knowledge of the sacred and the sacred knowledge, is, on the other hand, the basis of the project of modernity. Both of these views converge within humankind: they can be resolved either as failure or as success.

Modernity, defined by the "liberal solution," is called into question by those very forces it animated. The "instrumental solution" is made contestable by the increasing interrelatedness of different countries and the greater dominance of the global market. This is evident in the need to resolve the relationships between structured wholes, such as nation and state, but also within them, given the various aspects of one and the same societies and states. This issue is reflected in its entirety in the Bosnian drama. It is impossible to resolve it at the global level unless it is resolved here in this country, which is experiencing its greatest tragedy at the turn of the millennium. The issue of tolerance based on the premises of different traditions that determine the totality of both Bosnia's and the world's history is vital to the survival of both this country and the world as a whole. An appropriate language must be found to shape a principled tolerance, wherein it would not be necessary to accept the philosophical anthropology that defines the liberal self.

Lack of Knowledge of the Root

Tolerance implies a division between the tolerator and the tolerated. Individuals who tolerate remark the difference between their own identity and that of the other. Based on this, they judge the other as different or wrong. The nature and level of tolerance depend on this judgment. The Others are always different, but they are not necessarily wrong in every judgment. The nature of the difference determines the type of judgment. Modernity seems to perceive religious and traditional differences as the main cause for the lack of mutual tolerance. Life is full of such differences: Buddhism, Daoism, Confucianism, Hinduism, Islam, and Christianity are not confined within clear geographical boundaries; they are in contact in all parts of the world.

Given its totalitarian interpretation of the world and its intention to organize it, modernity sees the diversity of traditions as evidence of their limitations. This view confuses the perceptions of unity and uniformity. Modernity therefore advocates and promotes the rationalist search for the shared elements of all religions and traditions. These are primarily the projects of historicism and phenomenology, which take religions as their subjects. Although, quantitatively speaking, these projects have achieved much, it is surprising that there is still little knowledge about the common root of different religions, their doctrines, rites, and symbols, and their link with the Truth, which is contained in their inner aspects and reflected in their outward manifestations. In its study of religions, historicism reduces everything that is important from a religious viewpoint to irrelevant or insignificant historical influences. The phenomenological study of religions, in turn, neglects the unity and uniqueness of the reality of manifestation of Logos: every religion with its corresponding tradition, both historically and metahistorically, springs from one and the same link of time and eternity, earth and heaven. One can hardly deny the good intentions of these projects to strengthen and spread understanding among people. They indirectly confirm and emphasize the importance of religion in political and social reality, with which the ideologies of modernity are preoccupied.

A related issue is that of the exploitation of religion for political purposes, which gives rise to diplomatic and political simplifications and distortions of religious similarities and differences. Passionate invocation and acceptance of brotherhood and unity does not help to understand why Mary is the symbol of the Soul of the World to both Muslims and Christians, and why Jews and Muslims do not display the cross, and the like. Reasons to respect the Other cannot be deduced from any sentimentality or any rational simplification: it needs a knowledge of the Other, which goes beyond mere tolerance. We should acknowledge and underline that tolerance is better than intolerance. However, when it comes to tolerating the religion of the other, which is different from that of the one who tolerates, it cannot be enough. Directly or indirectly, this attitude incorporates a view of the nature of the religion of the other, who is being tolerated together with his religion as such, as flawed or corrupted.

Understanding the different worlds of divine forms leads to adopting other religions as genuine. Their members in this case are not merely tolerated, but recognized and acknowledged on the basis of their link with the same principle according to which the one who recognizes them judges them as different. This certainly does not mean that something that is erroneous or corrupted should be tolerated by appeal to someone's belief or faith. Unless tolerance is transformed into knowledge of the reasons for recognizing the genuineness of other religions, it poses a constant risk of quarrel, exclusivity, division, and, ultimately, the merciless denial of others. The age of modernity is increasingly burdened with its experience of such occurrences and its inability to prevent them. Its overall experience bears witness to its helplessness in the face of the demand to prevent the use of force in the service of evil. But is there any room for hope in the postmodern age? "Postmodernism, in contrast, in its more extreme versions provides no such check. On the contrary, it leads directly to nihilism which can produce an intense and burning flame but which hardly moves society towards peace and justice."[21] If this is so, then critical reflections on modernity and the will present in modernity, is the first prerequisite for change in this course from bad to worse.

The transcendent unity of religions has its "root" in the Absolute, which is at once Truth and Being. The source of every revelation and every truth is in that one and the same Absolute, in which the teachings of all religions are the same. Below that level there are correspondences, but not identity. "The different religions are like so many languages speaking of that unique Truth as it manifests itself in different worlds according to its inner archetypal possibilities, but the syntax of these languages is not the same. Yet, because each religion comes from the Truth, everything in the religion in question which is revealed by the *Logos* is sacred and must be respected and cherished while being elucidated rather than being discarded and reduced to insignificance in the name of some kind of abstract universality."[22]

Atrocities Repeated: Hiding Behind the Appearance of Knowledge

Despite the belief in the capacity of the autonomous and rational self, the Holocaust was not foreseen. Once it had become the most cruel experience of millions of Jews, an experience accompanied by screams, smoke, and ashes, but which left behind barely visible traces, the world of politics "undertook" the construction of a narrative to justify its reluctance to face the event before its horrors had become unbearable. This belated confrontation with the event was accompanied by the penitent vow: Never again! Just fifty years later, the pledge was shattered by the screams of the killed, tortured, and persecuted, and the smoke rising from their homes and mosques throughout Bosnia. The issue of guilt and responsibility emerged in a similar manner to that which reflected the immediate experience of the Holocaust. The Bosniacs felt that the crime committed against them was identical in principle to that committed against Jews. The repetition of the pattern of relationships in these two paradigmatic European cases is important as confirmation of the claim that everything that may be regarded as knowledge must be thoroughly re-examined. Faced with the insistence and clarity of the new experience, people may conclude that they did not know, but does this result in a change of their attitude towards themselves and the others?

> Now I think I understand what I couldn't understand before: how it happened that people who lived near German concentration camps didn't do anything, didn't help . . . maybe the best explanation as to why people didn't stop the massacre is given by a Polish villager from present-day Treblinka[23] who, in answer to the question whether they were afraid for the Jews, answered that if he cut his finger it hurt him, not the other person. Yes, they knew about the Jews, the convoys, the fact that they were taken into the camp and vanished.

Poles worked their land next to the barbed wire and heard awful screams. "At first it was unbearable. Then you got used to it," said yet another villager, a Pole. They were Jews, others, not-us. What had a Pole to do with the fact that Germans were killing Jews?

So we all get used to it. I understand now that nothing but "otherness" killed Jews, and it began with naming them, by reducing them to the other. Then everything became possible. Even the worst atrocities like concentration camps or the slaughtering of civilians in Croatia or Bosnia. For Serbians, as for Germans, they are all others, not-us. For Europe, the Other is the lawless "Balkans" they pretend not to understand. For the USA it's more or less a "European problem": why should they bother with the screams of thousands of people being bombed or simply dying of hunger, when the screams can hardly be heard? Let Europe do something, aren't they working the land next to the barbed wire?[24]

The events in Bosnia could not be foreseen either. All the knowledge generated by accelerated development was not sufficient for a confrontation with evil. Again, a narrative was created to justify the belated intervention that did not answer the question of the "them and us" enigma. Though it gave no answer, yet it cannot not remain very far from the knowledge of those who can never be free of responsibility for the killings and suffering. For though the killed and the persecuted may be distant and Other, they are essentially members of the same humankind mirrored in each individual. Tolerance, ideology, and tradition are today indeed notions that concern Bosnia directly, but they cannot be understood outside the "us" that is the ontological unity confirmable only in multiplicity. No view can encompass all the aspects of this question. It is, however, necessary to recognize that no approach or answer, regardless of how it may be shaped, can be a reliable guarantee against new unpredictable events. Refusing to face this increases the probability of new events in which the experiences of both the Holocaust and Bosnia would recur.

A Multitude of Narratives and the Spreading of Confusion

The very fact that the events in Bosnia gave rise to comparisons with the Holocaust is reason enough to claim that we do not know the real nature of the Bosnian tragedy.

This claim is clearly confirmed by the existence of numerous narratives regarding the causes, course, and effects of those events, in all areas of analysis and presentation—among the media, politicians, diplomats, scholars. There are essential disagreements on the very nature of the war. The narratives range from those presenting it as a civil war to those that see it as a war of aggression against a sovereign country. There are, however, no plausible efforts to examine and present forms of those narratives in a comprehensive phenomenological approach. The work of David Campbell may be an exception in this regard.[25] He took a sample of nine books dealing with the causes, course, and consequences of the Bosnian tragedy to examine the construction of different historical narratives.[26] His examination shows that the authors of the narratives produced different accounts—often quite conflicting—of one and the same event. International decision-makers were thus able to find support in an appropriate narrative for almost any view they wished. The evidence of killings, concentration camps, hundreds of thousands of refugees, and the like, however, forced them to remain indifferent to the end. The inability to bring a quick end to the events witnessed by the whole world compelled the most important international players to see Bosnia's reality in a way different from that offered by available narratives.

Some of the selected authors believed it was a civil war. They agreed with regard to its nature, but not with regard to its causes. For some of them, the blame for the civil war lay with the Bosnian Muslims, or more precisely their ethno-political oligarchy, which decided to proclaim the country's independence. Others blame it on the centuries-old hatred among ethnic groups in Bosnia, which in given circumstances erupted into a war. In both cases, the narratives resort to a construction of history and identities which, as they believe, justifies their presentation of the event. Opposed to these are the accounts of the war as an aggression by Serbia, whose leadership commanded the army of the state in dissolution. In this case, one is dealing with an international conflict for which international players undoubtedly bear part of the responsibility. However, these narratives, and the decisions based on them, offered the possibility of presenting genocide as "ethnic cleansing," and the aggression as a "civil war."

Introduction: The Arrogance of False and Inaccurate Knowledge

The Bosnia that can be said to be known is actually not Bosnia. This assertion, derived from ancient Eastern wisdom, is not mere rhetorical conjecture. It is a paradigm that simultaneously introduces and proffers responses to the paradoxes of the life and knowledge of Bosnia. The admission of ignorance is the highest form of knowledge. Discussing that which is known is mere "indulging in idle speech." Knowledge does not need knowledge, any more than light needs light. Ignorance needs knowledge, just as darkness needs light. One cannot pour anything into a full glass. The arrogance of false and inaccurate knowledge lies at the heart of the Bosnian temptation.

Let us imagine a meeting of the most renowned Bosnian thinkers and writers on a certain Saturday in the spring of 1991. Now let us also imagine one of those present addressing the others as follows: "Less than a year from now, Bosnia will be racked by a terrible war. It will be directed from centers of power outside Bosnia, yet it will be presented as a war between the components of the Bosnian unity. The most horrifying methods will be employed in this war—rapes, mass slaughter, persecution, destruction of religious sites. The world for the most part will observe it, and in various ways assist the perpetrators of these atrocities to achieve their goal of the total destruction of Bosnia."

Let us ask ourselves how the participants in the meeting might have responded. The majority of them would have most likely rejected such a possibility and proclaimed its proponent to be eccentric or foolish.

Let us now imagine those same participants gathering again in the spring of 1997. They have neither freedom of movement nor freedom of access to their property in Bosnia. The internal borders of Bosnia present a greater obstacle to their movement than any other borders in the world, from Bosnia to the remotest cities in the East and the West. The majority of them will keep silent about what was said at the 1991 meeting. The predictions of the war have been confirmed by actual events in the cruelest way imaginable. However, the question of changes in the consciousness of those participants is still far from being answered even today. Events never occur without a cause. The interdependence of cause and effect manifests itself over time, and thus can be observed.

It must be acknowledged that in 1991 the participants in the events in Bosnia did not have the ability to identify the way in which historical events repeat themselves according to seeming laws, and thus to foresee the war. But faced with the Bosnian conundrum, none of them had the courage and integrity to say that he did not know what was awaiting Bosnia. If, after the experience of a war that they had not foreseen, those same participants were able to admit that they do not know what lies ahead for Bosnia now, this would be a significant indication that there was a chance for true knowledge to burgeon in such a void. Only with this admission would it be possible to expect the course of events to shift from eating the fruit from the tree of knowledge, which was transformed into eating the bitter leftover roots of that tree, to the possible novel discovery of what has been lost in Bosnia's identity. This generation had neither sufficient knowledge nor sufficient skills to defend Bosnia. Though one can now claim that Bosnia has not been defeated, one cannot say that it has been defended. Bosnia remains distant from us even today, although we frenetically pursue her, growing increasingly distant from her within our own selves.

In the Aftermath of the War

The question of Bosnia's future cannot be the same now as it was to the participants in the spring of 1991, for it is now being asked in the aftermath of the war. What can this question offer us today? Are the seekers after knowledge, those posing the question, and the issue at stake, in a different relationship from before? This relationship between learners and learned is knowledge. Is a different knowledge possible from the knowledge that these participants had prior to the war against Bosnia?

This leads us to the conundrum of knowledge as the attitude of an individual or of a group of people toward the objective of discovery. Both of these possibilities require reexamination, given the experience of the war. Only after a painstaking and thorough reexamination of knowledge as the attitude of the individuals toward themselves will it be possible to inspire such changes as will perhaps, in a slow and lengthy process, result in what we call "knowledge of a group," "a nation" or a "community of nations."[1] And this very collective knowledge, where the cry of an individual seemed to be a "call to the deaf," was part of all that can be summed up in the phrase "the destruction of Bosnia."

It is worth pointing out some of the most important elements of the collective ignorance about Bosnia. The misreading and misuse of history had a substantial influence on those who made decisions concerning Bosnia. It is therefore of great importance to examine the essential aspects of the way history was misread in order to create the illusion that political decisions were well-founded.

First, every national history in this part of Europe was produced within the framework of a political agenda for the creation of a nation-state. These histories are therefore invariably focused on promoting the view that there is a distinction between the collective "I" and "they." At the heart of this distinction lies the principle that there is no true friend without a true enemy, and that as long as we do not hate what we are not, we cannot love what we are. This model requires all hatreds to seek allies within the broadest global context. Hatred could thus contribute to the establishment of "borders of civilizations," as a prerequisite for global predominance, in the context of this separation between "us" and "them," by those who are convinced that their speed and power in pursuit of the outside world, which is escaping from them, legitimizes their right to subordinate all other people in the race.

Second, the identity of Bosnia is primarily determined by traditional wisdom while the contemporary understanding of civilization is almost completely divorced from wisdom. In consequence, political analyses and decisions fail to recognize and support what is crucial to the preservation of the Bosnian paradigm. This is part of the global state of afffairs that is reflected in present-day Bosnia just as in any other part of the world.

The Mystery of "Wrong"[2]

It is an uncontestable historical fact that conflicts between Muslims, Catholics, and Eastern Orthodox Christians have never been instigated from within Bosnia itself. This assertion is not meant to imply that Bosnian history has been flawlessly harmonious and exemplary. Nowhere in the world has such a history. But the paradigm that had survived in Bosnia for a period of over five centuries bears witness to the fundamental paragon of humanity from time immemorial. To be in the world means to partake of multiplicity, which cannot deny its ontological unity. The paths and ways of life may differ, but they all face the judgment of Truth in the same manner. For a period of over five centuries, both churches and mosques existed side by side, each on the same firm footing, in the towns and villages of Bosnia. The exclusivity of the belief that the church comprised within itself the entire and proper sacred doctrine, and that this doctrine should not mingle with any other, did not imply the denial of the rights of others to hold the same belief about their mosque, or synagogue, or a different church. We may not be able clearly to demonstrate today in rational discourse how this feeling was shaped through the centuries, but, in the long-lasting sense of "wrong," we can find a significantly more profound source of understanding the sacredness of different paths.

Yet the history of Bosnia is viewed at the level of rational discourse and within the framework of European plans to eliminate the Turkish presence in Europe. It was on this basis that Christian movements in the regions of Europe that had once been part of Turkey were supported for so long. Images of the suffering and bravery of Christian warriors in battles against Turkey were promoted, in which the simple image of this struggle equated Turkey with all non-Christian religions. Thus was constructed the myth of Serbian bravery and the Muslim threat. It is possible to recognize in many of the views expressed by European powers since 1991 the continuation of those old historical models in the empathy for the Serbs, who fought as an ally in the wars against Germany, and the deliberately promoted image of Serbian invincibility.[3] Participants in the Bosnian drama whose task was to be present in Bosnia on behalf of the world order admit that in their political action or inaction they relied on, or used as justification, suitable interpretations of history.[4] This can be stated with certainty about the books by Robert D. Kaplan—*Balkan Ghosts: A Journey through History*[5]—Rebecca West—*Black Lamb and Grey Falcon*[6]—and Fitzroy Maclean—*Eastern Approaches*.[7] It is possible to provide an extensive bibliography of books of different intellectual levels that underpinned the views of the "creators of modern politics."[8] The relatively limited military aid that arrived after the horrifying slaughter and destruction completely shattered the myth that from the beginning of the war had constituted an obstacle to the more resolute protection of Bosnia and its people and opposition to the criminal use of force. The shattering of this myth showed to what degree distorted readings of history were used in modern politics.

The resort to force to achieve long since established political objectives, and everything that followed the use of force, clearly demonstrated that modern politics lacked a fundamental understanding of the way in which humankind lives. Different myths are present in the consciousness of the majority, whose attitude toward the world can be symbolically illustrated by a full glass into which nothing can be poured. Anything that is added into the glass is a spillover that invariably entails undesired consequences.

The Model of Amnesty of Crime

Fervent attempts have been made to assimilate the war against Bosnia to new theories, models, or paradigms of the international state of affairs in the period after the bipolar division of the world was ended. There are attempts to portray this war as a "clash of civilizations," whereby the principal instigators of and participants in the war are in various ways exonerated from their guilt. In such views, future conflicts in the world will neither be conflicts of different ideologies, nor of different social classes or otherwise defined economic groups. They will, instead, be conflicts between peoples who belong to different cultures. Tribal and ethnic conflicts will arise within individual civilizations, but the fundamental threat will result from clashes of civilizations themselves. The main proponent of the theory of the "clash of civilizations," Samuel P. Huntington, believes that this is the nature of the "bloody conflict in Bosnia" as well. This sets the "destruction of Bosnia" in the context of the theory that the world is composed of "the West" and "the rest." Since Bosnia is in Europe, the logical conclusion of this theory is that it is composed of "non-European" elements.

The different communities of Bosnia, seen in the light of religious differences as the major determinants of one's affiliation to a particular culture or civilization, are Catholic, Eastern Orthodox Christian, and Muslim. In Huntington's theory, these three distinct elements of Bosnian unity are defined as: Catholic—part of "the West," Orthodox Christian—"Russian Orthodoxy;" and Muslim—"Islamic." Three civilizations or three religious transnationalisms thus confront one another in Bosnia, finding support for their activities in this part of Europe through the three religious communities. Since this definition does not rule out the second element as non-European, the Muslim element in Bosnia remains as "non-European," as "the rest" in relation to Europe. And it is this aspect that is of crucial significance to an understanding of the possible future both of Bosnia and Europe, and of the world as a whole.

Rationalism vs. Wisdom

"Non-European" elements in Europe are nowadays mainly reduced to the presence of Muslims. The contestable nature of such feelings and opinions is quite obvious. Christianity and Judaism are no less non-European in their fundamental attributes than Islam. However, the predominant perception of the deep-rooted division of the world into the West and the Orient, whereby the West is associated with Christian and the Orient with Islamic elements, when reduced to political conflicts, generates a permanent source for a pattern that is, historically speaking, easily transformed into genocide against the weaker.[9]

This example, which illustrates the inability of the modern age to judge two sacred traditions by the same standards, can be used to indicate the sources of the theory of the clash of civilizations. The contemporary understanding of civilization does not grasp the truth that there is but one traditional wisdom, notwithstanding its capacity to adopt an infinite multitude of forms and its presence everywhere on Earth and in every era. Wisdom is the "vertical" relationship of humans with their ontological principle, or the transcendental cause and effect of everything. This relationship can be maintained through an infinite multitude of forms, where one form does not exclude the other, and each one of those forms facilitates the attainment of wisdom. On this basis, it is essential to distinguish political projects from sacral traditions. When they are equated with one another, every sacral tradition is pushed into the most abject humiliation and, at best, abandoned to a political and powerless will subjugated to sentimentality and morality.

The presence of different cultural poles and civilizations is the reality of the world. Yet this fact cannot in any way result in a negation of the ontological unity, to ignore or neglect which means to lose the authentic poles of every culture, obscure the center of human individuality, and allow the world be "led" into conflicts based on simplistic ideological projects. The only response to this is the restoration of the memory and knowledge of traditional wisdom whose treasury is the entire world and the entirety of history. Only an ignorant Christian could think it strange that he can find the most glorious confirmations of his religion in the sacred prophecies and heritage of Muslims, and vice versa. Only an ignorant Hindu or Buddhist will marvel at the fact that Islam and Christianity in essence offer redemption, the blessed example of the perfect man, holy name, in an almost identical way. However, their surprise at facing the same elements behind utterly different statements will only be a reflection of the superficiality of their comprehension of their own traditions once they hear the prayers of American Indians.

Does the absolutization of the fact that it is possible to portray the current state of the world in terms of the paradigm of seven contemporary civilizations—where this division fails to be transcended by the universality of wisdom—imply the continued tenacity of the ideological perception of the world?

Ideological Reading of Holy Prophecies

To observe the world from any individual or collective perspective means to select a model, paradigm, theory, or matrix. This is a prerequisite for understanding what is happening in the world that is being observed. It should, however, be noted that each of those approaches functions only within rational limits. Yet the phenomena around us that are interpreted through these models are not manifest only in rational categories. The rigidity and unalterability of these models also acts as an obstacle to humans altering their own world and adjusting to a "recovery" from the conditions they have experienced, even though they were not able to understand them in advance or to foresee them. Insistence on these rational models is very often a destructive force in the context of the relationship toward oneself. Without these rational means, however, it is not possible to understand changes in the world. Although these means serve as a yardstick of reality, they are in and of themselves invariably contingent and susceptible to change:

> . . . philosophy, in the sense in which we understand the term (which is also its current meaning) primarily consists of logic; this definition of Guénon's puts philosophic thought in its right place and clearly distinguishes it from "intellectual intuition," which is the direct apprehension of truth. It is important, however, to establish yet another distinction on the rational plane itself. Logic can neither operate as part of an intellection, or else, on the contrary, put itself at the service of an error; moreover unintelligence can diminish or even nullify logic, so that philosophy can in fact become the vehicle of almost anything: it can be an Aristotelianism carrying ontological insights, just as it can degenerate into an "existentialism" in which logic has become a mere shadow of itself, a blind and unreal operation. Indeed, what can be said of a "metaphysic" that idiotically posits man at the centre of the Real, like a sack of coal, and which operates with such blatantly subjective and conjectural concepts as "worry" and "anguish?"[10]

The abundance of distorted readings of sacred prophecies will illustrate this as well. Although the advocates of different ideologies will invoke the fundamental determinants of civilizational stimuli, they will never accept that prophecies contain those sources of wisdom that never allow them to be confined within any exclusively rational model. In creating the conditions that obscure or impede the expression of the principle of unity in diversity, distorted readings of sacred prophecies are accompanied by a falsification of history, which is assigned the role of justifying political decisions. Scientific progress would not be possible without the constant replacement of one paradigm that has become powerless to explain new or newly discovered facts with another paradigm that takes those facts into consideration in a more comprehensive manner. In order for a certain paradigm to be accepted as new, it is sufficient for it to have certain advantages over the paradigm with which it is competing. It should not and cannot explain all the facts it encounters.

This universal and widely accepted truth also includes the important acknowledgement that any understanding we have of the conditions in the world around us is incomplete if it is linked only to the "measurable" world or the world of exclusively rational categories. Conflicts that produce destruction similar to that in Bosnia, or to what we call the Holocaust, show that those horrible events cannot be avoided if we believe only in rational models.[11]

It should be acknowledged that theories that take into consideration the interrelatedness of cause and effect are unavoidable for political decisions that we can accept as valid from the viewpoint of the times we live in. However, given the examples that are constantly being tested, the question as to whether such an understanding of the world can find a way to avoid the "clash of civilizations" becomes important. Is the path that is, as it were, based solely on the evolutionary idea inevitably paved by conflicts and human suffering?

Knowing and Being

The participants in the meeting mentioned earlier in this essay did not know how to recognize possible events in their environment, way of thinking, or social trends. Their inability to do so was the result of lack of wisdom, which may be defined as their conviction that they knew. The events of the war proved that far from being "full" of knowledge, to the point at which nothing could be added, they had been full of ignorance. Everything they had been incapable of conceiving was demonstrated to them to see, hear, and feel. Those events certainly form part of their experience today, but it cannot be said with equal certainty that it also forms part of their knowledge, to be transformed into wisdom. The profane life is, as wise men would say, but an illusion stemming from ignorance. Nothing of this kind in fact exists. Every phenomenon is in a relationship with the higher world, that realm of unshaped potentiality or archetypes. The fact that phenomena can be perceived independent of their transcendent principles does not necessarily imply that they are distinct from and independent of that relationship with the principle.

What has been experienced in Bosnia can manifest itself in at least two dimensions. The first dimension is the terrible aftermath of the suffering, which leaves havoc behind it without any significant alteration in the knowledge of those who have witnessed it. And the second is that in the wake of the suffering, the illusion that "the glass is full" is seen for what it is, and wisdom is attained by acknowledging the lack of knowledge of, above all, what manifests itself as an infinite multitude of different facts and phenomena. Nothing that we can do can undo what happened; it can, however, become knowledge of the kind that can be used to shape future events.

Can the human path founded on an understanding of the world whose core is the evolutionary concept and on an absolute predominance of materialist prosperity liberate humans from the kind of suffering that Bosnia has experienced recently? The very fact of asking this question—a question which, it is clear to see, most people do not understand—brings into salience the limitations of the contemporary conception of knowledge, where civilization loses its link with the principles of a higher order. This relationship can be recollected only if we clearly identify the prevalent and pernicious dispersion of the ontological unity. To recollect means to gather what has been dispersed—and this is the fundamental and sole meaning of traditional wisdom. Its framework can be any authentic religious tradition.

However, the contemporary understanding of religious traditions has separated them from their original purpose, which is to enable humans to distinguish the real from the unreal, to embrace the real and to redeem themselves in the absolute identicalness of being and knowledge through authentic spiritual conduct in every aspect of their life. Simplified paradigms or maps are necessary for human thought and action; and such models make use of rational conduct. Without them, thought and action would resemble the oscillation of a particle in the wind. However, the absolutization of rational models poses a danger as well, since the flaws of the models—without which they are not possible—have consequences of vast proportions. All such models include prejudices, peculiarities, and assumptions that determine our perception of reality and its facts, as well as our judgment of their mutual relationships.

Conflicting Predictions

The purpose of rational models is to arrange and generalize the knowledge of reality; to explain the causal relationships between phenomena; to predict future developments; to distinguish the relevant from the irrelevant; and to determine the ways and means of achieving the set objectives.

With such models of assessing the state of the world as a starting point, it is possible today to identify completely contrary, yet equally probable, predictions of the world's future. According to Francis Fukuyama, the end of the bipolar division of the world marks the beginning of the era he calls the "end of history," or the disappearance of all the causes of large-scale conflicts. This heralds the victory of liberal democracy as the foundation of ruling systems that will transform global antagonisms into global harmony. This is, in fact, the end point of humankind's ideological development, and the universalization of Western liberal democracy as the ultimate form of human government.

A second model sees the world's reality as determined by a multipolar division into several civilizations; a division which nevertheless, in Samuel P. Huntington's view, comes down to "the West" and "the rest"—"the rest" encompassing the diversity of non-Western civilizations. These civilizations will act antagonistically, and antagonisms can develop into global conflicts. This model focuses on Islam as the most significant nucleus around which the powers confronting the West will assemble.

A third model predicts the possibility of various conflicts not only between states but also within them. The world order will disintegrate in a horrible war of everyone against everyone; in this view, the current more than one hundred and eighty nation-states cannot represent the building blocks of a stable world order, for they are not internally homogeneous in a manner that would provide for durable and stable relationships between the actors.

All these models include in different ways the view that Western values are essentially irreconcilable with those of the non-Western world. This can be considered as the fundamental and defining premise that is built into each of the existing models. It is a prejudice in its nature and should be treated as the most important potential error. On this rests the sustainability or failure of all the models observed. The Bosnian experience is of crucial significance, not as proof of the validity of, let us say, Huntington's model. On the contrary—it is proof of its untenability. If the sources and postulates of traditional wisdom are eliminated from the political stage, religious systems are transformed into politics governed only by a different language. In this context, clerical habits become the most effective way of concealing the satanic presence in the promotion of the argument that differences among people find their most complete expression in hatred and animosity.

The Quest for the Center

"Global unification," "European unification," and the "unification of Bosnia" seem to be the most common patterns of contemporary considerations of the state of the world. They appear so familiar that suggesting they should be thoroughly reexamined strikes most people as surprising and unnecessary. However, in order to understand the Bosnian question one must first focus on a radical examination of these syntagmas. Only what has been recognized as dispersed can be united. The very term unification implies the potential to restore authentically to unity that which is in multiplicity. Unification, thus, invariably includes two poles—the center, with which union or unification is to take place, and the multiple periphery, which is being united with the center. Thus, unification is not possible without bringing the center of each dispersed individual entity into a relationship with the center around which unification is carried out or with which all individual entities are identified. The stimuli for unification can stem either from the force of attraction of the center or from the imposition of such forces on the individual entities as will bring them into a relationship with the center. At the level of conscious existence, individual entities can establish or restore their lost awareness of their relationships with the center, and recognize themselves in it as in the higher principle, and thus be in a unique relationship with it. However, when a center and peripheral phenomena are recognized in any such activities, unification always manifests itself as a strengthening of those two poles—the center and the periphery. If unification is enforced by external forces, the resistance of individual entities grows stronger. If it is the product of internal stimuli, then the transformation of individual entities and their awareness of their individuality in relation to the center and of the necessity to sacrifice it for the link with the center also increase.

When it comes to the unification of the world, the question arises as to what the center could be around which the current components of the global mosaic would unite. It should be noted here that every community of people, large or small, every religious community, large or small, every civilization, by the very fact of its existence confirms, in different ways and with different intensity, its connection with some external pole. Unification would imply that those centers must be connected willy-nilly with a certain external pole. The greater the external pressure, the greater the resistance at the centers. External pressure will produce new energy at the center, while the source of pressure will necessarily lose its power in the process. Clearly, the question of unification of the world will remain puzzling and distant as long as it is linked in advance with any exclusive view of the world, entailing the defeat of and mastery over other views. It is sufficient to consider any contemporary world view to see that they are antagonistic in their external forms. "Liberal democracy" is today perceived by most as the best system of government, but there is also a large number of those who will never be able to accept this belief. The more they are pressured to accept it, the greater their resistance will be, and, seen over time, their strength as well. For there is no compulsion in belief!

The unification of Europe is for the most part perceived today as based on the following three elements: (1) the unity of the geopolitical area, (2) Christian history, and (3) the power and potential of liberal democracy. These postulates of European unity exclude numerous elements of the European totality, assigning to them the position of the Other and rendering them incapable of finding their place in the region through the relationship with its supposed center.

These remarks can be summed up by examining the source of social stability. Bosnian society is indubitably fractured today, and looking for ways to unify it is part of any rational or intuitive focus on the future. To modern thinking on social stability, and the same applies to the liberal-republican perspective, its source is the autonomous and enlightened self of the individual who is a free moral judge. This modern idea of individual and society is, however, denied by many experiences of the twentieth century. It is in Europe that the individual and collective identity has very often degraded from the autonomous self, which included the will for power, towards ethnic, racial, and territorial givens, which resulted in the violent denial and destruction of the Other. The necessary alterations to the perception of identity, which would include a shift of focus from the autonomous self to the transcendent source of moral authority, calls for a riddance of the prevalent perceptions of religious plurality, perceptions that spring from the imposed modern idea, which is currently going through an indisputable crisis.

No Answer to the Question of Harmony and Opposition

What could bring about the unification of Bosnia? The answer to this question presupposes a recognition of the possible centers of individual Bosnian elements and the center with which those elements could connect. After losing its independence as a state towards the end of the fifteenth century, Bosnia and Herzegovina survived as part of a series of complex state communities—the Ottoman and Austro-Hungarian Empires, the Kingdom of Serbs, Croats and Slovenes, the Kingdom of Yugoslavia, and socialist Yugoslavia. The religious and ethnic differences of Bosniacs, Croats, and Serbs were built into Bosnia's unity in a complex manner. The Croat and Serb communities are part of larger religious communities, and the existing borders of Bosnia and Herzegovina do not form a barrier to their range or their internal links. The Bosniacs do not have any significant connections outside Bosnia and Herzegovina. All three of these communities seek to define, develop, and strengthen their own unity, which results in different views of history and of the future. Given the way these communities intermingle and intertwine, the unifying tendencies of all three are mutually opposed. The greater the insistence in connecting the center and the periphery of each of these communities, the greater the antagonism in relation to the other two. The disintegration of Yugoslavia was caused by the very postulate that "all Serbs should live in one state", which provided a complete definition of both poles of Serb unification. The strengthening of their effect was impossible without a response by both of those poles within all the other communities. Hence, the relationships between the pole of Serb unification, the pole of Croat unification and the pole of Bosniac unification were strained to the limit.

The war had the effect of reinforcing this dual division within the entire Bosnian population. As a result, a separation into several complex elements is currently evident, where the internal antagonisms between the center and the periphery are at the same time opposed to the centers and peripheries of the other two communities.

As for Bosnian Serbs, they still focus on the alluring aspirations of a pan-Serb center, aspirations that are directly opposed to the unification of Bosnia. The aspiration to pan-Serb unification, therefore, has two levels. The first level is that of unification of Serbs around a "second-order" center in Bosnia, intended finally to become identical with the pan-Serb center. Such aspirations can be recognized in various forms within Serb national politics as a whole as well as within its individual elements. A similar development is visible among Croats. When viewed as a BiH-wide project, the unification of Bosniacs is opposed to the aspirations of both Serbs and Croats. This was clearly confirmed by the course of the war, in which the internal aspirations among Bosnian Croats and Bosnian Serbs were effectively harnessed and governed from the centers of neighboring states.

The Dayton Peace Accord postulate that the unification of Bosnia and Herzegovina can be ensured by recognizing the consequences of centrifugal effect within Bosnia and Herzegovina in the form and content of oligarchic systems has proven to be an illusion, since the center that would gradually establish and reinforce the links between the communities has neither been recognized nor, in consequence, strengthened.

The Reasons for Bosnia

Although Bosnia was shaken to its foundations by the destructive activities directed against it, the situation after the war and the Dayton Peace Accord show that the same centrifugal aspirations have been preserved. But so have the reasons for and necessity of the survival of Bosnia and Herzegovina. All attempts to construct acceptable models to explain events in Bosnia and Herzegovina, which would also be able to explain upcoming developments, remain for the most part so ineffective that numerous exceptions make them hardly viable. Those models do not take into consideration in sufficient measure all the relationships of Bosnia as a whole with the surrounding geopolitical factors—primarily with Serbia and Croatia—or the consequences of the differences resulting from the problem of the unification of Europe and the world.

On the other hand, the naiveté of the assumption that the main partic-ipants in the war can also become the principal builders of peace is over-looked. The institutions of authority, in which elements of the elite, organizers, and executors of genocide participate, directly or indirectly, can-not develop into a center that would be powerful enough to attract the scat-tered fragments of Bosnia. This fact is increasingly reflected in the need simply to forget, instead of understanding, both the causes and the effects of the war, since the current peace builders are complicit in causes and effects alike. Hence, it is quite understandable that a host of "courtier" intellectuals is gathering again around those seemingly united participants in centrifugal activities in Bosnia, intellectuals who know everything, and can therefore spend days analyzing and interpreting everything that has been and will be. Their idea of debate is merely to attach labels to phenomena whose internal and external centers they fail to recognize and therefore do not bring into re-lationship with one another. The real center, around which unification would be feasible, thus remains almost completely unknown, but no one ac-knowledges this, which is the first prerequisite for eliminating that lack of knowledge. It seems to be taboo.

This is why all the numerous theories, models, and syntagmas sound so utterly unconvincing in the face of Bosnia's reality, which is, rather, reflected in the deep fears and refusal of people to face what is happening here today. Thus, an academic analyst, explaining the situation in Bosnia, will categori-cally state that the war against Bosnia cannot be explained unless one accepts that it was essentially irredentist, meaning that it was launched with the aim of establishing new borders that would include one entire nation. This was in-deed the aim asserted by the *Memorandum of the Serbian Academy of Arts and Sciences*, which took into account the history of such postulates from the time of *Načertanije* and even earlier. However, this account of the anti-Bosnian war should be challenged by asking what is the cause of the irredentism. If the an-swer is—nationalism as a political ideology—then the next step should be to ask what are these persistent reasons for nationalism. The answer that it is the struggle for power should be met with yet another question: why is that? And finally, only when faced with the answer that it is a question of "human na-ture" is it possible to pause and ask oneself: If human nature, which is ulti-mately one and the same, is also at the basis of a war such as this, would it then be possible to recognize within it an essence that would be both the cen-ter and the periphery at the same time?[12]

If the answer is positive, then it is for this very essence that one should seek a language that would overcome the existing antagonisms.

Politics and Prejudices

The situation in post-Dayton Bosnia allows for a reexamination of the most important political decisions with respect to their motives and foundations. In the overall attitude of the international community towards the war against Bosnia, two significant prejudices can be identified, recognizable in every decision, as well as in the Dayton Peace Accord as a whole. The first springs from claims and beliefs about Serbian invincibility on the battlefield, and the second from the view that the relationships between ethnic and religious communities are essentially determined by hatred and conflicts. Both of these assumptions testify to the claim that "knowledge" is an obstacle to recognizing the real aspects of phenomena.

After three years of suffering for almost the entire Bosnian population, while the world was an "irresponsible witness" to slaughter, incarceration in concentration camps, rape, destruction, justifying its irresponsibility by citing the dangers of becoming embroiled in a conflict with the Serbs, the whole myth of invincibility was shattered within just a couple of days by air strikes. Almost nothing remained of this myth, and the very same West that had been so terror struck by Serb invincibility dramatically had to prevent a total collapse of the entire structure that had been built on the foundation of that myth and horrible atrocities. The many claims that enormous military force would be needed to halt the war against Bosnia, and that it might become a quicksand from which they would be unable to extricate themselves, proved once again that politics and prejudices are inseparable. However, the demise of this myth also showed that in their mutual antagonism and insincerity, European countries had merely exploited this myth when balancing the prosperity of their own countries against any moral responsibility.

The second claim, about hatred and the unsustainability of common living, upon which entire concepts of the destruction of Bosnia—as well as most Western decisions on action or inaction—were based, has survived in the acceptance of the consequences of the war without identifying the culprits. The entire Dayton Peace Accord subscribes to this prejudice, though it attempts to conceal it through a series of statements. The right to return is indeed provided for in the Accord, yet the attitude of the signatories and guarantors of the Accord towards that issue shows that the partition of Bosnia into ethnic entities has been largely accepted.

The borders between the war-constructed "Bosnian entities" are now more solid and impassable than any other borders in Europe. The forces that seek to turn those borders into their own oligarchic fortresses are still present on both sides, without being held accountable. Forces aspiring to alter the resulting myth of the rigidity of these borders do not exist on the political stage. And it is this that again points to the need to reexamine the adequacy of "knowledge" as an important obstacle to the elimination of Bosnia's political sclerosis. This can primarily be done through a complex reexamination of the multitude of centers and peripheral dispersions acting in and around Bosnia today, as well as through an assessment of their possible development. And once again, through a shift from the idea that it is impossible to change the current situation on the basis of its return to individual consciousness, which is totally subjugated to the illusion of "irredentism," "nationalism," and "power," its eventual outcome being a weak and helpless individual.

Human Perfection Between the Center and the Periphery

The idea that the individual self or the human inner being may be the center around which people should unite may to many seem utterly incomprehensible and naïve under current circumstances.[13] However, everything within the scope of our analytical thinking bears witness to the powerlessness of the knowledge of this very majority in the face of the constant possibility and actual realization of slaughter, concentration camps, rape, destruction. In connection with this, we should recollect not only the social psychology of George Herbert Mead, but also Huston Smith's notion of the self as established by an internalized morality, as well as the evidence of structural comparisons between the development of individual identities and the changeable natures of collective inclusion and solidarity.[14] "However," notes Adam B. Seligman, "when that form of solidarity predicated on the shared strong evaluations of the individual can no longer maintain its sense of familiarity (due to purely structural factors, i.e., increased system differentiation and role segmentation), the individual as basis of personal identity may disappear. In this disappearance the preconditions for trust do themselves disappear as well. And as people return more and more to group-based identities (often of an ascribed or primordial nature), we may well ask if, in some cases—and in what is almost a case of historical reversal—risk is not giving way to danger and the problems which were once encompassed by a calculus of trust and mistrust are not redefined by one of confidence or lack thereof?"[15]

The transcendental unity of religions is an unpopular syntagma among both contemporary politicians and religious leaders. In simplified perceptions, this syntagma appears as an unreasonable denial of religious differences. Individuals as creatures of God created between the fairest stature and the lowest of the low, are thus reduced to closed circles of forms and interpretations, which deprives them of their principal position in the earthly world. If God is one, then humans are in essence one as well, with the potential of realizing themselves in their relationship with the Most Supreme Being. This potential cannot depend solely on one form or one history. Those who recognize the human capacity to distinguish the real from the unreal and embrace the real cannot fail to find the perfect example of following and achieving human perfection. However, what is missing today is a systematic dialogue between those who bear witness to the path towards one and the same in different traditions. Although Bosnia in its entirety represents a unity in diversity, it remains inexplicable why throughout its history there has been no systematic research of this unity in diversity and the testimony of one and the same knowledge in different historical events. This knowledge has survived as an aspect of the sense of the sacred and of wrong, but has not reasserted itself against the prevalent rational models and the profane knowledge of everything.

In that very inability of religious affiliation to be more than mere morality and sentimentality lies its denial. And the failure of people of different sacred traditions to establish a firmer alliance in Bosnia located within the very cores of their sacred traditions speaks not against those cores, but against those who do not fathom them in their full unity.

No earthly plurality can be preserved in its entirety without a constant restoration of the relationship with its center. If that center is a false or unreal image, then the dispersion outside it will manifest itself in any attempt to connect with the center as a betrayal of the primal purpose of its creation. Each relationship between the center and the periphery will thus inevitably generate evil energy.

Recollection and Return

The Bosnian experience is evidence that the arrogance of the prevalent knowledge in the contemporary world is a constant source of suffering. That knowledge is not what it pretends to be is continually demonstrated by the suffering that humans, in their deception, fail to avoid. This failure ensures that wisdom begins with the acknowledgement of ignorance. And this acknowledgement returns the individual to his/her true self as the most important mystery of all events.[16] This is the recollection or return of the scattered elements to their center. And the human core is one and the same, regardless of the religious paths and forms through which scattered and forgotten humans aspire to reestablish themselves within it.

The inability of ruling politics to develop an awareness of the lowest common denominator of the common links with the center does not stem from any desire for it, rational or not. It is, rather, a logical consequence of the human condition in which there is no relationship with the center. It is a manifestation of the arrogance of the kind of knowledge that does not contain a single drop of wisdom.

The inability of churches and priests to establish a dialogue and to proclaim, loudly and resolutely, the ontological unity of humanity and the inviolability of human sacredness bears witness to a most malignant betrayal of the very sacred pledges on which these organizations and their members rely. All that the churches emphasize, with appeal to sacred prophecies, is betrayed in reality, where human life and honor are worth less than the most worthless nameless phenomena scattered in the world.

The treasury of traditional wisdom, encompassed by the totality of the heavens and the Earth and testified to by the lives of holy men in all parts of the world not only remains the concealed, but also the only possible source of overcoming antagonisms and human desolation and disorientation.

Given that the nearest projection of human interiority is what forms the outer world, which manifests itself in direct contact through specificity, the boundaries become both clarity and mystery. If one accepts the postulate that there is no world beyond its most distant material boundaries, this is reflected in a closing off of human interiority also; and this is related to the premise that it comes to an end at some boundary in the depths or the heights. Society and the world then become the final determinants and arbiters of human destiny, which means that the outcome of human will lies only in its achievements in society and the world.

If it is postulated that all the boundaries of the material world are evidence of only one level of being, it necessarily follows that the world is open to higher levels. This openness cannot be limited or confined, but leads to the Absolute. In consequence, every human individual is wholly open to perfection. In principle, all the different languages, meanings and symbols—regardless of whether they have taken shape within the revealed religions or in metaphysically-based teachings—can be straitjacketed into one level of being, or open to the Absolute. To be Muslim, Christian or Jew, Daoist, Buddhist or Hindu, means to have the potential for openness to or sealing off from the absolute. Openness means that the eternal word comprises every language in unicity as the first confirmation of the Ineffable, and that belonging to one of the sacred teachings or ways offers the individual or community a complete orientation towards the absolute, without excluding the same potential for every other heir to and member of other traditions. In this case, each individual self in these other traditions simply discovers its "lost treasure." Translation from one meaning or symbol into another reinforces affiliation and liberates from the fear that is rooted in ignorance. The total experience of different traditions is the treasury of all people and all communities, provided that their mutual recognition derives from and leads to Perfection. Does not the book *A Treasury of Traditional Wisdom* demonstrate this perfectly clearly?[17]

Paradigm

The Human Enterprise

The various external influences that have operated on Bosnia have, more often than not, been innately hostile: interpretations of Bosnian history have tended to be slanted or distorted by the constructions that these forces have placed on Bosnia's history for their own purposes. Nevertheless, in its struggle for survival, Bosnia has endured: its present state reflects the numerous distortions produced by external and internal forces and by subsequent internal weakness. This constitutes a "paradigm," standing as a challenge before the world and, most importantly, before the Bosnian people. This challenge demands a new perception. Careful reappraisal and analysis is a prerequisite for the revival of Bosnia's capacity to adapt and compete, thus enabling it to overcome both external and internal forces of destruction.

The history of Bosnia, like any other history, can be viewed on the one hand through the prism of the ideals that lie at the basis of its essential identity, and on the other, through the betrayals of those ideals. Where those ideals are present and manifest, the forces that converted them into reality, and where they are betrayed, the powers that have opposed them should be identified.

The most salient components of the Bosnian identity are Catholicism, Eastern Orthodox Christianity, Islam, and Judaism. The essential similarities of these four sacred traditions transcend their differences. It is beyond dispute that their essence, the aspiration to realize humanity's search for perfection, is one and the same. Historically, all four traditions trace back to a common ancestor, the prophet Abraham. The Arabs, including in the direct line of descent the Prophet Muhammad, are his posterity through his eldest son, Ishmael or Ismail while the Jews, or the Children of Israel, are his descendants through his younger son, Isaac. To that younger line—as Islamic tradition also acknowledges—belong the Virgin Mary and her son Jesus, the Messiah, who are at the heart of Christian teachings on the Redeemer.

More crucial, though, than these corporeal bloodlines is the belief, present in all four traditions, that the "intellect," or the Holy Spirit, enables every human to achieve perfection and redemption: to rise from the level of individual reason to the supra-individual. Bearing witness to this potential are the exemplars of God's messengers, whose lives in their entirety are offered to humanity as tradition. Their lives, like their sayings, have become the very word of Truth, expressed in diverse forms and languages. This diversity, however, does not negate the unity manifested in each of the traditions and each of their messages.[1]

The truth is thus pursued by various paths in this finite world:[2] the different paths are named after those who have revealed the Truth in human language. Human understandings and interpretations stand in contrast to the original revelation and its existence through time. The Truth is infinite and eternal, but in the finite and temporal world it is accessible only through its manifestations in multiplicity. These incorporate the different interpretations which, being the consequence of individuality, represent the inherent right to simultaneous and individual interpretation. A responsible attitude towards the Truth demands acceptance of the contingency of every interpretation—which means of the legitimacy of differences in interpretation. The messengers of the highest order, who bring news of the Truth itself—messengers such as Abraham, Moses, David, Solomon, Jesus, and Muhammad—are followed by varied forms of acceptance and interpretation of their message, and by the development of corresponding social relations, establishments, and institutions.

The revelation of the Truth is conveyed in different languages, eras, and conditions. Its interpretations then have to meet various demands, in which awareness of the Truth as unshakable and unchangeable is frequently diminished. We note a widespread tendency to reduce the diversity of paths and ways of life into uniformity, subjugated to those individuals or groups claiming to be closest to the Truth itself. It is on this basis that various rejections of the original tradition arise. They manifest themselves in the separation of the ruler from God's rule, treating the ruler as parallel to or equivalent to God, and finally promoting him to a higher level than God, until God is reduced to god, one among many phenomena.

The human search for perfection, however, resists this relativization of principle, noting its distance from acceptance of the Truth as perfection. Desire for perfection leads back to the original messages, and to acceptance of the principle that each individual can understand them on the basis of innate faculties. At the same time, this means accepting that, since all interpretations are relative and conditional, none can be imposed. It is logical to conclude that God Himself created a path and a way of life for every individual and every people.[3] Upholding this as a principle implies accepting and acknowledging the paths and ways of life chosen by others.

In other words, one truth may give rise to different *world views*. It should be noted that the three essential elements of any world view are a cosmology, a social philosophy, and a metaphysics. Cosmology—as demonstrated by fundamental knowledge—is alterable. There is no cosmology that can be said to represent ultimate knowledge. No cosmology is, therefore, sacred in its systematically presented content. A similar conclusion can be drawn regarding social philosophy. The interpretation of social relations and institutions, as well as their creation and maintenance, is a continuous process. None of these is unalterable, or, therefore, sacred and not subject to revision or negotiation. Cosmology and social philosophy alike are an arena of constant construction and deconstruction, in which adjustments are made according to changes in human perception.

Metaphysics, however, in the full sense of the term is a teaching that is not subject to change: it is the knowledge of principles, which are eternal, though manifested in an unlimited number of ways. This requires the human self to be determined by two elements: its givenness, which is not subject to either choice or change, and transcendence, that heteronomous source of evaluation and selection to which the self submits voluntarily. One's relation towards others is determined by the first or both of these elements, which in Bosnian tradition corresponds to the definition of an individual who is not "related" at all with the factor of social coherence: "he is not of my kin nor of my congregation!" "Kin" here corresponds to the given, unchosen and unchangeable elements of individuality, and "of my congregation" to the heteronomous source of moral identity of the individual and the community. The idea of the liberal or secular self places this transcendent moral source within the self itself: it is the free and autonomous individual who can himself choose among different goods the one that meets the individual and collective interest.

Different interpretations of the truth about the Messiah have spread across the world since his coming. They are reflected in the origins of Catholicism, Eastern Orthodoxy, Protestantism, and other established Christian communities. In the Bosnian region, at least two of these different interpretations, Eastern Orthodoxy and Catholicism, were present, with their accompanying communities. There was, however, a third interpretation equally present: the "heretic" Bosnian Church, or the institution encompassing the communities of the Bosnian Christians. The power that some of those communities had was at times used to prevail over the others and force them to accept the doctrine of those in power. In this Bosnian model, as an ideal of the highest order, the duty of those who espouse it to recognize and protect the rights of others is central to the identity of Bosnia. This ideal was based primarily on the awareness of transcendence, which corresponds to the higher level of manifestation of the link between people of different traditions. This is the "my congregation" element, the sacred source of identity of any self, regardless of differences in terms of "kin." This is the human achievement that makes Bosnia different: Bosnia is of a higher human level, though exposed to destruction and negation in which the self is degraded to its baser elements, determined solely by "kin."

The Source and Courses

The sacred traditions that constitute Bosnia's identity—Bosnian Christianity, Catholicism, Eastern Orthodoxy, Islam, and Judaism—are different in form, although the differences are often very small. However, it is the very awareness of small differences that has seriously exacerbated tensions at the individual level, to make them known and to preserve them. This includes resorting to external similarities that enhance external differences, as well as establishing links with the distant and unfamiliar, in order to preserve distinctiveness from the familiar. Thus, there is a frequent tendency within these sacred traditions, all rooted in the very being of Bosnia, to insist on the differences of forms, with the concomitant loss from the intellectual horizon of the shared essence—the right of every individual to redemption. Distinctive traits and differences in the meanings, symbols, and concepts that determine the entirety of the individual connection with the center often serve to mask it. Ideology is thus presented as intellectuality. The aspiration for the supreme ideals is manipulated in accordance with the need to establish simplified systems of ideas, justified on the grounds of religious and moral necessity, but offered as political and national programs, in which the scale of values is reduced to a fraction of the values required by the principle of unity in diversity.

It can be claimed that Bosnia has become the context for the quest for the centers that lie at the heart of religious particularities. However, these centers are always seen as confined to rational conceptions of the world—where religion, as genuine intellectuality, is reduced to mere sentimentality and morality. This adulterated concept of the center cannot provide an environment in which loyalty to the Truth would prove that differences are conditional and that the existence of a multiplicity of paths is the norm in the quest for that same truth. This is typical of the age of modernity, where the self with its autonomous reason is the center of social change, which in turn, operates on the self. If social circumstances alter, whether or not change is accompanied by violence, a framework is established for the self to advance towards its highest potential. Human beings themselves are sufficient for this: they are both the opener and the opening towards the "end of history."

Passing over the rather vague data we have on the Christian presence in the Bosnian region, which is connected with the complex contrasting and conflicting understandings of the message of the Messiah in the first millennium after his incarnation, it can be claimed that Catholicism in Bosnia is principally represented by the Franciscans. Their presence is closely linked with that of the Bosnian Christians, and there has been a long-standing dialogue between their two views of the Messiah's presence. The Bosnian Christians incline to the view that individuals have the right on their own, without the ultimate judgment of any church, to attain the inner sense of the revealed word of God. The Franciscan view is that ultimate judgment relies on the saintly capacity of intercession, such as was bestowed on the founder of the order, Francis of Assisi. This position underlies the ever closer attachment of the Bosnian Catholics to the Pope, and the center of his power, as the vital external center. This same dialogue, however, produced attempts to find answers to the same questions in regard to the depiction of Muhammad as the Seal of Prophecy—the final message, and thus the message resolving the fundamental controversies between interpretations of the Messiah. Thus, Bosnia's dialogue on Christology branched towards a different core tradition, symbolized by Mecca, as the Valley of Fragrance, the symbol of the renewed covenant with humankind.

In contrast, Orthodoxy does not accept either of these two centers, but seeks an ever firmer connection to national and state programs, in which political programs are interwoven with interpretations of the Messiah's message. But where Judaism is concerned, since the Christian and Islamic traditions of Bosnia are only branches of the tree whose roots lie in the *religio perennis*, incorporating the original treasury of the Jewish people, the small community of Jewish exiles readily found its place in Bosnia's unity of diversity. The followers of Judaism possess a tradition capable of establishing dialogue with all others, although at the same time preserving connection with the Truth through their own language and doctrine of symbols and ideas.

These individual identities, fundamentally related to one and the same end—human redemption or perfection—have established dialogue without reference to the need for mutual protection, or to the necessity of establishing political institutions able to ensure their protection. The phenomenon that we refer to as modernism, where national ideologies are incorporated into immense and powerful totalitarian structures,[4] is fundamentally contradictory to Bosnia's precious, fragile unity in diversity.

The Orthodox community in Bosnia accepts the national ideology, seeking to modify its components wholly in accordance with the Western European developments of the eighteenth and nineteenth century. It adopted the ideas of liberty, fraternity, and equality, but applies them only within the framework of its own national identity, which it regards as an extension of the medieval Orthodox Serb kingdom, symbolized primarily by Stefan Dušan's despotism. Everything that opposes this ideology—that is, the presence of different religious, cultural, and political entities—represents Others, who are an obstacle to the establishment of this ideologized understanding of liberty, fraternity, and equality. Thus, the center of the Orthodox community leans towards the Serbian national leadership that is outside Bosnia and sees the country as a purely peripheral region: one that the advocates and followers of the Serbian national ideology believe should be more closely linked to the national center by the establishment of a united Serbian state.[5]

The Bosnian Catholics in response have adopted a reactive version of this ideology. They, too, take the line of transforming their historic relationship with Croatia into acceptance of the ideology of Croathood within which the center shifts towards the proponents and advocates of the ideology. This claims that Croatia's political destiny is being realized, in a strict sequence dating back to the Middle Ages, by its modern search for an expanded nation state. Tomislav's kingdom, like that of Dušan, has become the critical historical moment from which the nation was launched on its course towards the climax promoted by latter-day politics. Being equal in principle, these two national ideologies naturally conflict with the interwoven, copresent Muslim dimension.

The latter is similarly related to historic Bosnia, but has failed to establish the same national ideology. Through such national ideologies, the unity of diversity is reduced to the hard-line and exclusive individuality of national homogeneity in the form of national states. The most complete expression of this model is offered by the national politics of Yugoslav President Slobodan Milošević and Croatian President Franjo Tuđman, who tried to legitimize their aspirations to the complete redrawing of the borders between the Serbian and Croatian nation states by urging the Bosnian Muslims to reduce their part in Bosnia to a demand for their own national program: that of establishing the Muslim state. This is, as the two leaders believed, the most effective way to destroy the remaining elements of Bosnian unity, and to prevent its revival in the form of a complete and effective political concept. This greatly diminishes the likelihood of creating a political mindset based on the acceptance of unity in diversity, present in the history of Bosnia's religious relationships, but insufficiently developed at the level of political culture.[6]

Attraction and Repulsion

The global changes that took place between the first and second halves of the twentieth century, and that can be noted in these differences of outlook, found their reflection in Bosnia, too. To the extent that the impact of the ideologies of the modern age—the most important of which are liberalism, communism, and socialism—was felt within Bosnia's different components, that impact must be recognized in the weakening of those elements of Bosnia's identity that can be defined as tradition or as the sacred. Religious interpretations, symbols, and ideas become ever more subjugated to national ideologies.[7] The voice calling for humanity to remember its shared, sacred elements, becomes ever weaker: the voice calling for strong, defined borders grows more powerful. Secularism, which is originally a denial of the unity of the material and the spiritual, as well as the reduction of humans to solely spiritual aspects, reaches a point of grotesque distortion precisely in the denial of any need to connect with the plane of supra-individuality, without which religion is nothing. Given this absence, religion is powerless. The subsequent adjustments that have taken place within ideologically driven religious systems are a gross denial of the essence of intellectuality treasured by religion.

The response was the appearance of groups and individuals who accepted neither secular simplifications nor the ideologization of religious systems. However, the majority of these individuals and groups were defined more by emotion than by knowledge, were more interested in opposition than action. They became the voice of opposition to the Communist empire, known in Western liberal circles as "political dissidents," "outsiders," and "prisoners of conscience." In the widespread upsurge of religious awareness in the former Eastern Bloc, in which modernism took on the unexpected and quite different components typical of the second half of the twentieth century and the collapse of Communism, these individuals and groups were left in a vacuum, lacking political power. They attempted, clumsily, to convert their feelings of opposition into a substitute for the fallen ideology: this was snatched at eagerly by individuals and institutions of the lingering complex bureaucracies of ideological (totalitarian) states.

In this confusion of sentimental and moral reactions to the crudeness of imposed rational systems, and the perilous combination of a new political ideology with the old organizations of the ideological (totalitarian) society, political abuses abound. Again, the fullest representations of this model are found in the politics of Milošević and Tuđman—and also in that of the leader of the Bosnian Muslims, Alija Izetbegović, who has been allocated the role of symbolizing the forces advocated by those who would destroy Bosnia. These forces, abandoning the Bosnian unity of diversity and reducing the Muslim struggle for existence to striving for a "Muslim state," are the justification for the devastation of Bosnia. This is the simple external dimension of this phenomenon. It is, however, inseparable from the global trend that can be named postmodernism. The causes of the Bosnian tragedy are closely linked to the precipitous descent of the autonomous self into its baser nature: "The fear and hatred-induced acts that brought about the war cannot be explained rationally. They were evoked by human destructiveness and self-centeredness. Sinfulness and intransigence are at the motivating core of the war."[8]

The growing need for religion within the separate groups making up Bosnia has coincided with the decrease in real power of the ideological (totalitarian) system embodied in the ideological (totalitarian) state, and has animated the yearning for new national ideologies. At their heart lie the goals of establishing ever more powerful national states. This calls for the present borders to be redrawn, and leads to confrontation with each religious and national group opposed to these changes. This in turn produces "national unities" based on the undisputed dominance of one leader and one political party with the aspiration to become the principal element of the whole nation, and to transform this matrix of complex and interwoven entities into structures where state and territory form a single entity.

Out of this process resulted the driving force of disintegration of the former Yugoslavia, and the war against Bosnia.[9] The real lords of this war have been from its very beginning Slobodan Milošević and Franjo Tuđman with their respective elites, countered by the opposing, but in principle identical, behavior of Alija Izetbegović and his followers. An integral aspect of their systems—an aspect of particular intellectual importance—is that of placing religious meanings, symbols, and ideas in a subordinate position, serving and upholding the new ideologies. In this context, the will to power is the driving force of social action. Voluntary submission to the transcendent authority disappears altogether, leaving the ideological project with no more than its mask to convince the majority of the people that ideological power is upheld by religious reasons. The voice of opposition to these new ideologies, which have relied principally on the military to achieve their goals, has remained weak in Bosnia itself. Equally weak were those forces that could have sustained and supported the purposes and powers of the international order, and their desire for social stability and respect for human rights in Bosnia, as a part of Europe.

The security of the world is vitally linked to the security of Europe and its role as a factor of peace or war. It was possible to stop the war against Bosnia only by substantially obstructing the elites and forcing them to follow a comprehensive plan for a military and political settlement. Bosnia was thus again placed in the position of a de facto protectorate within which the existing forces of destruction were restrained but not eliminated. The restraint imposed by the presence of outside forces can only be substituted by the growth of political forces that would respect the nature of their individual sacred elements, but at the same time bring them into harmonious unity on the basis of a comprehensive policy linked to the most important centers of power in the world.

Ignorance

There is, then, a critical need to understand and to build a perception of the Bosnian identity as capable of transforming the root of its historical existence into a comprehensive policy. This need, however, remains misunderstood from the viewpoint both of political liberalism and of sacred tradition. The first perspective, represented by the military, political, and economic presence of the international community in Bosnia, underpins the belief that the foundation for establishing and strengthening peace in Bosnia lies in political institution-building, and in stimulating economic recovery and development. This is a necessary but insufficient condition. False perceptions of the sources of trust between the different participants in Bosnia's unity can be eliminated neither by exclusively economic, nor by scientistic or militaristic interpretations of the country's identity.

Those forms of integration or aggregation at various levels that are capable of providing a foundation for political and economic effectiveness cannot be merely reduced to the standard rational model of fulfilling self-centered individual aspirations to material goods.[10] Various elements are at work here that cannot be explained away as purely rational motives. It is not that they are antirational, but nor can they be grasped by any study that fails to consider the nature of sacred tradition, which regards reason and rational behavior as merely forms derived from a suprarational level of being.

Contacts between Bosnia's distinct component groups are maintained today largely through the mediation of the international community. The individuals, institutions, and organizations representing the international community encourage and support connections between these components. As a consequence, they become increasingly distanced from one another and increasingly focused on external relationships and interests. It is assumed that the political and religious institutions and individuals of the ideologized (totalitarian) entities of Serbs, Croats, and Bosniacs, are the reflections of deep ethnic, religious, and political differences. Thus, the basic elements of trust, which lie beyond the scope of the rational modeling of economic behavior, are inhibited by the mutually exclusive political elements between which members of the international community act as mediators. Members of Bosnia's component groups find it easier to establish connections with the outside world than with ideologized (totalitarian) individuals and institutions in their immediate environments. This outlook produces an increasingly rigid and closed mentality. The sense of unity of language, ethnogenesis, land, and history, and of the close relation between their sacred traditions, becomes ever more distant from the outlook of individuals and groups. Numerous utopias surface in which the distant is seen as near and the near as distant, while small differences are encouraged to grow into insurmountable obstacles.

At the same time, the hope of creating an alternative way of thought, an alternative policy, and an alternative history, itself appears to be a utopian dream. Limited outside support, often linked to the functions of bureaucratized and outmoded organizations, is treated as though it were vital to safeguarding those at risk. The mentality of fear and the uncritical acceptance of diverse forms of foreign presence helps entrench the blockade against open dialogue and the development of associations and institutions based on trust. This mind set is treated as accepted wisdom at both the individual and the collective level, and seen as the answer to every issue. What it really signifies, however, is submersion in ignorance. Ignorance spells doom for humanity—when ignorance is regarded as knowledge, the consequences for humanity are truly grave.

These mutually exclusive (totalitarian) ideologies result from the adoption of the rational model as sufficient in itself and from the demand for universal subservience to this model and the subjugation of others to its dominance. Attaining the maximum interest is the justification for the development of rational models such that this goal will be achieved in the most effective way possible. The sense of "moral restraint" is dwindling ever more in the attempts to "conquer" nature and force it to yield up everything it holds at any cost.

Any reversal of the current state of affairs in Bosnia demands a heightened awareness of this ignorance, with open dialogue on all issues in place of the arrogance of the current accepted wisdom—not least because the experience of the present century offers sufficient proof of the effects of ignorance. Recognition of this defect could be the critical step towards reviving the core identity of Bosnia. Without a renewed willingness to acquire and accept the ideas behind the concept of Bosnia, change cannot take place.

This change of outlook could result in a transformation from total reliance on salvation from without, to perceiving the inner capacities for dialogue common to all the components of Bosnia's identity as a potential source of trust. This is the only way in which external support, currently accepted as the only salvation for Bosnia, could be converted into a facilitator of these internal changes. This intangible characteristic of the social entirety that evades neoclassical economic theory, and finds its most complete expression in culture, both complements and makes possible the project of economic recovery and sustainable development without which the goal is unattainable.

While no achievements can be made in this domain given the prevailing climate of political thought, the present truce will remain no more than plaster over the wound, with no guarantee of healing. The ideologizing—and idealizing—of history will intensify. Allegiance to the restrictive scale of values prescribed by ideological exclusiveness will continue to prevent individuals and groups from entering the field of open dialogue and strengthening trust.

The Future of Trust

Bosnia today is comprised of distinct groups whose varying capacity and reach is predicated upon their military resources. Territorial ratios of 20, 30, and 50 percent of the total area of Bosnia and Herzegovina approximately correspond to these group divisions, the first and smallest marked by the presence of the Army of Bosnia and Herzegovina, the second by that of Croat Defense Council, and the third and largest by the Army of Republika Srpska. These three territorial units retain their integrity by impeding the freedom of refugees to return to their homes and freedom of movement in general. They are the reflection of the persistence of the three national politics which, each in their own way, are a revival of totalitarian ideology. Distorted readings of history are exaggerated by these politics, which compete with one another in building their own separate histories. These are linked with pitifully minor aspects of cultural individuality, which are touted as essential demonstrations of "separate national cultures."

The subordinated institutions and organizations of the religious communities, in common with every other captive institution, are expected to serve this purpose. The degree of their political and social value is measured by their readiness to subjugate themselves to the corresponding national political totalitarianism. This situation is directly contrary to all forms of action founded on faith in the possibility of dialogue between the Bosnian entities in the broad range of their relationships and similarities. Collective differences must give way to the right to individual distinctiveness that is not contrary to the Truth, and yield to the need for relations based on trust.

The distinction between forms of thought and action that exacerbate conflict and distrust, and those that look to a future of strengthening and expanding trust between the inheritors and participants in Bosnia's unity in diversity, has thus far remained beyond the intellectual horizon. Since the prevalent concept is one of reduction to a purely political dialogue between totally separate, ideologized ethnic entities, all efforts to strengthen trust are interpreted as the denial of these entities. Thus, the political stage reveals the paradox of opposition between virtually indistinguishable political oligarchies. The one area where all can achieve consensus bears no relation to the resolution of differences: it lies in their joint opposition to all efforts at transcending the borders to which they have confined themselves. From the standpoint of these forces, open dialogue in which every participant in Bosnia's unity of diversity can take part is aimed not only directly against themselves, but also against the very essence of the Serb, Croat, and Bosniac entities. "Everything can be divided," they claim.

These forces have arrogated to themselves the full right to interpret forms and modes of division, which presupposes absolute knowledge of the entities thus being separated. This is the most pernicious manifestation of "knowledge," as a consequence of the ideologized concept of the world. The people of Bosnia need the contrary assertion: "Everything can be joined." This unification does not demand the exclusion of individual differences: it is at the core of every group.

The collapse of the bipolar division of the world, and the disintegration of Communism as a totalitarian ideology, led to the devastating war against Bosnia. This phenomenon and its wide-reaching consequences cannot be explained outside the effects of Communism. The concept of a society entirely subjected to the Communist ideology denied many individual and group identities, most significantly those of culture and religion. Opposition to the totalitarian ideology developed for the most part along the line of fostering these identities. Outsiders, dissidents, and prisoners of conscience, under Communist rule, sought those dimensions of individual and group identity that were contrary to the Communist concept of society. Since the Communist image of society incorporated the goal of social integrity and economic development as justification for the tacit abandonment of those dimensions of human integrity that are inseparable from culture and religion, the opposition largely ignored the fundamental issues of the modern world while emphasizing individual and group differences in the light of that rationalized image. The decline of the Communist ideology as the basis of the social system left a vacuum inviting other potential forms of structuring the institutions and organizations of society and government. But inherited hostility towards a defunct state and a strong feeling of individuality cannot be substitutes for a new social ideology.

The continuing presence of the international community, primarily taking the form of substantial support for reconstruction and development, meanwhile gives rise to a dependency mentality, which leads in turn to a decreasing awareness of the need for long-term, well-planned actions. Decisions based on the insights of systematic studies are notably rare. The consequences are readily seen in the increasing distrust in the future of Bosnia among young people.

Any change of the current state of affairs requires full insight into all social dimensions, and the metamorphosis that they would need to undergo for awareness of trust to overcome the prevailing conditions of reservation and distrust. This cannot be achieved through political action alone without prior research, nor can it be attained by means of intuitive knowledge seeking to impose itself in the domain of rational consciousness.

The Message

The insight of poet Mak Dizdar reached the most distant—which in traditional wisdom means the deepest—frontiers of Bosnia's identity in the modern age. In the final poem of his book *The Stone Sleeper*—a book that reflects the Bosnian unity—the open nature of this country representing, through its link with the basic principle, a symbol of the inexhaustibility of Bosnia's identity, is explored through the illusion of incompleteness. The Bosnian self rises above the persistence of slaughter and the extinction of culture:

> *. . . to hear me walking through*
> *The city again*
> *Quietly stalking you*
> *Again*

> *And secret and sly as a Western spy*
> *You'll burn my home to the ground*
> *Till all*
> *Fall*

> *And then you'll say these dark words*
> *This nest is done for now*
> *This cursed cur*
> *Is slain*
> *With pain*

> *But by a miracle I will still be present dreaming here on earth. . .*

And from afar
I'll let it be told
This truth of mine
Unerring
And old

　　　　　　　　　　　　　　　　(Mak Dizdar, *Message*)

In this endless illusion of the supremacy of darkness "a message of flowers will still remain in blossoming strands:"

(You know nothing about the town in which I dwell
You've no idea about the house in which I eat
You know nothing
About the icy well
From which
I drink)

　　　　　　　　　　　　　　　　(Mak Dizdar, *Message*)

During the last decade of the twentieth Christian century, when the torrent of killing and extermination was flooding Bosnia from north and south, east and west, fascination with the Internet was spreading across the world. It appeared that the latest communications and computers were changing the very foundations of the world. Yet these new links form a metaphor for the repetition of old laws: those who are incapable of "only connecting," despite the communications that make it possible for them to see and hear each other, merely exacerbate their own remoteness. They believe that communication with the far distant will perhaps heal the pain of the gulf between them and those who are physically close. We have reached the point when the remembered experience of acute mental and physical pain forces us to recognize that we are at a crossroads: the choice is either to opt for becoming ever more remote from one another, to the point of disaster, or to turn away from the ashes and the devastation towards a new direction, which may be our redemption.

The sense of Bosnia, the Bosnian feeling, has never become systemized knowledge in which the connection of each group identity with the same center, the *locus*, would be manifest. Connections with distant environments and interests have meaning for the people of Bosnia only if they spring from their own firm sense of reliance on the pillar or axis rooted deep within them and within the *locus* of the land.

The ability to communicate with every part of the world is an illusion that deflects our gaze from our forgotten or neglected responsibility to discern the essential elements of unity in the core identities of Bosnia's component groups. The quest cannot succeed if the seekers are ignorant of the relationship between reason and intellect. The divisions brought about by killings and devastation can perhaps be overcome through discovering and strengthening trust among these peoples of one and the same country, whose villages and cities are configured in undeniable unity. If not, then the obsession with a purely physical transcendence of divisive borders via links to remote compilations of data is only one of the ways of closing the door on humanity's quest for perfection. However, if the connection to a common center is discovered and established, this will make it possible to recognize the sources of trust and the potential for dialogue between all the participants of this unity in diversity. This unity, whose leaves branch out across the world, will effect the blossoming of that "message of flowers" that springs only from a common center. It follows from this recognition, however, that Bosnia's circumstances must be considered in the light of the balance of forces that contribute to the preservation of unity and those that act to the contrary.

The partition of Bosnia is an indisputable fact. This is not what was envisaged by the Peace Accord, which includes provisions that would enable the current situation to be changed, but contains too many internal inconsistencies for this to be carried out effectively. It is therefore important, in any consideration of the situation in Bosnia, to be aware of the possible limits of these changes. If the options come down merely to their advocates and those who will implement them, the question arises, who are the destroyers, and who are the builders of what remains of Bosnia, whether in its current reality as a state or as a concept?

Three Elites

While leaving for another occasion a comprehensive consideration of the plan to destroy Bosnia and Herzegovina, it can be claimed with certainty that three elites are recognizable as the destroyers: the Serb, Croat, and Bosniac elites. Placing them in this order illustrates the cause and effect nature of way in which these elites acted. For any extended—or, as it is more often called, Greater Serbia—the denial and destruction of Bosnia was a prerequisite, so that the dismembered country could serve as the raw material with which to establish this hypothetical new ethno-national Serb state. The counterreaction to this plan was the demand that in the course of this dismemberment as large a portion as possible be allocated to the hypothetical extended or greater ethno-national Croat state.

The latest formal version of this plan was the agreement between Milošević and Tuđman, reached in Karađorđevo at the beginning of 1991.

The major obstacle to the plan lay in the very nature of Bosnia and Herzegovina: the population distribution showed Bosnian Serbs living in 95 percent of the country's territory, Bosniacs in 94.5 percent, and Croats in about 70 percent. Drawing borders between ethnic entities would necessitate mass expulsions and, as the latest war testified, the use of genocide to achieve the desired partition.

The destruction of the state structures of Bosnia and Herzegovina was, therefore, central to this destruction of a country. The concept of the so-called Muslim State became central to this plan:[11] advocates and implementers of this concept were sought, and given every encouragement when found. The main element of this strategic model became the destruction of every form of trust between the members of Bosnia and Herzegovina's unity in diversity. The sowing of hatred emerged as the essential means of achieving the destroyers' ultimate aim: the destruction of Bosnia and Herzegovina.

Neither Defeat nor Victory

The peace agreement reached in Dayton and signed in Paris at the end of 1995 halted the war against Bosnia and Herzegovina. On the basis of this agreement, it can be said that the state has not been defeated; but neither has it been defended. Its multiethnic structure has been distorted across the entire country by expulsions and killings; above all, almost everywhere in Bosnia and Herzegovina the Bosniacs have been destroyed or reduced in numbers by genocidal methods. The cessation of war had the effect of legitimizing many of the effects of the destruction. Three ethno-national governments were established, each with their corresponding territory, ethno-national armies, and other elements of statehood: police, financial systems, education systems and so forth.

None of the elites of destruction had achieved its ultimate goal, but each could be said to have achieved some sort of success. From this sense of success sprang the resistance to any elimination or alleviation of the aftermath of destruction. Most refugees and displaced persons cannot return to their homes and property; and when they do return they do not have access to the most basic of rights: protection of their lives, dignity and property, freedom of speech, movement and association; the right to work, the right to free practice or expression of their religious, national, or political identity, and so on. Meanwhile, the political stage is, for the most part, still dominated by those same elites who dealt in the cruelties of the war: they have not yet forsaken the ideologies that were the basis for the plan to destroy Bosnia and Herzegovina.

The current situation is understood and interpreted by the destroyers as an important, albeit limited, success in achieving their primary goal of building ethnically pure national states from the ruins of Bosnia and Herzegovina. This view is supported by the existence of Republika Srpska and of ethnonational armies; by the weakness and obvious dysfunctionality of Bosnia and Herzegovina as a state; by the lack of even the slightest trust between the separate elements; and by various other factors. The parties therefore see their interests as lying in the preservation of the status quo as essential for achieving their aims at some later stage. They try to obstruct at all costs the efforts of the international factors—the presence of foreign troops is frequently claimed to be the activity of the *International Community*, although it is only under the most favorable circumstances that the campaign of these forces can be called that of a *community*—in order to demonstrate the impossibility of Bosnia and Herzegovina.

Coercion and Anxiety

The destroyers continue to regard every action aimed towards the affirmation of the original elements of Bosnian unity as politically directed against "ethno-national rights" and the status quo of the peace agreement. Any demand that trust should be strengthened between the peoples of Bosnia is interpreted as a political sleight of hand aimed at imposing what is most often called "a unitary Bosnia". Every single meeting and discussion—and these are, it is worth noting, growing more frequent by the day—is presented as just the collaboration strictly necessary for economic affairs or trade relations and the like.

While these are necessary, they fail to take account of the needs that have their roots in history, culture, and religion.[12] The vital campaign for economic renewal is being conducted, for the most part, without any contact with culture. It is a known fact that economic development can flourish only if planted in the ground of those forms of culture that promote and strengthen trust between peoples. Any continuing efforts to show that parts of Bosnia and Herzegovina's history reveal a genuine advance towards establishing a unity in diversity are interpreted through the lens of ideologized readings of history. The demonization of Bosnia's entire past and culture continues without check, and at the same time the prospect of a shared future, as the justification for trust arising from dialogue about just such a future, is rejected. On this basis, events in Bosnia are reduced to just two aspects: first the present, caught between a dark past and an uncertain future; and second, the "unfinished" nature of the war not long ended and the current peace. This is reflected in the instinctive exodus of the young and gifted, who, their prospects severely limited, are leaving Bosnia to make their future abroad.

Advocates of the Status Quo

The current economic, political, and cultural environment of Bosnia has become the playground of the advocates of the status quo. These are the people whose involvement in the rule by the ethno-national oligarchies and their close connection with them have won them positions and privileges unthinkable under the conditions of liberal democracy and a free market. (Or, to put it more simply, under the conditions which apply in a state structured so as best to ensure the general good of its members.)[13] They are also those who, in the absence of the rule of law, have been able to acquire connections, profit and influence, which in "normal" countries would be regarded as illegal. And again, they are those who, under conditions of gross social inequality, use their influence with the state-owned media to present themselves as the saviors of those who have been displaced, humiliated, and deprived of all rights. And yet they are immune from any responsibility towards those to whom they make these promises.

In the current absence of a coherent social order, one that would be in evidence throughout the legislative, executive, and judicial authorities, and given the flood of foreign humanitarian aid directed mainly at the victims, changes to the status quo would mean significant loss of privileges for some. Therefore the ruling oligarchies de facto oppose any change, although their rhetoric pretends otherwise.

This growth and expansion of hypocrisy is visible among all three oligarchies. Each tries to claim the credit for preventing total defeat, instead of acknowledging that defeat and their responsibility for the killing and destruction of those in whose names they are supposed to speak. This is often described in terms implying that the leader or leader has acted as savior of the people. The general disintegration and absence of any sense of moral responsibility encourages the basest forms of personal gain, while emphasis is simultaneously placed on the threat presented by other people.

The Incentive to Build Afresh

The destruction of Bosnia and its termination by the peace agreement raised awareness among the people of Bosnia and at the broadest international levels of the unresolved threat of ethno-national elites prepared to use ethno-national ideologies to achieve their ends by way of state and parastate organizations and criminal perpetrators. The current situation in Bosnia and

Herzegovina can thus be viewed as the basis for building Bosnia and Herze-govina afresh. Liberal democracy is reputedly the means of ensuring general recognition and respect for all individual and collective differences, and the state as a whole is seen as the guarantor of individual and collective rights aris-ing from this postulate. It will be possible to test these premises and examine their truth on the basis of Bosnia's future.

Bosnia and Herzegovina is, in any view, a concept of the highest order. Its entire history has been that of a country of diversity, first religious, and then ethno-national. It is thus a paradigm for the world as a whole. If the paradox of simultaneously recognizing and resolving differences cannot be solved in Bosnia, then we are faced with the likelihood that it cannot be solved anywhere in the world.

Bosnia and Herzegovina is today literally a global issue. To address that issue, the involvement of the global community is needed. But this is not enough. The vital prerequisite for any possible future of Bosnia and Herze-govina that is in accord with the best aims of humanity, is the discovery or re-discovery of those elements of Bosnia's past that will deepen confidence in the chance of building a harmonious future.

Waiting for Change

There is no coherent or convincing interpretation of the paradigm of Bosnia. This lack is favorable to the destroyers, and goes against the builders. The concept of "ancient hatreds" between the peoples of Bosnia is more often re-futed by the instincts of ordinary people than examined systematically and re-liably at an intellectual level. Thus, the theory of hatred continues to be a powerful weapon in the hands of morally irresponsible and intellectually shal-low readers of history, and those who reduce religion to the level of simple ideology. Although it is possible to adduce many examples of perfect mutual trust among the morally resolute in Bosnia and Herzegovina, there is no de-cisive action to produce intelligent and constructive testimony to the possi-bility of a future for Bosnia and Herzegovina's unity of differences, in politics, the economy, and culture.

The possibility of unity is most frequently championed from the stand-point of simple ideas of tolerance, which too often come down to indifference to crucial religious elements, and opposition to any efforts to acknowledge those elements. Such a viewpoint fails to take account of the potential of au-thentic Catholicism, Orthodoxy, Judaism, and Islam to play a decisive role in enabling the discovery and encouragement of relationships involving "univer-sal mutual recognition." This may well be key to creating a society in which the most important aspects of human nature can express themselves freely, with simultaneous protection of the rights arising from acknowledged differences.

Bosnia and Herzegovina is awaiting changes in its situation of a kind that will lead towards the organized facilitation of dialogue on and confidence in a community of all its people, who are willing, ready and capable to take responsibility for preserving this country as a place that will be beneficial for all its people; a community that belongs, in the totality of its membership, to different sacred traditions, different ethno-national groups, different political visions, and different concepts of the past, present, and future. There are not a few signs that this need can indeed be fulfilled.

This option, however, demands constant revisiting of the issue of the treatment of unity of differences in the contexts of tradition and liberalism. If tolerance is a possible yardstick of this treatment, this revisiting should then be accompanied by a reexamination of the views of both tradition and liberalism.

5
Europe's "Others"

Introduction: Oblivion Instead of Understanding

A mere fifty years elapsed between the Holocaust and the genocide in Bosnia.[1] As in most instances of manifestation of evil, here, too, evil is still present after its apparent withdrawal into the proffered oblivion instead of understanding. For most people today, the truth about the Holocaust seems to be just a figment of the prolific human imagination, rather than something that happened in recent European history. Similarly, the truth about the genocide in Bosnia already appears as a painful misunderstanding without any internal logic. The history of Bosnia, like that of any other part of the world, is not ideal. It is true, however, that for almost one thousand years the villages and towns of Bosnia were inhabited by people of different cultures. If we agree to limit culture to "meanings, symbols, values, and ideas," including phenomena such as religion and ideology, as opposed to social structures,[2] an understanding of the interconnectedness of the cultural and social spheres is of central importance in answering the question whether the interconnectedness of the Holocaust and the genocide in Bosnia, and the predominant understanding of both, can form the basis for identifying the living germ in the present that will reveal itself fully only in the future.

Over a period of more than five centuries, Bosnian towns were inhabited by Christians (both Orthodox and Catholic), Muslims, and Jews. Their way of life was such that their cultural differences endured and developed, interwoven and interconnected. Within this diversity were two conflicting dynamics of history. In the first, it was their interconnectedness that was of greater importance for the future, and in this context the "meanings, symbols, values, and ideas" of cultural differences were to be understood as only superficial differences, of which the final outcome and scope could not be conflicting. In the second dynamic, the particularities and differences of "meanings, symbols, values, and ideas" were irreconcilable, and the connections were at risk of being ruptured and broken. These two elements of Bosnian culture were present throughout its history, the first ensuring the survival of Bosnia's unity in diversity over more than five centuries,[3] and the second manifesting itself in numerous discords and conflicts, including the recent war against Bosnia as probably the worst manifestation of this type of understanding of culture.

Both the Holocaust and the genocide in Bosnia can be explained logically and convincingly by using the model of "struggle for recognition." If the "meanings, symbols, values, and ideas" of one culture are postulated as absolute, then a different set of relationships are understood as opposition by the Other. Any opposition is at the same time a reexamination of the absolute postulates, which is understood as animosity and non-recognition. On this basis, individual existence is transformed into a demand that others recognize the individual in the same form as he perceives himself. Recognition of the self of the one claiming recognition means subordination of the others, who are seen as hostile as long as they do not accept the understanding of the first. At this level there vanishes the ontological principle that every self actually has an equal need for recognition, and that recognition cannot be received from others until the self admits to itself and to others that, despite their differences in "meanings, symbols, values, and ideas," the very fact of existence implies the sanctity of all others. No existence can have an advantage in principle, and only when all differences are transcended in order to attain the ultimate reality does it become possible to eliminate the demand to recognize others through subjugation, ultimately manifested in their destruction.[4]

Different Interpretations of the War

The experience of the war against Bosnia, which must be recognized as partaking of the same nature as the Holocaust, offers itself to the European mind as a possibility to reexamine the present and future state of Europe.[5] It should be emphasized that qualitative parity, which does not exclude differences in intensity or quantity, represents an important prerequisite for understanding the nature of events in time. A full circle is determined by just two points. By the same token, the ability to recognize and interpret events lies in the knowledge of the principles constituting the basis of events in time. Interpretations of the war against Bosnia are again placed between two extremes which determine the position of each individual in relation to the war itself and its effects.

The first interpretation of the war against Bosnia emphasizes that it was the result of irreconcilable differences between the distinct entities present in

Bosnia. At the level of different sacral traditions, this means the irreconcil-ability of Christianity and Islam. This interpretation resorts to European his-tory in its entirety, where every conflict with different systems of government that have a connection of any kind with Islam have been interpreted as part of a deep historical conflict between Christianity and Islam.

The second interpretation presents the war against Bosnia as the manifes-tation of a combination of "elites, ideologies, systems, and perpetrators," using force and genocide to achieve political objectives. In this interpretation, the war against Bosnia is a simple war of conquest, which used all available means to achieve the objectives of conquest, including mass killings of those who op-posed those objectives. Every element of the combination of "elites, ideologies, systems, and perpetrators" used all available means, including current and his-torical prejudices, against the Muslims. At the same time, the Muslims were encouraged to treat others in a way that would justify a war a against them.

An analysis of the basic premise of the first interpretation brings into salience the key task of understanding the transcendental unity of sacral tra-ditions. If the two sacred traditions, Christianity and Islam, are indeed what they claim to be, they cannot differ in their transcendental origins and pur-poses either. This origin and this purpose must be one and the same. It is per-fectly clear that their manifestations in the world of phenomena or in human history can never attain unity at the expense of diversity, or diversity at the ex-pense of unity. Were it so, it would be necessary to accept that the antago-nisms at work within diversity could be ultimately resolved in a horrific attempt of one to annul the other. This is the fundamental question of human discourse, primarily of intellectual discourse, or of the fulfillment of human responsibility. Those who fail to recognize unity in diversity or diversity in unity, deny their own existence as evidence of the meaning and purpose of being human.

The second interpretation provides clear indicators of the fragility of the world order, when founded outside the awareness of ontological unity. It proves again that any policy that excludes responsibility for the rights of oth-ers, which is a logical consequence of treating one view of humanity as absolute, must culminate in the most unspeakable denial of humanity itself.

Muslims as the European Other

Neither the Holocaust nor the genocide in Bosnia can be understood outside historical manifestations of the fundamental aspects of the struggle for recog-nition in Europe. The basis of this struggle is Christianity, which manifested itself as a unifying and homogeneous force for as long as Others were present as a true cultural power. Having Christianized the pagans in the North, and expelled and converted Muslims in the South (Spain, Sicily, and the Balkans), Europe was left internally culturally divided, with many differences that Christianity failed to transcend. The "struggle for recognition" continued as the driving force of history, while Others were present throughout Europe in an endless multitude of cultural differences. The presence of Christianity, related to the development of modern humanism and democracy, proved itself insufficiently powerful to overcome the antagonisms of different identities in Europe, which were ever more crystallized as different forms of social integration which became increasingly present and more active.

Raising awareness of a new threat from the Other is readily propelled by internal differences and antagonisms in Europe. This is all the easier if the Other can be described in a language that has been already confirmed by history and thus made a significant part of cultural heritage. In European culture in general, the historical meaning of the words *Muslim* and *Islam* is totally distinct from their doctrinal meaning, and these terms can thus be easily reduced to a negative image, used as a tool to enhance the European tendency to declare its values as absolute, and therefore decisive, criteria.

Only now, in current circumstances, when "Islam" is no longer present as a political power in Europe, is a way of perceiving differences acknowledged that does not produce reductive models of cultural differences, but rather points to the ultimate causes and effects beneath the surface of world events. It is thus possible to identify two views of Islam in Europe today, which are mutually incompatible but at the same time of such importance for understanding the future that they should be promoted to the level of fundamental contemporary intellectual questions.

In view of the long-standing ideological and political antagonisms within Europe and in relation to its immediate neighbors, the term "Islam" was used to denote any political power that did not accept the European understanding of culture at the level of social systems. Anything that was different from this identification of culture with the social system, irrespective of the extent to which its historical roots and ultimate orientation and outcomes may have been related to European soil, was considered Other and "non-European." For this reason, ideological systems and the powers of social action were directed against them. A logical result was occasional alliances of "elites, ideologies, systems, and perpetrators" in criminal campaigns of destruction of others. In such circumstances, the reality of the "first" was divorced from their cultural models, whereas the models of the Other were equated with their reality.

The most common example of this pattern can be illustrated by reference to the dominant European terminology. Anything that occurs in areas inhabited by Muslims (the word *Muslim* denotes a person who submits to God, and *Islam* is the totality of this submission) is identified with Islam. Thus, the dominant European perception identifies Islam with violations of human rights, tyranny, economic backwardness, abuse of religion for political purposes, terrorism, and the like. All these horrors of the living conditions of Muslims are equated with Islam. This is the origin of the widely used terms "Islamic terrorism," "Islamic fundamentalism," and "the Islamic threat." On the other hand, however, in cases when the perpetrators and advocates of such acts originate from cultural areas not inhabited by Muslims, they are not called "Christian extremism," "Christian terrorism," "Christian fundamentalism," or "the Christian threat," though their elements may be exactly the same.[6]

Terrorism, violation of the sanctity of human life, tyranny, the imposition of religion by force, irresponsibility towards the most vulnerable segments of society, and all other similar phenomena are as alien to Islam and Muslims as they are to Christianity and Christians, Hinduism and Hindus, Buddhism and Buddhists, or any other sacred tradition and its followers. The betrayal of human ideals in such forms of evil transcends the expression of any sacred tradition in history. And this is the basis of another, complementary, approach in the European perception of Muslims as Other.

Unity Underlying the Diversity of Symbols

When speaking of sacred traditions, "meanings, symbols, values, and ideologies" are based on the creative role and the sacredness of the Word. In essence, the Word is action, and, therefore, movement in space and time. Symbols and values may be universal, but their meanings and ideas change over time. Thus, all their manifestations in particular historical periods, or in particular areas of the world, may be absolutized, or transformed into unalterable states, only in the context of the protection by force of static ideologies and social systems. However, their transcendental source, which is always identical to the ultimate purpose, remains ever present in them, just as it is present in other symbols and values, despite the rigidity they acquire through received meanings and ideologies. On this basis, we can claim that neither Christianity, Islam, Judaism, Hinduism, nor any other sacred tradition,[7] can be mutually opposed in the essences underlying its adopted symbols and values. To claim the contrary would mean that there is only one authentic sacred tradition, or none at all. As each follower of a sacred tradition believes in the truth of his sacred symbols and the values supporting them, to interpret just one of them as exclusively sacred would be tantamount to proclaiming the right to destroy every other.

When the Muslim Holy Book says that "Islam is the only faith in God," it means only that, from the viewpoint of the universal sacred tradition, submission to God as the ultimate truth is a prerequisite of any tradition or, in religious terms, of any salvation for humanity.[8] It is therefore understandable why the salvation of Christians and Jews as those "who obey God" is confirmed on the same basis, and why God "created a path and a way for each nation." This creates the possibility for any cultural differences to be accepted not as inner opposition, but rather as unity in diversity, the pattern permeating the totality of existence. No form of human society as a whole, nor any of its parts, can escape this pattern.

In Europe today, Muslims are perceived as Other in the full sense of the Hegelian model of the struggle for recognition. But they are not the only Other, as is clearly demonstrated by the nature of the Holocaust, the best known explosion of the tensions created by the dynamics of this struggle. Between Muslims, as currently the most numerous and visible European Other, and the dominant forces of social dynamics in Europe, there are many Others. Many are likely to become Other under different circumstances, even if they are Christians or social groups within the same ethnic or linguistic community. This is essentially a question of identity, which in the postmodern age will grow ever more complicated and decisive in humanity's desire to survive in the face of the hostilities it has produced.

This gives rise to fundamental intellectual questions. On these questions depends whether the existing differences between cultures in the world will bring humans back to their ultimate roots and potentials, or whether they will manifest themselves as forces leading humans to the basest forms of existence, human degradation, and obscurity. Is this not clearly demonstrated by the abuse of people for the purposes of those in power, embodied in the complicity between elites, ideologies, systems, and perpetrators of genocide, present in recent decades throughout the world, and also in Europe itself? Is this not demonstrated by endangered minorities, women, children? Are the widespread tyrannies of scientism, militarism, economism, not part of this?

The Struggle for Dominance

Samuel P. Huntington's model of the clash of civilizations reduces cultures to existing social systems. It is undeniable that cultures and social systems are interconnected, and often inseparable. However, if it were impossible to discern the universal bases of culture, then the idea of universal human rights itself would be nothing but an intellectual construct. And no one can justify this premise today, regardless of whether his view is based on a sacred tradition or on the ideas of modern humanist philosophy.

The world is indeed divided into a multitude of different "meanings, symbols, values, and ideas." However, this division is transcended by the unity of the essence of human beings, which cannot depend on "meanings, symbols, values, and ideas." Only a reduction of culture to absolutized values and ideologies can transform differences into the right of the stronger to compel others to recognize him in the way in which he sees himself in his ideological image of the world. Even if it were to be supposed, however, that the strong would wholly prevail over the Other, turning them into the servants of a powerful master—to take a long-term view—such a relationship would not resolve the existing contradictions, since it does not accept the ontological fact that existence itself is a testimony and evidence of God as the source of both unity and multiplicity. This vision of "the end of history" merely rechannels cataclysm away from the periphery, where civilizations clash, inwards to where "minor differences" appear as obstacles that are even more difficult to overcome in that ideologized "homogeneous humanity." Since these internal differences can never vanish, alliances of elites, ideologies, systems, and perpetrators carry the permanent potential for conflicts between cultural blocs, based on the current, mainly political understanding of religion, to be redirected towards new genocides.

The prevailing absolutized ideological interpretation of sacral traditions actually means a denial of the absolute nature of the metaphysical unity of the sources of all traditions. Sacred traditions are thus identified with politics or with the political contest for domination, which is literally a betrayal of those sacred traditions. They lose all their links with their unconditional center and, totally subjugated to conditional interpretations and ideologies, are reduced to "civilizations," which do not have within them either the language or the means for a dialogue of living participants in a unity of differences. And logically, therefore, they must clash.

Europe meets all the conditions for moving towards the future in either of these directions. Which of the two will really become its historical course does not depend on the immutable internal laws that govern historical processes. When such a claim is made, what is actually emphasized is that the current perceptions of Europe's and the world's future are built into that future. But perceptions are not immutable. Is the European experience of the Holocaust and Bosnia changing the European perception at the end of the second Christian millennium?

Departure from the Principle of Unity

The different forms of the struggle for recognition that underlie the genocide in Bosnia followed faithfully the matrix of the initial perception of Muslims as the Other of Europe. In equating the reality of countries and societies in which Muslims live with Islam on the one hand, and accepting the European political and cultural arena as directly opposed to Islam and Muslims on the other, the destroyers of Bosnia took into account the "Christian justification" of their actions. However, killings committed by appeal to Christian reasons can only be contrary to Christianity, since they deny the truth of existence as the Divine Revelation. If, however, explicit and conclusive grounds against the Holocaust and the genocide in Bosnia are not discerned in the very foundations of Christianity, oblivion and lack of understanding will directly favor a new eruption of both, with time and place as mere accidents that no barriers of civilization can ward off.

That is why in the world of today, to which the word ecumenism has become perfectly familiar, the question arises: Does the dialogue between different entities in the world proceed from the premise that different paths and ways of life are a gift of God before which every man is responsible? Responding to this question underlines the key importance of the sources and nature of trust between different cultures. This is the first prerequisite for a constructive view of the future of the world, encompassed by the principle of *solve et coaguli*. Prevalent interpretations of the ideologization of cultures deprive them of their fundamental aspects, their source corresponding to the transcendental essence of humanity. Every culture maintains its relationship with this source through a continuous reexamination of its interpretations and forms. When it loses its link to its reference, a symbol dies, becoming a mere handful of dust. None of its interpretations is final, for if they were, they would exhaust the endless possibilities of humankind's freedom in the Absolute, as the archetype for each individual and humanity as a whole.

Although the pattern of religious antagonisms is predominant in the modern understanding of international relations, there are no significant factors preventing other differences—such as those of language, history, society, ideology, and others—from becoming the source of equally fierce antagonisms and conflict, as can be clearly illustrated by numerous examples from the history of Europe. This possibility should be eliminated, primarily, by having the courage to understand the most extreme manifestation of current antagonisms. The "clash of civilizations" is a reality that derives from modern humanity's departing from the principle of unity in diversity. This departure is an obstacle to transcending conflicts. The essence of the human presence in the world holds this potential within itself, wholly independent of the historical forms taken by culture. This essence does not depend on cultures, and cultures do not depend on it. When cultures are detached from it, they deny it.

An Anti-Muslim Ideology

The widely present and generally accepted notion of Muslims as "Islamic extremists," "Islamic militants," "Islamic terrorists," "Islamic fundamentalists," gives rise to a mind set in which all the conditions are met for the creation of an entire anti-Muslim ideology. All the elements of this ideology can today be found scattered throughout a host of publicist, essayist, political, pseudoscientific, and pseudo-religious interpretations of modern world phenomena. From this it is but a single step to the creation of a political elite that would draw these scattered elements together into a comprehensive anti-Muslim ideology. And after that step it will be easy to identify or establish the organizational conditions for and to incite those who are to carry out the orders of such an elite. In that way all the conditions for a new genocide would be met.

If a comprehensive analysis were to be made of the circumstances preceding the genocide committed in Bosnia and the actual course of the genocide, it could be readily concluded that the matrix was followed with mathematical precision, but that there was a lack of ability to recognize and prevent the course. The nationalist policy of Greater Serbia, followed closely by that of Greater Croatia, instigated at every level of social action an atmosphere charged with elements of anti-Muslim ideology. The politics of the "solution to the Serb question" added to this ideology many interpretations of history for the purpose of achieving political goals. A careful reading of the basic policy guidelines shows that these documents took it for granted that they would find support in the many European misconceptions about Muslims, as well as in distorted readings of history based on European, mainly British and French, political perceptions of the role of Serbs in earlier wars against Turkey, the Austro-Hungarian Empire, and Germany. This genocidal policy also relied on these numerous interpretations of history when it suited its goals. This is particularly evident in the falsification of the history of Bosnia, which for the most part has not seen any large-scale religious or national conflicts. This is why the national ideology of Greater Serbia continued for so long to promote and support every presentation of Bosnian history as an arena of hatred and war, although this was clearly contradicted by historical facts.

Even without misinterpretation, the history of Europe readily lends itself to anti-Muslim ideologies. This greatly adds to the credibility of the premise that another genocide against Muslims in Europe is entirely possible. This premise is of great importance for any serious analysis of the future of Europe.

Today, Muslims are able to meet their basic needs (employment, housing, education) in Europe to a much larger extent than in their countries of origin. However, they are also more exposed to animosity and discrimination than anyone else. This animosity and discrimination is based not on racial but on religious grounds, since the majority of Muslims living in Europe today are either quite similar or identical to Europeans. The source of animosity and discrimination is prejudice against Muslims. The nature of these prejudices today is similar in principle to those encountered by Jews in Germany in the 1930s, prejudices that found their ultimate expression in the ideology of the "final solution" of the Jewish question and the Nazi Holocaust.

Since current European laws on the right to religion as a fundamental human right do not comprise all the elements that would ensure the same religious rights for Muslims as for all others, the development of laws that would include those elements would be a step forward in preventing the development of an ideology of the "final solution of the Muslim question." Although Muslims cover a wide range of ideas and ideologies in their understanding of the world, the prevailing European perception most frequently reduces them to a group vaguely defined by the syntagma "Muslim fundamentalists." This denominator encapsulates the negative definition of the Other. It implies that all Muslims are fundamentalists, and hence dangerous.

However, only once the main intellectual trends among Muslims are recognized is it possible to identify the basis for a useful and mutually beneficial dialogue in Europe. For there are many more common than antagonistic areas between Western cultures and Islam. The issue behind the title thus enters into the area of relations between different religions. The achievements of European studies of religious pluralism, conducted within the framework not only of theology, but also of history and the phenomenology of religion, have, unfortunately, not contributed to any significant degree to the elimination of dangerous imputations against Islam and Muslims.

For and Against Unity of Differences

The following story from Sarajevo under siege illustrates possible different views on this attitude. Fred Cuny, who was trying to help Sarajevo's people to survive the numerous threats to their lives, was in the city during 1993,[9] when the city was surrounded by an almost impenetrable military stranglehold. People were being killed daily, and daily facing a desperate struggle for water, bread, or medical assistance. The diversity of narratives on the causes and possible outcomes of the situation had the effect of minimizing the role of international factors, and the situation was often interpreted as a "Muslim threat."

Fred Cuny was trying to help people to produce enough drinking water from the city river, which was routinely muddy and dirty. As an American and a recognized member of the community of internationals who were involved in providing humanitarian aid to Sarajevo, Cuny was able to come and go as he wanted. He often talked to the leading figures of the community to which he himself belonged. He once related a telling anecdote about a prominent British officer, one of the highest-ranking commanders of the international peacekeeping forces in the region, which is worth quoting. After Cuny tried to explain to him that it was necessary to bring into the city some equipment that was required to help people who did not have enough drinking water, the British officer pointed to the Bible in his waistcoat pocket, saying that he could not be on the side of those who were under siege, and that their side— by "their" he meant himself and Cuny—was the side of those who were surrounding the city. The American then said to the British commander of the "peacekeeping" troops: "I am a Christian from the American South. Since my childhood I've known what the Ku Klux Klan is, what racial hatred and persecution of others are. And I am not on the side you're pointing at."

This anecdote may also be read as a parable of the modern world. Modern military skills and equipment were employed in the siege of a city whose historical center comprised churches, mosques, and synagogues. Cannons, mortars, and tanks were deployed on the hills surrounding the valley where the city lay. Down in the old city were the defenders. The forces on the hills asserted that they could not and would not live with the Muslims. The defenders of the city themselves, for the most part, persisted in defending the life that had shaped their identity—the life of a unity of differences. One of the political leaders of the besieging forces sent a message to the defenders that he would stop killing the Muslims as soon as they stopped advocating that they all should live together.

Both these conflicting political views found their justification in relevant historical narratives and interpretations of the holy books. The first view was based on a denial of the situation as it was then. This view demanded both power and a narrative. On the other hand, the established reality of life does not demand constant justification by way of rational discourse and its corresponding power. Consequently, resorting to violence is the only way to secure the necessary authority for the side that is denying unity, which seems weak and unjustifiable. This means that "violence is taken as a species of inscription and an act of authority. Acts of violence, like acts of speech and writing, invest the material with meaning by giving it structure. . . . In its inscription of will on the world, violence is a signifying act, giving expression and authority to identity and will."[10]

The tendency to justify violence as a factor of identity by narrative elements relying on the holy books and the related tradition should be opposed with a counter-narrative. It is here that we can conclude that every nationalism is essentially antitraditional: every form of identity that transcends the limits of national ideology, by virtue of being on a higher level, must be reshaped or excluded in the context of nationalism. The sources and injunctions for tolerance to be found in the sacred heritage of different religious traditions are, therefore, the yardstick for establishing whether a given religious organization is in the service of nationalism or of a transcendent moral authority. If it does not serve such an authority, it cannot avoid supporting violence.

References to the Bible as support and justification for a negative attitude towards Muslims are not rare. However, it should be emphasized that it is not possible to justify a priori hatred towards anyone on the basis of the Bible, though there are quite a few individuals and groups who persistently claim the opposite. The fact that there are efforts running counter to this, themselves not without a basis in history, indicates the complexity of the situation in which Europe would find itself in possible upheavals.

It is impossible to speak here of the ethnic aspects of identity, towards which the autonomous self readily descends, as illustrated by the now large number of such cases in recent European history. This concerns the reliance on religious symbols deprived of their essential content. In such interpretations, Christ himself is brought to the courtroom where he is required to be an advocate of hatred and killing. The modern self is thus reshaped from the autonomous self, which is above kin, ethnos, homeland, and nation, into a baser self, in which his given elements, which can be symbolically called "kin," are not sufficient in their nakedness. What they need is a narrative that wraps them in the appearance of sacredness: this is achieved through references to "ancestral customs," "holy books," and the like.

Judaism, Christianity, and Islam: The Conundrum of the Sequence

In order to eliminate the threat to which Muslims are exposed as Other, the solution to the European enigma of the unity of diversity demands a clearer insight into the existing approaches to religious studies. The theological approach, which is prevalent in discussions between various Christologies in Europe, has not contributed to any fundamental harmonization of the knowledge of different forms of religion. Historicism, on the other hand, has facilitated the identification of an apparently logical solution to the relationship of Judaism and Christianity. If Christianity is the final and highest level in the "historical development" of the Revelation, then Judaism can also be recognized as the starting point of that development. The most obvious illustration of this solution is binding the Jewish and Christian holy books into a single Bible, including everything from the first words of the Book of Genesis to the last words of the Book of Revelation. According to this view, the Christian documents of the New Testament are the completion and logical continuation of the Old Testament.

But the question of Islam remains almost insoluble, since the revelation of Qur'an to the Prophet Muhammad comes last of all. It can be presented as a separate and irregular phenomenon, but the limitless potential of the truth to manifest itself regardless of space and time, since "the spirit bloweth where it listeth," would then remain incomprehensible. According to the historical approach, which was developed among Muslims from the earliest times, the Prophet Muhammad is "the headstone in the corner" of the pluriform structure of religion, the one that in Christianity corresponds to Christ. Thousands of books have been written in which this belief was explained. Their Muslim authors offer a large body of evidence for the place held by Muhammad, with reference to both the Qur'an and the Bible. The historical approach in religious studies has no solution to this contradiction.

Phenomenology advances a step from these approaches to religious plurality. However, even there the manifestation of religious elements in space and time is weighted towards the belief in human centrality. Placed in the context of religion or tradition, every phenomenon in culture becomes comparable to another phenomenon. This connection, however, remains inadequate unless a phenomenological order is previously established for all the manifestations of individual religious or traditional totalities. In this, as already noted, reasons can be found for the followers of one religious tradition to tolerate others. But in the light of the premise of the comprehensiveness of every religious tradition, whose root is Truth, this approach, which is manifested in tolerance, does not provide a principled explanation of that plurality. A full explanation emerges only when the metaphysical teachings of esoteric unity are accepted. This acceptance cannot be expressed in simple terms in the language of discursive thought or philosophy. A much more determined effort is required to establish a viable bridge between these two sides—tradition and philosophy—and to synthesize their languages.

In the case of Bosnia, tradition is the internal and most important aspect of an experience that reaches all the way to the current remodeling, tensions, and disruptions. As these changes are essentially linked with the spread of influence of modern ideologies, which are without exception anti-traditional, a more or less ideological tolerance of traditional forms is established. This tolerance is, however, coupled with the expectation that tradition and its forms, as remnants of an outlived stage, will disappear as we progress towards the "end of history."

Bosnia's plurality is composed primarily of Christian and Islamic elements. The Western ideological perspective has a less complex approach to Christian elements, perceiving them as more familiar and more easily adjustable to its notions of progress. Given the historical and emotional experience of conflicts with political systems that have presented themselves as Islamic, and contemporary discords of an economic, political, and cultural nature between the West and what is usually called the "Islamic world," those Bosnian elements that are associated with Islam are readily exploited in an anti-Bosnian narrative.

Crime as the Means of Achieving Unconditional Loyalty

Though sentimentality based on prejudices and an inadequate understanding of certain issues are part of the current and earlier instances of the denial and destruction of Bosnia, most frequently termed "ethnic cleansing" and "genocide," even modern sociology falls short of understanding this phenomenon. Current research and reflection provide no unequivocal and clear answer even to the question: Why did those who began the war so mercilessly kill, rape, incarcerate, torture, and persecute the Muslims?[11] The most frequent answers are that they aspired to the establishment of new states and the homogenization of ethnic areas, or that it was the result of the eruption of old hatreds. It can be shown, however, that none of these interpretations is true, since not one of them encompasses all the phenomena that were and are present. On the other hand, accepting any one of them may contribute to a continuation of such phenomena.[12]

If the use of the term "ethnic cleansing" is examined more closely, the fact that there are still some Muslims left on the territory where ethnic cleansing was conducted makes it impossible to accept that ethnic cleansing as such was the objective of the program that formed the context for the atrocities. If one assumes that the objective was the occupation of territories, the occupation should have eased off towards the end of the war, which was not the case. What, then, is the underlying reason? It is evident from the very nature of the term that there is a problem of definition, as well as the need for the phenomenon to remain obscure in character. Cleansing is a totally inappropriate term for it, for cleansing is originally a term of sacral nature, indicating the desire to separate one thing from another. This separation is possible only with a knowledge of the boundaries, which means to define the identities of both that which is being confined within and what forms those boundaries. In this context, cleansing would mean delineating the self from what limits it, based on a scale of values: what is less valuable is discarded or destroyed. This is, however, the ethical dimension of an essentially unethical phenomenon.

Though the call for this campaign can be designated and interpreted as ethnic cleansing, it is untenable in the face of a rational examination. Rather, its nature is sentimentalist. But even in that case, the external manifestation of a phenomenon demands a search for its deeper, underlying reason. Opposition to the use this term is most frequently expressed by an insistance on the idea of genocide. Genocide is a more just name, but even this name does not exhaust the content of this phenomenon. The intention of the perpetrators of the crime was not to destroy all Muslims. This was not their objective, though many of the perpetrators felt that the relationship between them and their victims would be untenable if the victims were to survive.

Understanding this phenomenon is aided by the realization that it is inseparable from the role of violence in the constitution and articulation of a political identity. The realization of the idea of "unity," "homogeneity," and "power" of the overall Serb or Croat identity is conditional on the destruction of all those aspects that are Other to that identity. The war against Bosnia, as David Campbell notes, "was more about political identities and their constitution than their inevitable antagonism."[13] People were killed because they constituted or symbolized a particular community. "As the means by which identity is inscribed and transcribed across a range of surfaces," notes the same author, "violence can be thought of as the practice through which questions of history are deployed in the present for contemporary political goals. The result is the performative enactment of the identities subsequently regarded as preexisting and the source of the conflict. In these terms, the strategically bizarre cultural violence against symbols of identity in Bosnia—mosques, churches, museums, and memorials—and the horrific violence against bodies—mass rape of women and the mutilation and rape of men—become comprehensible if no less unjustifiable."[14]

Only on the basis of different attitudes to the participants in the war against Bosnia will it be possible to attain a different, and probably deeper, understanding of this phenomenon. The premise of the national interest, which includes the establishment of a pyramid composed by a leader at the top and the postulated national unity below him, comprised by the conceived nation-state as a whole, demands that all individuals be connected into the system. But these connections are either weak or nonexistent. A prerequisite for such connections is, therefore, the disruption of the existing connections, or the destruction of any loyalty that is outside the conceived pyramid of national interest and the related identity. Accordingly, in order to construct the conceived nation-state, it is necessary to destroy Bosnian society. This goal cannot be achieved by political means. What it demands is a denial of the existing human bonds by virtue of which that society exists. In this context, the claim repeated on many occasions, that Serbia was untenable as long as Bosnia existed, is understandable.

For all of those who had been, directly or indirectly, involved in the bonds that formed the basis of Bosnian society, those very bonds were an impediment to the transfer of their full loyalty to organizations, ideology, and the leader of "one's own nation." They were, therefore, encouraged to solve their status by a complete disruption of any bond that was not a bond with the leader. And this demanded that they commit or endorse the worst forms of crime against those who participated in the society. Only in this context can one understand why Others—Serbs, Croats, Bosniacs—were denoted as the principal culprits in those projects.

There is no way to achieve full and unconditional loyalty unless members of the envisaged and sought after national homogeneity are implicated as either perpetrators of or accessories to crime. The more atrocious the crime, the greater their loyalty. This dimension is logically accompanied by other forms of complicity, which are always on the other side of morality. "Ethnic cleansing" or "genocide" is the external dimension of the phenomenon, visible to observers. The killing of a society, which is the essence of the phenomenon, remains, however, concealed behind the horror of the visible crime. The observers and forces engaged in bringing the conflict to an end focus their attention almost entirely on the visible crime. The centers and sources of criminal energy remain on the margin of the overwhelming horror. And not only that—those very criminals are often actors and guarantors in ending the conflict and keeping the peace.

6

The Extremes

Introduction

The turn of the second millennium in Europe was marked by the widespread killings, persecution, and destruction that took place in Bosnia. It may be that this is an anomalous occurrence in the temporal evolution of uninterrupted progress, as Francis Fukuyama saw it,[1] but it is also an important milestone on the path of which the end is known to no one. Seen in the context of this dilemma between happenstance and the possibility of the end of history—a possibility with which humanity has been obsessed, as a vision subordinate to reason, ever since the Renaissance and the Enlightenment—Bosnia apparently remains torn between what it in fact is and the image of it that is put forward in numerous ideological and sentimental interpretations. The most important features of these two extremes can be identified. The first includes the traditional identity of Bosnia's entire history, which remains largely inaccessible to interpretations based solely on discursive thought. The second is the attempt to conduct a scholarly examination of a phenomenon of which an integral element is also "the most atrocious crime in Europe after the Second World War"[2] in terms of a convincing rational model that would include various political, economic, and cultural aspects.

Throughout Bosnia's history there have been attempts to institute the right to religious diversity. From the first indisputable references to the Bosnian state towards the end of the twelfth century[3] to the most recent era, Bosnia never ceased to be a country where different Christologies clash, are reexamined, and become reconciled. In the earliest period, the intention was to ensure the right to the interpretation of religious prophecies independent of the direct influence of large church establishments. Implicit in this very tendency, however, were demarcation from these establishments and strained relations with them. This is why the entire history of Bosnia is brimming with instances of attempts to establish dialogue between those who advocated this attempt to gain freedom for a small country and a small people on the one hand, and the major factors of the world order on the other. This process gradually gave rise to a Bosnian religious diversity that was composed of the members of the separate Bosnian Church, Eastern Orthodoxy, Catholicism, Islam, and Judaism, primarily as moral communities based on different religious revelations. The exoteric diversity of religious forms thus became the most important element of Bosnia's entire history.

It can be said that the Bosnian people constitute one nation, given the fact that they share the same country, the same language, and the same history, but the assertion must be accompanied by the recognition that this unity has borne with it a diversity of religious identities throughout. They survived on the basis of tolerance that had neither permanent sources nor permanent forms: they underwent numerous changes of feeling and perception, which was invariably reflected in the relationships of the different identities. These forms of tolerance were to undergo their major transmutation at the turning point in Bosnia that marks the retreat of the traditional way of life in the face of modernity.

Religious diversity in the premodern period in Bosnia cannot be interpreted or protected without taking into consideration the intuition, probably more significant than understanding, of a qualitatively different kind of human knowledge and the way of life that it implies. The sense of the sanctity of human life that springs from the uncreated and uncreatable substance of every self, through which one and the same God is present in every man, almost never disappeared from the horizon of traditional man. In this view, the possibilities of the self are limitless, but cannot be realized without a heteronomous authority and without transcending every form and every individuality. Although this realization is conditioned by the perfect human agency—Moses, Jesus, and Muhammad—its entire root lies in the unity of truth, in one and the same God. To leave the human horizons without this absolute transcendentality and immanence of God means to reduce and confine the human self to finitude. Phenomena, ideas, and urges then assume the status of that absolute transcendentality and immanence, thus becoming idols that determine the degree of freedom or slavery.

The most essential aspect of tolerance—if we use the term in its modern sense, which does not exist in the traditional experience—was not taking on sufferance, a mere putting up with, the Other who is "wrong and mistaken." It meant acceptance of a different expression of the one and only Truth. No other interpretation of tolerance can represent the framework within which different religious communities survived over many centuries in almost all parts of Bosnia. Neither political realism nor indifference towards others can be the principal source of this centuries-old plurality.

The Bosnian Paradigm

The Bosnian model from the late twelfth century until this turn of the millennium can be described as an attempt to establish a unity of religious differences. "Unity" in this case does not mean oneness. Failure to distinguish between these two terms may be a source of misunderstanding from the very outset. Bearing this in mind, it is necessary to expand on the relationship between the two. Unity can consist of different elements, which are always more or less complex forms. As such, they are characterized by limitations, divisibility, and connectivity. This further means that they have an exterior and an interior. They can have a harmonious and nonexclusive relationship, or they can clash and cancel each other out. The highest degree of their connection is an organism or an organic community of individual organisms. The condition of these relationships in time can help in determining whether aspirations towards harmonization or towards exclusion are prevalent within them. The highest manifestations of their unity are humans and the cosmos. In this analysis, the term unity stands for the existence of religious diversity. This research aims at identifying the tendencies characteristic of such a situation in the context of the Bosnian paradigm.

Seen from the present, the religious plurality of Bosnian society invokes three hypotheses about its origin and reason for survival. It may be an "instrumental" condition, lacking the means of change. Another reason for its enduring is the absence of both attraction and rejection among its components. And last, it can be a consequence of the strength and heightened awareness of the inner elements of each of the present religious traditions, which impose and govern the indispensable diversity. These are the possible perspectives of the duration of the separate identities making up the unity.

The highest plane of this exoteric situation of religious differences is their esoteric oneness. Oneness means absoluteness. It is not limited by anything, which means that neither is it contingent on anything. No form of existence can either add to or subtract anything from it. Oneness as such is the founding principle of every individuality and every unity. It is the source of all knowledge, and everything that lies outside it can only be its more or less clear image. As such, oneness is both transcendent and immanent. Otherwise, it would not be oneness: it would include duality, which also means limitation. This would breed an insoluble relationship between things that limit and those that are being limited. That is why oneness is perfect non-duality. It is a metaphysical concept in its origins, and unity is its projection in space and time.

Sarajevo as the central city and capital of Bosnia has sublimated the Bosnian unity throughout its history, a unity that is in diverse ways reflected in every Bosnian settlement, and the most visible sign of this unity of differences is to be recognized in the coexistence of mosques, churches, and synagogues. Here, as in every city, public places cannot be segregated: they equally belong to everybody, to every individual and every community, regardless of which sacral center they may belong to. It could thus be claimed that the sacral center is divided into several manifestations. The reflection of a different religious revelation—Torah, Christ, Qur'an—beams from each one of them, transmitting itself throughout space, reaching to every individual and every community. In this way differences in the world of multiplicity and motion remain connected, through different revelations, with one and the same Revealer.

When sacred histories coincide temporally and spatially, inescapably they constantly "touch" and "intertwine" everywhere with the current from the center of a different revelation. None of these revelations can find grounds for the denial of another without denying itself on the same grounds. It is only once we accept, on the basis of both knowledge and being, this oneness manifested in multiplicity that we can explain how the cluster of a coherent urban ensemble forms and develops, composed of houses, streets, neighborhoods and certain quarters of the city where the inhabitants are predominantly Orthodox Christians, Catholics, Muslims, or Jews, but also other quarters where the population is mixed and almost wholly intermingled. In the long-term view, diversity is inconsistent with the denial of the Other. But the denial of the Other is at the same time the denial of the individuality of the denier, as we can conclude from the Bosnian experience.[4]

Central to the topic of this paper is the question whether the indisputable unity of different religious traditions in Bosnia has its own esoteric oneness.

This question can be answered from two perspectives. The first is a philosophical perspective whose basis is discursive thought, and the second is a traditional perspective in which intuitive thought prevails. Their languages are related but not equal. Every attempt to reduce these two perspectives to either one of them will result in a failure to answer the question, or in a truncated answer at best.

On the Border

The great schism that occurred within Christianity, the imperial religion, in the twelfth century had a major impact on the Bosnian region. The two universal churches that emerged from the schism have never reached agreement on the territorial boundary between their respective religious jurisdictions.

Thus, Bosnia remained a country to which both of these churches laid claim. The divisions that sprang from this schism, in terms of liturgies and gravitational centers, were quite different in this country from the form they took in its more or less immediate European neighborhood. Every form of acceptance had always involved some kind of rejection, and vice versa. It is thus possible to identify numerous resemblances and differences in the Christian experience of the Bosnian people that do not exist in the neighboring countries. It is beyond doubt that the medieval Bosnian state was essentially linked to the Christian experience. However, it was at the same time both Catholic and non-Catholic, both Orthodox and non-Orthodox.[5] This could explain the religious plurality and polyphony in which the Bosnian Church was but one form and one voice, extremely important, yet never the one and only.

Then, in the fifteenth century, in the long and complex course of changes, Bosnia became part of the huge Ottoman Empire. Given the multireligious nature of that empire, Bosnia preserved the basic pattern of its original identity within it. This pattern, it is true, was fundamentally reshaped, but it did not lose its original character. Bosnia as a whole gradually took the shape of a country whose culture was composed of Catholicism, Orthodoxy, Islam, and Judaism. Both spatially and temporally, the country was to become full of religious plurality and polyphony. In the west, its borders marched with those of Christendom, in which a religious plurality that would include Muslims was unthinkable until the nineteenth century. Coming from the west, the Bosnian border marked the beginning of a space and time where Muslim culture existed alongside with that of Western Christians. In the opposite direction, though, from east to west, the Muslim presence was sharply cut off by the Bosnian border: there could be no Muslims to the west of it. The Balkan territories of the Ottoman Empire included numerous religious, ethnic, and linguistic communities, among which the Ottoman imperial perspective assigned to Islam a position of political privilege. This not infrequently led to the denial of the equal rights granted in principle to Muslims, Christians, and Jews as communities of the revealed books.

The Renaissance perspective of human potential in making use of what is proffered by the self and the world, which took further shape in the Enlightenment, reduces humans to the horizontal flow of time. They are not determined by the mystery of the soul of the world as the spirit's mediator in governing every phenomenon, but are, both individuals and members of the community, participants in the chain of causes and events that they can influence. This excludes the dimension of verticality or revelation: humans cease to be the bridge between Earth and Heaven, the *locus* of the revelation of the uncreated Word and God's image. Humans thus assume the role of the shaper of that flow. They see the start of their interference as marking a turning point in space and time; further movement from this point is seen as the logical march of history towards its end, as Georg Hegel pointed out in his shift of perspective from the Holy Spirit to the Temporal Spirit.

History thus becomes a power per se and is understood as the subject of change. Into this view, it is sufficient to recognize that embryo of the collective in time past that can be denoted as a protostate, follow it up to any present moment in time, and then read change and acceleration into it in terms of the "known" logical procession. This type of modeling of change reaches its fullest expression in ideological images of the world—in liberalism, socialism, conservatism, and nationalism. Population numbers, territory, language, religion become the criteria to be applied in identifying the forms and substance of that nucleus. However, these criteria never attain the clarity of a definition. The situation differs from case to case—things that are important in one place may become irrelevant elsewhere, and vice versa.

The nineteenth century saw the emergence of aspirations to give shape to a rationalist construction of the "Serb nation," which included the idea of the decline of Turkey and was preceded by, or concurrent with, similar ideas of the "Greek nation," the "Bulgarian nation," and so on. The supposed decline of the Ottoman Empire ushered onto the stage the ravaged and vulnerable territories that in every ideological picture seem tailor-made for the establishment of a nation-state that would serve to realize the ancient desire for the protostate, which, from the ideological perspective, had been thwarted a long time ago due to the interference of evil and injustice. Each of the three envisaged nation-states already referred to—the Greek, the Bulgarian, and the Serb—the nations in question were Eastern Christian, and were linked by important doctrinal and emotional relationships. However, as their power increases they come into conflict over territories and political domination in those territories. Religious similarity as a crucial element thus ceases to be an element in the process of constructing the nation-state as the cornerstone of identity. At the same time, linguistic and ethno-genetic differences increase in importance, as do medieval states and dynasties, with which the modern would-be nation-state seeks to establish continuity.[6] This establishes a dual criterion of Orthodoxy and language. Religion remains its primary element, but it can become considerably more flexible and usable only when supported by language. Equilibrium is found in the balance of power, which is most frequently a simple reflection of the numerical size of either of the peoples.

Promotion of the principle of the power of quantity leads to a total denial of those whose numbers are small: they are either absorbed among the more numerous, or destroyed. This is the crucial change in relation to the traditional perspective, in which principles do not adduce either power or force as their evidence. The common factor of all the emerging nation-states becomes the denial of Muslims and of everything that underpins their presence in the entire region. This denial almost always includes reductively equating Islam and Muslims with Turkish rule. Overthrowing that rule as a prerequisite for the establishment of national freedom is directly linked to the elimination from the scene of Islam and Muslims.

Processes following this pattern take place mainly in the regions that march with Bosnia to the east, but also within Bosnia itself when they cannot be prevented. On the other side of the border, to the west, a different process of delineation takes place among the Slavic population that today for the most part call themselves "Croats." Since the religion present in the nation-states of the Hungarians, Germans, and Italians, which were the envisaged goals of political and cultural activities within the Austro-Hungarian Empire, was not different from those of the Croats, here, too, linguistic differences become a factor of delineation, while the construction of the proto-state as the starting point for the development of identity is expected to lead to the establishment of a new nation-state. In this connection, there are identifiable aspirations to define the integral Croat state as a moral historical community, and not as a community of blood. The reduction of this pattern to Catholicism as the foundation of Croathood manifests itself as an anti-Bosnian tendency.[7] In the first of these processes, it is possible to recognize the desire to relativize or undermine the role of religion and to reinforce the language of history and political interest. The position of religion in the second perspective, however, is the reverse: its collision with the political ideology is an inevitable consequence of that reductionism.

Part of these two processes in Bosnia's neighborhood, which continued within different state contexts in the nineteenth and twentieth centuries, was the detaching of Croats from their western neighbors in order to draw closer to the Serbs, which was justified by their linguistic and political similarity and by the need to deter the Hungarian, German, and Italian threat. Both of these peoples would encounter a paradigm in Bosnia that was essentially opposed to the idea of the nation-state, primarily in the light of the definitions essential to both of these national ideologies. If religion is the most distinctive feature that differentiates Croats from Serbs and that makes them different nations despite the fact that they speak the same language, then in the case of the Bosnian Muslims, who live throughout Bosnia and in significant numbers even in parts of its eastern neighborhood, one should accept the fact that it is not possible to establish the postulated nation-states for Serbs and Croats on Bosnian territory. This problem can be solved in two ways. The first is to abandon the ideology of the nation-state as the only valid ideology. The second is to establish a state or states in which nation is not equivalent to a religious, ethnic, or linguistic community. This generates the need to formulate a unity of differences that would not exclude religious, national, or state communities.

Contrary to this solution there persists the familiar and rationally explicable project of establishing one state for one nation, for which the European experience has provided ample evidence. Since Serbs, like Croats and Bosniacs, do not live in a homogeneous community in a single territory, the establishment of the state postulated in this way demands a demographic restructuring of the neighboring territories. Killings, expulsions, and destruction are the only possible way of doing this; otherwise, a single state for an entire nation is not feasible. Accepting this as impossible brings into salience the need for cooperation among nations and states, in which existing borders would also reflect a harmony of differences. They would remain borders, but at the same time they would be bridges. This renders the issue of tolerance crucial.

Two Perspectives on Tolerance

Bosnia is the only ancient and culturally structured European country in which a religious pluralism that includes the presence of Islam has survived for over half a millennium. On the basis of this pluralism, regardless of the quality of the relationships among its different elements, a more or less unified society was built. In no other part of southeastern Europe where some form of religious plurality was present is there the continuity of a unified society.

It should be noted at the very outset that nowhere in the entire history of Europe has a balance been established between the different Christian churches of a kind that has endured without interruption for several centuries. The presence of Jews, without which the history of European pluralism cannot be understood, was eliminated at different times in a similar way to that of Muslims. The Holocaust was certainly an exception in that brutality was so concentrated into atrocities of such magnitude, but it was still part of the same cause and continuity. This is why Bosnia's pluralism can be understood only in terms of its specific nature, given the presence of Islam. It is fair to say that there has been a historical equilibrium between the three factors of Bosnian society—Islamic, Jewish, and Christian. Nowhere else has such a balance been achieved in the form of a stable society. It may also be viewed as a balance between Islam, Catholicism, and Orthodoxy. These patterns appear largely unconvincing to the contemporary observer, sometimes distasteful, and often even repugnant. However, the fact that Bosnian society has existed for many centuries can be neither understood nor described without taking into account these differences.

The emphasis of Judaism lies on the importance of and adherence to the revealed Law. Only in the social extension of the mystery of the Temple and the Ark of the Covenant, later represented by the synagogues of the Diaspora, is it possible to bear witness to the covenant with God and commitment to the revelation. From this follows the preparation for redemption that will take place through the Messiah.

Christianity does not deny the Law, but sees it as absorbed and realized in Christ himself as the revealed Word of God. And since he is the revealed Word, his mother is the recipient of the revelation, which is a unique phenomenon in the totality of religious experience. Jesus becomes the body in which the Word has been realized, and thus the condition and purpose of all human expectation and attainment of redemption. As such, he is rejected by the Jews, which results in two faces of the exoteric manifestation of one and the same essence. Never and nowhere do they achieve lasting equilibrium.

Islam is the name of the submission of all that exists to its supreme and ineffable principle. It is the way of existence of humans and the cosmos in relation to that principle, which reveals the truth about it through the Prophet Muhammad. In this case, the receiver of the revelation of the Word and the Word itself are not one and the same thing. The revealed book is, therefore, the Word of God, with which Muhammad's human life is in perfect compliance. He transmits the Law and upholds it perfectly. The Jewish emphasis on the Law and the Christian emphasis on faith thus converge in Islam's founding the entirety of both individual and social life on faith and the Law. In this view, the Law is accepted without this entailing the rejection of Christ: in the revelation that was disclosed to Muhammad, God purified his mother and raised her above the women of all the worlds;[8] and Christ himself is the Word of God bestowed upon Mary.[9]

It follows from this that Christians, Jews, and Muslims living together represents an equilibrium underpinned by the very nature of the Divine revelations. In this view, others are not "in error." Their potential is one and the same perfection, but there are different ways of attaining it, which are revealed, true, and orthodox, although exoterically different. This is not about tolerance, but about the sacred recognition on the basis of the esoteric sameness of different exoteric manifestations of truth. The revelation explicitly corroborates this: *Surely they that believe, and those of Jewry, and the Christians, and those Sabaeans, who so ever believes in God and the Last Day, and works righteousness— their wage awaits them with their Lord, and no fear shall be on them, neither shall they sorrow.*[10] This clear position, which identifies humankind's salvation as their highest potential, confirms the esoteric oneness of different divine traditions. These individual and shared characteristics are linked to their sacral centers—synagogues, churches, and mosques—and through them to one and the same "Holy of Holies."

The prevailing perception of the Other as those who are in error goes contrary to this understanding of the relationships between differences. Although, they profess and follow what is wrong from the viewpoint of the absolutized configuration of the self that judges, they have to be tolerated, because political circumstances do not allow a different attitude. This necessity can be solved in three different ways: through a solution based on political realism; through the possibility of plurality characterized by unconcern with the differences that are private and outside the public domain; and on the basis of accepting the human self with its unquestionable right to freedom and indisputable equality in principle in relation to any other that participates in society as a whole. These are the three perspectives of tolerance. They can be linked to the esoteric unity of religious differences, which presupposes the relevance of religion for every individual, but which does not resolve the issue of the segment of humankind for which religion has no significance.

Historicism Instead of Principle

Research into Bosnian culture reveals that there was no significant preoccupation with history in earlier periods. Every individual, on the basis of his/her connection with tradition, is responsible to the sacred knowledge and knowledge of the sacred. This does not depend on either space or time. No imaginary history governs either individual or collective destiny: the direct "contact" with God, which takes place through every phenomenon in the self and the outer world, is the most important element of the drama of life. No success or failure on the part of either ancestors in the past or descendants in the future can absolve one from the responsibility of the individual present, which is not a time of simple sensitivity and enjoyment, but is actually a constant contact with Eternity.

The ideal identity is defined by the *logos*, which is identical to the perfect human. This has never been, nor could it have been, a state of consciousness and existential activity that would encompass all the individuals and all the communities in Bosnian society. Not one sacred tradition has ever advocated the possibility of paradise on Earth: it is only an ideal to which individuals conform, transferring their knowledge into their being, and vice versa, establishing a link with and upholding virtue. In this view, morality is based on the immutability and constant presence of the sacred knowledge and knowledge of the sacred. Virtue is a condition and consequence of intellectuality or connection with Knowledge, as opposed to non-virtue, which is, above all, a consequence of ignorance.

This state of consciousness and conduct in the Bosnian way can be described with the term "wrong" (*grehota*), which has already been elaborated on. This term can be used to denote the general responsibility of individuals towards themselves and the outer world. "Wrong" encompasses the whole of knowledge and identity through which it is possible to deny access to salvation in perfection. "Wrong" wholly transcends any exoterically shaped religious dogma and its related morality and rites. It does not depend upon them, but they are always in touch with it.[11] "Wrong" is often incompatible with rational models. It can be said that in the ideological image of the world, based on the notion of the autonomous self, "wrong," which otherwise permeates the individual who is connected with tradition, becomes in an untenable position and fades away, rather as plant or animal species are becoming extinct before the eyes of equally indifferent witnesses. "Wrong" is the intuitive and primordial sense of human responsibility, an immediate expression of the quintessence of human being, comparable to the sense or knowledge of beauty.

The modern notion of the establishment of a nation-state is accepted as the basis of the historical course towards paradise on Earth. Since "history judges" on the basis of its "lines of force," what is needed for its direction is an elite, and the elite is sublimated in the leader, or ideology, which connects the root nucleus of that state in ancient times with the envisaged state of the "end of history," or a new paradisiacal condition of the nation. Seen in the context of the destruction of Bosnian society, this perspective rests on two pivots of decisive importance. The first is the idea of the Serb state. Ideologically postulated, and justified by historicism, "Dušan's kingdom" is defined as a nucleus that can reach its full development only in a new Serb nation-state. This means that obstacles should be eliminated from the whole of the territory that can in any way be related to the set goal. The justification for this may be "ethnic homogenization," "historical or natural rights," and the like, all of which cram the propagandist books of Serb nationalism. This programme requires the borders of this envisaged state to include "all Serbs," with a concomitantly reduced presence of all those who are not Serbs. Demographic restructuring based on ethnic homogenization was an essential element of the Serb uprisings in the early nineteenth century and of the Balkan Wars in the early twentieth century. One of the methods employed was genocide, an attempt to eliminate Muslims. Such campaigns were continued during the Second World War and the 1991–1995 war against Bosnia.[12]

Bosnia lies at the very core of this project. In its maximalist claims, the whole of Bosnia was to become part of the territory of the envisaged Serb nation-state; in more realistic approaches, some parts of Bosnia could be "ceded" to the elite of the Croat national project, as happened in 1939 under the well-known Cvetković-Maček Agreement, which was repeated, with tragic consequences, in the Milošević-Tuđman agreement in 1991. In the case of Bosnia, the central issues are its religious plurality and its inability to fit into the national history that has been fabricated to serve the project.

Complementary, and hence in principle equal, is the project to establish the Croat nation-state. This project, too, envisages a state that would include all Croats. This state, too, has a maximalist and a minimalist perspective. And here again, the reasons for its existence lie in a historicism that recognizes its state proto-nucleus in ancient times, in Tomislav's kingdom, which is a modern historicist construct. Between this kingdom and the present-day there were sufferings and obstacles to achieving the goal of the nation-state as an earthly substitute for the heavenly Jerusalem, which is first embodied in the leader, and then in the nation and its state territory.

These two perspectives meet as action and reaction, as thesis and antithesis, on the Bosnian territory, which, in the interest of both sides, has to be denied every validity and historical foundation. For both sides, Bosnia is a "historical monstrosity" and a "colonial creation."[13] As such, Bosnia is represented as a major obstacle to achieving the set goal of a nation-state for all Serbs and Croats respectively.

Karađorđevo: The Leaders' Agreement on Crime

The ideological premises of the Serb and Croat national blueprints outlined here explain the dominant interpretations of the process of dissolution and destruction of Yugoslavia. Yugoslavia as a state was originally designed as the realization of the Serb national will: the unification of all Serbs in one state, as the culmination of historical development from Dušan's kingdom to its resurrection. The Kingdom of Serbs, Croats, and Slovenes, renamed the Kingdom of Yugoslavia in 1929, survived amid a bitter and cruel dispute between two national ideologies that were identical in principle—the Serb and the Croat. At the foundation of this dispute lay their attitudes towards Bosnia. These two perceptions are by nature completely opposed to the plurality and polyphony of Bosnia: the establishment of a homogeneous Serbia, whose antithesis is a homogenous Croatia, is impossible without the denial and destruction of Bosnia as a unity in diversity. The promotion of the "national interest of Serbs and Croats" thus incorporates the denial of Bosnia's existence in its entirety.

It is therefore understandable why both Milošević and Tuđman should have embodied and perpetuated such an understanding of historicism above all through their consensus regarding the denial and destruction of Bosnia in the course of the dissolution of Yugoslavia. In early 1991, the two of them met at a place in Vojvodina called Karađorđevo, seeking to reach agreement on dismembering the Bosnian state so that they could build an expanded Serbia and expanded Croatia from the pieces. In late 1991, this agreement, seen through the lens of the "Croatian national interest," was explained by Tuđman in a meeting with representatives of his political subalterns in Bosnia:[14]

Accordingly, Bosnia and Herzegovina has no future as a sovereign state.

And even if it could survive as an independent state, gentlemen, what would it mean?

With the current Muslim policy, it would become more closely linked to Serbia than to Croatia, in the political sense.

The establishment of borders—are we going to establish borders between Croatia and Herzegovina so that a Croat from Herzegovina could not go to his Croatia, or vice-versa?

Are we going to set up customs controls? Do we want things like the ban on selling petrol, issued with good reason by the Government? Finally, do we want money, and all that together; these are all problems that arise in the usual legislative-administrative sense, which create new relationships that would be untenable, in my opinion, for Croatia, given the shape of its borders, and the Croat part of the Herzegovinian and Bosnian territory alike.

Therefore the survival of the sovereignty of Bosnia in present circumstances from the Croatian point of view is such that not only do we not have to support that idea, we must not even openly raise the issue; but why not accept the offer of redrawing the borders when it is in the interests of the Croat people, here, in this Republic in Bosnia and Herzegovina? I can see no serious reason to the contrary, indeed, in the talks that I have personally had with both Izetbegović and Milošević. Besides, one of our people in Bosnia has drafted a proposal for such a delineation of borders, where the Croat areas, both those that you have brought into this community of Herceg-Bosna and the community of Croat Posavina, and probably, for geopolitical reasons, the Cazin-Bihać area, would go to Croatia. This would almost optimally satisfy the Croat national interests, not only for the time being but also for the future. The remaining areas, which would remain inhabited mainly by Muslims with some Croats Catholics, could form a statelet around Sarajevo that would be reminiscent of that historical little country Bosnia, which would be a buffer zone between Serbia and Croatia, and which would necessarily rely on Croatia in such conditions. This would also satisfy the international factors which, most certainly, seriously count on that Serb gendarme, as you have already mentioned, against that Muslim element, Islamic element on the territory

of Yugoslavia, whose aspirations are to form an Islamic state in Europe with the
support of Tehran and Tripoli.

From this point of view, any cantonization, with the survival of Bosnia and
Herzegovina, is not a solution for us in terms of delineation.

So this is where the problem lies. That is why I think that you have missed
out a bit. You have pursued a policy of maintaining sovereignty, while the
neighbouring areas were more in favour of joining Croatia. After all, people
from those areas are participating in the defence of Croatia.

The question arises: these people ask for Croatian passports, there is a
whole series of issues, you know. If we were not to satisfy these demands, we
would create a rupture within the Croat national identity, which is such as it is.

Accordingly, it seems to me that, just as we used this historical moment
to create an independent Croatia, which is internationally recognized, it is
time we gathered the Croat national identity within maximal possible borders. It is of lesser importance from that point of view whether it would be 30
or 28 municipalities.[15]

The two sides—Milošević's and Tuđman's—perceived themselves as the
absolute embodiment of "national interests." Identified with the historical
course as the decisive will and force, they were aware of the balance of power
between them, and regarded Bosnia as a pliant object within which those who
are more powerful could even act as "the bestowers of gifts." According to
Tuđman's testimony, the negotiations in Karađorđevo included a discussion
on the indisputable and obvious parts of Bosnia that would lie on either side
of the new border between these national states. But the negotiations also included giving away other parts. "I want to tell you", Tuđman said to his associates, "exactly what Milošević said: 'You take Cazin, Kladuša and Bihać, I
don't need that, that's Turkish Croatia.'"[16] This shows how the ideology-based
picture, in which the ideological unity of differences is completely denied, was
viewed as material that was available for use regardless of human destinies, for
they were insignificant in relation to the set goal: the final solution of the
national question in the form of establishment of the national state.

Ideological Distortion

On the basis of these indications, the tension that is destroying Bosnian plurality can be shown to be of an ideological nature. The ideological concepts of
establishing nation-states include the formulation of historical trends within
which it is possible to present the denial and destruction of Bosnia as a pattern through which historical injustices are to be redressed. The subjectivity of

the national *self,* which passes judgment about the nature of Bosnia, thus proclaims itself identical to the deified history, and the different nature of Bosnian society an obstacle and opposition to the realization of that absolutized national *self.* In this view, the fact that Orthodox populations in Bosnia regard themselves as Serbs, and Catholic as Croats, and that they cannot live in the national states which include all Serbs and Croats respectively, is to be presented as the very essence of Bosnia's existence.

If Bosnia exists as a state, then the Serbia that is postulated by the Serb national program is not possible. The same goes for the Croatian national program. Denying and destroying Bosnia is therefore equivalent to confirming and establishing the national states that are demanded for all Serbs and all Croats respectively. The forces that resist such denial and destruction must be presented as enemies of Serbs and Croats, and the nature of those forces construed as repugnant to the universally accepted perceptions of development and progress in the liberal democratic world. When members of the Bosnian people who are at the same time members of the Serb and Croat peoples respectively resist the denial and destruction of Bosnia, they are presented as traitors. This creates a process of inner dissolution and delineation on the basis of religious, or in other words of national, tensions.

All forms of trust, cooperation, and awareness of the reasons for tolerance conflict with general national programs. The final outcome of a program envisaged and directed in this way was to isolate the Muslims and demonstrate that they alone advocated an integral Bosnia. They would then be accused of trying to preserve the Bosnian state exclusively for their own purposes. The factor of Islam is involved in this process, because the Muslims' insistence on the Bosnian state, which in its entire substance, these anti-Bosnian interpretations claim, is accepted neither by the Bosnian Serbs nor the Bosnian Croats, is to be presented as an essentially Islamic ideological construct. Accordingly, every form of public or covert behavior on the part of the Bosnian Muslims that includes world views contrary to Western liberalism, democracy, and capitalism, and which are essentially linked to secularized Christianity, is perceived as support for the anti-Bosnian programs. Bosnian Muslims may be accused of taking up the cause of the "Islamic threat," which renders Bosnia as a state unacceptable and offensive to the most important factors of the world order, and which is used to justify the incitement of both Bosnian Serbs and Bosnian Croats against that state. At the same time, it is to be seen as a major ally in the activities aimed at destroying that country for the sake of the envisaged new national states for all Serbs and all Croats, respectively.

"Historical Lines of Force" as a Quantitative Criterion

On the basis of the ideological construction that, according to the deified role of history, is the result of a concatenation of circumstances recognized through the messianic position and assumed role of the national leader, the conditions were created for the achievement of the highest goal: the establishment of the national state, desired and urged for centuries but, as a result of hostile powers and historical immaturity, not yet achieved. After putting forward sweeping interpretations cloaked in historicism and national interests, Slobodan Milošević and Franjo Tuđman, as embodiments of historical development and national welfare, reached an agreement on partition. They regarded their goal as the indisputable, supreme national value, the attainment of which justifies killings, expulsions, and destruction. When in early 1991 he was asked about this goal, which became the first god of the ethno-national pantheon, Franjo Tuđman's answer to Stipe Mesić was: "Stipe, you don't understand what historical lines of force are."[17] This was his reply to the question whether it was reasonable to call for the destruction of Bosnia as a state and the allocation of parts of its territory to Serbia and Croatia. This was at the same meeting during which Tuđman explained the content of his talks with Milošević in Karađorđevo to his associates, displaying the geographical maps of the partition on which the two of them had reached agreement.

"National interest" is always related to a programmatic formulation expressed by a limited rational model. For this reason its realization in practice presupposes sentimentality as the basis of the actions of those responding to the call of the elite to take part in the pursuit of the set goal. Since the goal has been declared indisputable, obedience towards the leader and leadership is an unquestionable virtue as well. In this case, the means of achieving the goal need not be clearly defined. It is not necessary to say explicitly to the executors that killings, persecution, and torture of others are the only way to prove their loyalty to the leader. What guides them in that direction are the "historical lines of force," which are, given their deification, at the same time justification for crimes. In the eyes of the masses motivated by such sentimentality, so long as the other side has committed even the most minor of misdemeanors, the world becomes a mere battlefield for the clash between "us" and "them," a clash of which the outcome will determine the supreme goal, treated as a life or death issue.

In view of the preceding expositions on the nature of Bosnia's ethnic and religious plurality, at the turn of the millennium at least six important prerequisites for the reconstruction and strengthening of Bosnian society on the basis of dialogue and trust are identifiable.

First, Bosnia's religious plurality, which in principle includes Islam, Christianity—Catholicism and Orthodoxy—and Judaism, has an esoteric oneness in the understanding of which there are important reasons for a harmonious dialogue and trust. Reliable and comprehensive knowledge about this is lacking, responsibility for which lies not only with the totalitarianism of national ideologies but also with the secularized religious organizations that fail to remain independent and to distance themselves from the national programs.

Second, the collective identities in the form of ethnic and religious communities participating in Bosnia's unity of differences are possible as absolute human freedom if the sanctity of each individual within them is of central importance.

Third, the liberal notion of the autonomous self as the basis of equality and liberty, on which a harmonious society composed of plural identities can be built, offers tolerance that is founded on principles. The use of this offer presupposes a clear discernment between liberalism and nationalism.

Fourth, the esoteric unity of different sacral traditions that postulates religious plurality on the one hand, and liberal democracy, based on freedom and equality of the individual, on the other, can establish a relationship of understanding and complementarity. This demands a resolute emancipation of the advocates of universal dialogue and trust from the existing organizational collusion between nationalism and religion.

Fifth, the indisputable common interest of all participants in Bosnia's unity of differences, together with the tragic experience of co-opting historicism in the service of nationalism, demands the promotion of the basic values of sacral traditions and of liberalism with its postulation of human rights.

Sixth, the elimination of ideological and biased evaluations of different sacral traditions based on crude examples of the historicist and phenomenological methods is an essential prerequisite for remodeling the current inarticulate plurality of Europe into a harmonious unity of ethnic and religious differences.

$$7$$

In Bosnia or Against It?

Introduction

The war in Bosnia and Herzegovina may be perceived as part of a wider process that also includes the break up of Yugoslavia. To this day no comprehensive model has been offered to interpret this process. Furthermore, what we see advocated and adopted are one-sided ideological interpretations that create an illusion of clarity of the process analyzed, but that are intended to prevent a methodical and all-encompassing explanation of the linkages involved. "The war in Croatia" and "the war in Bosnia and Herzegovina" is the terminology that results from such interpretations. It was in fact a "war against Bosnia and Herzegovina," the origins of which lay in a long, well-prepared and rationally based attitude towards that state. Only through such analysis can we fully comprehend the complexity of events.

The rationale for the destruction of Bosnia and Herzegovina lies in the three ethno-nationalist projects, their relations with each other, and their capacity to link up, individually and together, with forces in the outside world. These projects are not identical; neither did they develop at the same time, nor do they carry the same significance in the hierarchy of events. Yet, although of different form, they are identical in their underlying principle. These are rational projects, though masked by irrational rhetoric, religion, and emotive readings of history, as is conclusively proven by their focus on and reduction to quantifiable goals. A convincing and rational model of their relationship can be established, but it is also worth highlighting and clarifying at the outset the crucial dilemma: either Bosnia and Herzegovina is an organic unity, or it is a construct of separable parts. The model espoused here adopts the first premise. Compared with its neighbors, Bosnia and Herzegovina has the longest lasting internationally recognized borders, that have undergone the least alteration in the last hundred years. The linguistic, historical, and geographic integration of its population was of a higher order than can be found among its neighbors. The population was almost completely mixed and intermingled: before this last war Serbs and Bosniacs lived on about 95 percent and Croats on about 70 percent of the territory of Bosnia and Herzegovina. Those different identities did not, however, develop as territorialized entities—they were totally independent from any distinct territory that could have been considered as belonging solely to them. It is impossible to speak of Bosnia and Herzegovina as a single country while affirming distinct identities on the basis of territorialization.

The recent war against Bosnia and Herzegovina was preceded by an era in which the state was founded on ideology. National identity and that of the republics making up the state, together with all other dimensions of society, were perceived as subordinate to the ideological project. Any insubordinate ideas and trends were rejected, suppressed, and often annihilated. The weakening of the hold of ideology allowed these forbidden and suppressed ideas to come to the surface, the force of their expression being determined quantifiably by the numbers prepared to embrace them. This tendency is also evident in the recent obsession with presenting census data in the form of maps of ethnic distribution within the country's ethnic and religious plurality.

The analysis presented in this essay does not take account of those external forces most frequently denoted as "the international community."[1] During the course of the development and operation of the three ethno-national projects, American, British, German, French, Russian, and Chinese policies had a complex effect upon them. (The presence of other international factors is not negligible, but nor is it decisive.) This particular aspect of the matter discussed here calls for a separate approach and quantification.

Three Nationalisms

Three ethno-national projects were involved in the process of destroying Bosnia and Herzegovina—the Greater-Serbian, the Greater-Croatian, and the Bosniac.[2] They are determined by the mentality and the logic of the ideological totalitarianism that preceded them, even though they try to distance themselves from it as much as possible. Their insistence on their differences from the Communist regime is largely rhetorical and superficial. In these projects, the ideology-based state is replaced by ideas and actions leading towards ethnic homogeneity, which should be logically complemented by "national sovereignty."

The Greater-Serbia project tied in to the creation of a new Yugoslav state as the project which met the demand for all Serbs to be gathered in one state with their own political domination guaranteed by virtue of their being in the majority, which in turn would be justified by their ethno-national ideology in its most literal application.[3] This concept could be brought about only in a centralized system of power. The distribution of power among the Republics and Provinces endangered the basis of the rule by majority and for that reason the Greater-Serbia elite opposed it most resolutely. Demands for the restructuring of Yugoslavia to be based on the dilution or revocation of the autonomy of the Republics and Provinces became crucial to the growth and transmutation of the Greater-Serbia ethno-national elite in their advancement of their own ethno-national project. As the Republics and Provinces resisted this, and the usurpation of the idea of a Federal State by the Greater-Serb elite failed to neutralize their resistance by force, it became necessary to advance the strategy to the next level: the sovereignty of the Republics is disputed, as are their borders, while the accent is put on the need to redraw the borders on the basis of earlier projects and debates and to create new forms that would represent a comprehensive solution, first and foremost for all Serbs and all Croats. This is evident in the message Slobodan Milošević sent to Karadžić in 1991 in which he says "The Slovenes can quit Yugoslavia now, but the Croats only after we sort out the borders."[4] This redrawing of borders represents a way to achieving the demand for a new state encompassing all Serbs. The borders of this state would, in accordance with this thinking, separate Serbs and Croats since they "do not want to and cannot live together" any more, as Dobrica Ćosić remarks.[5]

During 1990 and 1991, the project manifested itself on the political scene in the form of the Greater-Serbia elite's aggressive demand for the restructuring of Yugoslavia. Though carried out within the institutions of the Federal State, the key players were in fact the Greater-Serbia elite led by Slobodan Milošević, whose supporters throughout the state institutions helped strengthen the presence and influence of the elite at all levels of state. Thus, step-by-step yet swiftly, the army, police, finances, diplomacy, and other forms of state control were restructured on the basis of their responsiveness to the project of the Greater-Serbia elite. The process also produces adverse reactions in those areas where ideas of plurality of the Yugoslav state cannot be subjugated to the demands of this elite.

In the subsequent course of events, the Croat response to the Greater-Serb project is of key importance. The demand for the separation of the Croat state from Yugoslavia is both legitimate and understandable in the light of the Greater-Serbia project that was to transform Yugoslavia into a tool for the implementation of Serb ethno-national power. The Croat response was not exempt from the start from the influence of the Greater-Serbia project: it very quickly formed as an ethno-national project with all its important elements—

the elite, the ideology, the organizational structure—in the service of the establishment of a state that would represent an instrument of the political identity identified with the ethno-nation. The demand for "all Serbs in one state" was reciprocated with the slogan "all Croats in one state." Thus, a reactive mechanism was established that would substantially decide the nature of the subsequent war.

This duality of the Greater-Serbia and the Greater-Croatia project draws Bosnia and Herzegovina into its very center. Bosnia and Herzegovina is not and cannot be by its nature an ethno-national state of the kind postulated by the Greater-Serbia and Greater-Croatia projects. Its plurality is "unnatural," "freak," and "unsustainable," as both Milošević and Tuđman agreed. The key obstacle to the realization of their plan therefore led them to the conclusion that reaching agreement on the partition of Bosnia and Herzegovina was the only means of achieving the envisaged ethno-national states. It is indisputable that the focal point of the war against Bosnia and Herzegovina is to be found in the Karađorđevo agreement.[6] Whatever the actual content of the agreement, the subsequent war confirmed the following beyond doubt: (1) the Greater-Serbia and Greater-Croatia elites agreed that Bosnia and Herzegovina was not viable, and worked for its destruction; (2) the ethno-national make-up of Bosnia and Herzegovina required the use of force to break up its deeply rooted plurality and achieve ethno-nationalized territories that would lend themselves to inclusion in the new states; (3) the existence of Bosniacs throughout the territory was the main impediment to the efforts to realize these goals, which brings the "Muslim question" to the heart of the Greater-Serbia and Greater-Croatia diplomatic and military partnership thus established.[7]

The end of 1990 brought to power the three parties organized as "the political will of ethno-national entities within Bosnia and Herzegovina"[8] in the wake of democratic elections. The Serb and Croat parties were under the inherent direct influence of the ethno-national centers in Belgrade and Zagreb and were by definition subjugated to their respective elites' unitary ethno-national projects. Thus, the wider Yugoslav approach to the crisis of the state was replicated in all the institutions of political power in Bosnia and Herzegovina. These two parallel processes, ethno-national centralization and the strengthening of power at the republic level in an uncontrolled process of decentralization of the federal state, were demonstrated in the efforts to put the Yugoslav People's Army, which was a priori structured as a centralized organization, into the hands of the Greater-Serbia elite under the pretext of the defense of the federal state. A similar process was instituted in all other relevant federal institutions and organizations; for external consumption word was put about that the state was being undermined by separatists, secessionists and nationalists, while all the time, covert organizational links were being established by every Serb element with their ethno-national leadership headed by Milošević. It is particularly important to the understanding of this drama to note that large numbers of participants in the existing ideological system, under the cloak of their opposition to the "destroyers of Yugoslavia," proved totally incompetent and passive in recognizing and opposing the process that was going on. An explanation for this may be found in the disappearance of that aspect of identity which had been linked to the collapsing ideology. The demise of the Communist empire also led to a reduction of ideological identities to their "baser" aspects, such as kin, ethnicity, territory, and so forth.

The assertion that the Serb, Croat, and Bosniac ethno-national projects were equal in principle in the process of destruction of Bosnia and Herzegovina does not imply their hierarchical equality, nor equal guilt. The relationship of cause and effect is as stated above. The second project (the Croat) initially was of a reactive, even defensive nature; from this position, however, emerged a partnership with the first (the Serb) in their joint opposition to and the destruction of Bosnia and Herzegovina. The third project (the Bosniac) was initially defensive, but in time acquired a character that conflicted with the demand to protect the coherence of Bosnia and Herzegovina; and though this is the consequence of complex relations between power and powerlessness, the aggressive behavior of the former two and the struggle for survival of the third, the ideas it absorbs from the former two define the third project as their equal in its fundamental nature.

Secession and the Centers

During 1990 and 1991, the entire Yugoslav political scene was dominated by a bitter debate about the reorganization of the state. Its negative aspect was the possibility of secession and dissolution.[9] Any review of this course of events must take into account the dynamics of the relations between the crucial power centers. Throughout its sustained ideological build up and its modus operandi the Yugoslav People's Army had been oriented to the preservation of the unitary state. Its resistance to the dangers of secession made the People's Army responsive and readily assimilable to those forces that presented themselves as the defenders of Yugoslavia's continued existence. The logic of the secession, presented as a detachment of peripheral regions, diverts attention from the reality of the "secession from the center."

The secession of Slovenia was to the advantage of the Greater-Serbia project in that it favored the process of reducing Yugoslavia's constituent elements to the Serb component. For this reason, the secessionist center was to encourage and support those developments that would make the reorganization of Yugoslavia through the processes of secession inevitable while simultaneously putting the integrationist forces at the disposal of the Greater-Serbia elite, as an inescapable consequence. Once this process was launched and absorbed into the prevailing thinking, then, given the"inevitability of secession," the constituent elements of the Yugoslav state were to be called into question. This approach made the dissolution of the Yugoslav state into its sovereign republics impossible, whatever form it might take: a substantial rearrangement of all internal borders was necessary in order to achieve the postulated national interest. If the secession of Slovenia were to be accepted within the context of the dissolution of Yugoslavia as a whole, then the elements of sovereignty of which the Republics had been divested would have to be restored, as indeed was noted in the findings of the Badinter Commission.[10] On the basis of both their constitutions and the structure of government, however, the Republics had the right to oppose dissolution. Any coordinated resistance to the demolition of the constitutional system within the republics, it was judged, would most probably counter the powers of secession in the Belgrade center. Hence, the logic of the Greater-Serbia project had to provide for a coordinated collaboration in the denial and resulting destruction of the established order in Bosnia and Herzegovina, to avoid the break up of Yugoslavia being a simple dissolution into the sovereign states that had comprised the Federal Republic of Yugoslavia.

This thinking, within the context of the possible restructuring of Yugoslavia, made Bosnia and Herzegovina a central issue to the Greater-Serbia and Greater-Croatia elites. The future of the Bosnian-Herzegovinian state became the key strategic issue for these elites, who reduced their policies wholly to onto-topology. The resolution of their mutual relationship was seen in the context of the aspirations of external forces to protect and strengthen their interests on either the Serb or the Croat side, or both. It was assessed that the capacity of Bosnia and Herzegovina to resist the Serb and Croat sides acting in unison was poor, and that any future conflicts should therefore be "contained," with intervention limited to humanitarian aid. It is important, too, to note that in its mediation between the "warring factions," the international community accepted the issue of ethnic plurality that had been brought into prominence, and the proposed solution by way of territorialization. It incorporated this solution as the basis of all of its approaches and decisions.

Ethnicization of Territories

As early as 1991, the ethno-national offshoots of Belgrade and Zagreb began to bring the question of ethno-national territories to the forefront. Following the memory and experience of the past division of Bosnia by the Serb and Croat ethno-national elites, they proceeded with the formation of Serb autonomous lands and later of Croat regions.[11] The "Muslim question" surfaced as the key issue, so it is not surprising that along with democratic rhetoric[12] and the advocacy of ethno-national rights there appeared an ever more recognizably criminal content that proposed the solution of ethnic homogenization by the expulsion and elimination of the population using the means already employed in numerous previous wars. Ethno-national elements in the government increasingly acted as secret agents of the dictate of Belgrade and Zagreb, while the Bosniacs were prompted to forms of action that would be a simple mirror image of the Greater-Serbia and Greater-Croatia logic—relinquishing Bosnia and Herzegovina and adopting a pragmatic solution by which they, too, would receive their portion and thus finally solve their national question by having their own ethno-national state. During 1991 this ideological and political frame of events manifested itself in disgraceful public rhetorical quarrels among the ethno-national elites, which the participants in the disintegrating Communist system treated with abhorrence while proving apparently unable to engage in a search for solutions that would counter the real basis for these public expressions—preparation for the war as the realization of the agreement between Milošević and Tuđman to solve the Yugoslav crisis by respecting fully "the interests of Serb and Croat peoples as a whole." Two moods were present on the political scene during this period. The first was represented by the ideological and disintegrating Communist system, which was unable to comprehend the nature and content of the political demands related to suppressed religious and ethno-national identity. The second was a weak and politically insufficiently sophisticated force of former outsiders and dissidents who carried a baggage of antagonism toward the ideological establishment.

Since Bosnia and Herzegovina was in the same constitutional and legal position as Serbia and Croatia, its destruction implied its political dismemberment into three components—Serb, Croat, and Bosniac. As the structure of the ethno-nationalist parties known as the Croatian Democratic Union and the Serbian Democratic Party was only nominally representative of the Bosnian-Herzegovinian elements of their respective ethno-national structures as a whole, their activity in the state system of Bosnia and Herzegovina was a reflection of the will of the neighboring states. The Party of Democratic Action, which was the largest Bosniac party, had therefore to be formally represented as the authentic ethno-national will of that third component in Bosnia and Herzegovina, so that it could be pressured in various ways into a position where its protection of Bosnian-Herzegovinian unity could be labeled as an attempt to "Muslimize" or "Bosniacify" the unitary state at the expense of its other components. The destruction of Bosnia and Herzegovina, in Milošević's and Tuđman's original plan, is the means by which their respective new ethno-national states will be established, which is succinctly illustrated by Karadžić's assertion: "Our aim is to scupper Bosnia and Herzegovina." This is why the separation and propagation of exclusively Bosniac ideas within the Bosnian-Herzegovinian state was first envisaged and then encouraged in support of this goal, carried out through the "withdrawal" of Serb and Croat participation in favor of the creation of "ethno-national territories."[13]

During 1991, it was evident that the Serb Democratic Party was establishing ties with the army and the police throughout Bosnia and Herzegovina and was being transformed into a paramilitary organization with close links to the Yugoslav People's Army, the Serbian police, and other elements of their ethno-national organizational structure. All military command positions on the territory of Bosnia and Herzegovina were in the hands of Serb officers, most of whom came originally from Serbia proper. They were linked organizationally with a Belgrade headquarters already de facto subjugated to the Greater-Serbia ethno-national elite personified by Milošević; they continued to use Yugoslav state structures as an instrument to counter any opposition to their project. They paid great attention to the prevention of any possible modes of using the existing state structures or creating parallel ones that would have the capacity to impede the process of subjugation. As early as spring 1991, a large number of Serb refugees from Croatia came to Bosnia and Herzegovina; this population movement was used to form closer links among the police and military formations already in the hands of the Greater-Serbian elite. It is fair to say that already by that time the legitimate institutions of government in Bosnia and Herzegovina had no control over the greater part of the police force and no influence whatsoever on the Yugoslav People's Army troops stationed in Bosnia and Herzegovina. The leadership of Bosnia and Herzegovina saw clearly that Milošević and Tuđman were acting in a coordinated fashion for the destruction of Bosnia and Herzegovina. From Milošević's and Tuđman's perspective, direct opposition to the integrationist response to their own destructive project was unrealistic and dangerous. A more promising strategy was to work on the Bosniac political leadership, enticing it to substitute purely Bosniac political goals for Bosnian-Herzegovinian goals, which they did with the slogan Like it or not, this is what will happen.

During 1990 and 1991, the Territorial Defense was disarmed to prevent any possibility of legal resistance to the use of force in the implementation of these projects in the destruction of Bosnia and Herzegovina. Widespread arming of members of the Serbian Democratic Party occurred in mid-1991, under the direct supervision of Slobodan Milošević and through the structures of the Yugoslav People's Army. Some members of the federal state leadership were aware of this and informed the Federal Prime Minister Ante Marković and the Federal Defense Minister Veljko Kadijević. They however were already either powerless or unwilling to do anything substantial about it.

In the summer of 1991, a series of meetings took place of well-known political activists from the whole of Bosnia and Herzegovina, including a particular secret gathering of some twenty Bosniac intellectuals who outlined and discussed projections on the forthcoming war whose most violent form, they agreed, would take place in their country with most horrendous acts perpetrated against Bosniacs. They then reached a decision to start as quickly and as decisively as possible on preparations for resistance, with the primary concept of defending the Bosnian-Herzegovinian state through all its available institutions while seeking allies among any forces willing to support the survival of the state.

Politics and Defense

Based on the knowledge that there was a distinct possibility of the disintegration of Yugoslavia and of the connection between the Greater-Serbia and the Greater-Croatia elites, it was necessary to develop, within a very heterogeneous and frequently conflicting dynamism of political wills in Bosnia and Herzegovina, a common policy of action. Insistent demands for sovereignty by both Slovenia and Croatia, both expected and incited by the Belgrade secessionist center, could have led to the break up of the Bosnian-Herzegovinian state, since elements of its legislative, judicial, and executive powers were connected to the Belgrade and Zagreb elites. This could reduce the demand for state sovereignty of Bosnia and Herzegovina to a de jure status devoid of de facto content. If the state of the then Yugoslav People's Army is taken into account, as well as the thoroughly implemented disarmament of the Territorial Defense units of Bosnia and Herzegovina, it is obvious that defense capabilities were very weak and any attempts to alter them accentuated the threat of the incitement of and support for the desired disintegration, so that the dissolution of Yugoslavia would in practice lead to the break up of Bosnia and Herzegovina too. It is now clear that these weak defense capabilities were at the time judged to be insufficient to counter the consensus of the Belgrade and Zagreb elites on the destruction of the Bosnian-Herzegovinian state.

Hence, based on the agreed decision of part of the Bosnian-Herzegovinian political leadership, two political courses of action were undertaken in parallel. The first was linked to the aim of achieving international recognition for

Bosnia and Herzegovina, which was possible through a referendum, as was later concluded by the Badinter Commission. This imposed numerous political caveats and compromises. It was judged at the time that any position to the contrary would have led to the internal break up of Bosnia and Herzegovina before anyone even had a chance to cast a vote on its statehood in the context of the dissolution of Yugoslavia. The second course of action was directed towards the preparations for defense. These preparations were critically influenced by the political framework within which it was possible to carry them out and the prevailing unreadiness of the political power centers within the ideological system to act on the distinct possibility of war. The probability that the Yugoslav People's Army might join in a war against Bosnia and Herzegovina was seen by almost all key participants in the Yugoslav ideological system not only as infinitesimal, but also as a product of the imagination of nationalist visionaries, reactionaries, and historically immature individuals and groups. Yet, simultaneous with this thinking, there was underway a process of integration of the Army with the ethno-nationalist apparatus striving for "Greater-Serbia" on the borders of the smallest possible "Greater Croatia."

Success and Failure of the Resistance

The political framework of these events is known practically down to the last detail. It is worth noting, though, that a clearly defined political position towards the key attitude of the Serb and Croat elite—more precisely, those ethno-national elites represented by Milošević and Tuđman—was adopted by the Bosnian-Herzegovinian leadership, which was supported in this by all the Bosniacs and by substantial segments of the Serb and Croat peoples. This political position was that the state of Bosnia and Herzegovina and its legal status could not differ from that of Serbia and Croatia. If Croatia, therefore, were to table a request for independence, Bosnia and Herzegovina would do likewise since the independence of Croatia would make it necessary for Bosnia and Herzegovina to seek the same status. Bosnia and Herzegovina could not survive within Yugoslavia without the presence of Slovenia and Croatia, since such a Yugoslavia would in fact become Greater Serbia. The stability of Bosnia and Herzegovina positioned between Serbia and Croatia is possible if it has equal status. It was not possible to convince the majority of political observers and actors that the Serb and Croat elites were acting in unison towards the destruction of Bosnia and Herzegovina, despite the fact that a number of events at the beginning of 1991 indicated such an alliance. Croatia was generally seen as a natural ally without whose support it would be difficult or even impossible to oppose the Greater Serbia project.

This is precisely where the paradox of mutual cooperation and enmity began to develop. Croatia could base its demand for independence on its then constitution. That demand meant in principle that Bosnia and Herzegovina had the same option and the same right. This however called into question, at the time indirectly and indecisively—but only for tactical reasons—the already adopted strategy of partitioning Bosnia and Herzegovina in mutual protection of "the interests of Serb and Croat peoples as a whole." Not even the leaders of the Serbian Democratic Party, faced with the evident dissolution of Yugoslavia, could logically and persuasively counter the stated position of the Bosnian-Herzegovinian elite that they were willing to accept any proposal for the reorganization of Yugoslavia in which the position of all Republics would be equal, not precluding any options—a federal system, a confederal system, or independence for the constituent republics.

In parallel with the illegal activities of "defining" ethno-national territories in Bosnia and Herzegovina and the transformation of the elements of governance to subjugate them to the party structures, we also see a demand for the administrative restructuring of Bosnia and Herzegovina in accordance with the ethno-national interests of the two elites. In these demands, representatives of the Serbian Democratic Party and Croatian Democratic Union acted in unison and coordination. This assertion is supported by a message Franjo Tuđman sent to one of the leaders of the Croatian Democratic Union in Bosnia and Herzegovina at the time: "You must always demand the same as Serbs do, but after they do so." This restructuring was to take the form of defining ethno-national territories through changes to existing municipal boundaries, followed by an integration of these new municipalities into regions, as was indeed done in 1991. Since the population was so intermingled as to make impossible the creation of contiguous ethno-national territories, such demands at the political level were, as subsequent events would show, merely a preparation for the destruction of Bosnia and Herzegovina's integrity by forces acting in the service of the two ethno-national projects.[14] On the territories thus created, a complete ethno-national structure was built to the following pattern: (1) ethno-national uniformity realized through a single ethno-national territory; (2) a single ethno-national party, a single political-military system and a single leader, who is nonetheless totally subjugated to an ethno-national entity transcending state borders, which in turn have to be dismantled to allow the creation of a single ethno-national state. Hence, we see the Yugoslav People's Army presence on the territory of Bosnia and Herzegovina reduced to the Army of Republika Srpska, which in essence is just a part of the Yugoslav Army, and the formation of the Croat Defense Council, which again is essentially a part of the Croatian Army.

The reaction to these movements occurred amid dramatic efforts to preserve the legitimacy and legality of the Bosnian-Herzegovinian state. The constitutionally established Territorial Defense became a framework for official efforts to defend Bosnia and Herzegovina against destruction and it remained in principle the armed force of all the Bosnian-Herzegovinian people. It was later transformed into the Army of Bosnia and Herzegovina and with unexpected rapidity developed into an important factor in Bosnia and Herzegovina. It was conceived from the very beginning as a Bosnian-Herzegovinian force.

This very fact was the greatest obstacle for the ethno-national elites participating in the creation and implementation of the project for the destruction of Bosnia and Herzegovina.

The growth of this military force continued until mid-1993, on the pluralist basis defined by the constitution which reflected the organic unity of Bosnia and Herzegovina. Thus, the constitutional system, international recognition, and the Army of Bosnia and Herzegovina represented the decisive factors in the defense of the Bosnian-Herzegovinian state. The ability of Bosnia and Herzegovina to build up its defense so speedily and decisively in the face of the already well-developed forces of its destroyers had not been anticipated in either of the two coordinated anti-Bosnian-Herzegovinian projects—the Greater Serbian and the Greater Croatian.

The pressure from the beginning towards the physical dismantling of everything that constituted Bosnian-Herzegovinian unity into its "component ethno-national parts" would from mid-1993 give rise to a process of demolition within the Army of Bosnia and Herzegovina and its reduction to a "Bosniac force," but not in the sense in which the Bosniac people and its national interests are inseparable from the Bosnian-Herzegovinian entirety. This reduction was carried out in a particularly unprincipled manner, through the subordination of the Army to the party and the influence of oligarchies, implicitly accepting the legitimacy of the military concepts which are at the very foundation of the project of destruction of Bosnia and Herzegovina.

The Patriotic League

The inner circle of Bosniac members of the Bosnian-Herzegovinian leadership was more or less aware from the spring of 1991 that there was a great likelihood of war and that not resisting it was both morally and politically unacceptable. Any illegal activity to prevent such an occurrence or to prepare an organized form of resistance through movements outside state institutions and organizations would, in the opinion of key people in Bosnian-Herzegovinian political circles faced with such a threat, have contributed to a successful completion of the project of destruction of Bosnia and Herzegovina. They were therefore faced with the task of finding a form of action that would not further dismantle the constitutional state of Bosnia and Herzegovina. A number of officers of the Yugoslav People's Army then spoke up, warning of internal processes of Serbianization in the Army and of ongoing preparations for it to act as a tool of the ethno-national project and under the political leadership of the ethno-national elite whose nerve center was in Belgrade. The chosen strategy of the Bosnian-Herzegovinian leadership was to coordinate informally all participants in the Bosnian-Herzegovinian state system on a platform of resistance to the project of destruction. It concluded that the potential offered by the state system should be used as the essential framework for such action.

This approach was named the Patriotic League. It is fair to date its existence to the spring of 1991, though it was never an organization that could be labeled as parastate or paramilitary, as could be said of the Croat Defense Council and the Army of Republika Srpska. It was simply a forum for the patriotic forces of Bosnia and Herzegovina that gradually withdrew from the Yugoslav People's Army in the awareness that the Army was becoming a vehicle for the destruction of Bosnia and Herzegovina. Unable to serve in any other way under the circumstances, these forces gathered around a segment of the political, patriotically inclined, state leadership of Bosnia and Herzegovina, monitoring and analyzing from a military point of view the events unfolding in their own country and around it. In the process of dissolution of Yugoslavia and the disintegration of its institutions, these forces represented an important axis which was to enlist, through the Republic's organizations and institutions and with clear perceptions and a developed plan of action, in the Territorial Defense of Bosnia and Herzegovina, at a time when the country was already polarized by the forces of destruction. This segment of a broad alliance of patriotic forces was to become the foundation for the unexpected and astonishing creation of the Army of Bosnia and Herzegovina, the formation of which prevented the destruction of Bosnia and Herzegovina as a state.

If we can say today that Bosnia and Herzegovina was not defended, we can equally say that it was not destroyed either. This is the consequence of the feats of the unexpected and astonishing creation of the Army of Bosnia and Herzegovina, which in its origin was precisely what the name denotes. Its original political concept was the future of Bosnia and Herzegovina, in which members of the Patriotic League placed their faith and to which they remained faithful as a guarantee of their country's future. At the outset of the war, the Chief of Military Counter Intelligence (KOS), Aleksandar Vasiljević, tried to deter Alija Izetbegović by presenting him with intelligence material about the Patriotic League; to the latter's assertion that these were just worried individuals linking up into a network for the defense of the state should the need arise, General Vasiljević retorted: "We do not fear weapons, which are to be found all around, as weapons alone will never find the troops; we fear the troops that always find weapons for themselves."[15] If it is fair to say today that Bosnia and Herzegovina lacks a persuasive and consistent interpretation of its integrality around which a patriotic alliance of the greatest number of its people could gather, it is worth noting now, as it was indeed worth noting at the time, that the possibility that this might happen was the greatest anxiety of its destroyers, and that its integrality provided a source from which emanated something the destroyers never expected at the outset. Only from this integrality can we expect an emergence of the alliance of the forces capable of attaining the ultimate goal: the liberation of Bosnia and Herzegovina as the country of all its people joined in a common belief in their own future, a country of Bosnians who in this their identity betray none of other identities they may claim by right, whether these be called Serb, Croat, Bosniac, Orthodox, Catholic, Muslim, or Jewish.

War Against Integrality

A comprehensive interpretation of the nature of Bosnia and Herzegovina is not possible outside the framework of the phenomena encompassed by politics, ideology, and tradition. The age of modernity and its deconstruction in post-modernity determine the reality of the war against Bosnia and Herzegovina as well. It has been said here that the Greater Serbia and the Greater Croatia projects initiated and directed the war, whose goal was the destruction of Bosnia and Herzegovina's integrality. These two projects are essentially ideological. It is possible to discern within them the most important elements of modernity and post-modernity. However, in the absence of such examination, outmoded approaches and narratives, for the most part, substitute for the different interpretations that are in fact needed.

The perspective of both Miloševićism and Tuđmanism is the ideological ethnicization of the Yugoslav region, at a time when the ideology of socialism had lost all its important strongholds. In this perspective, Serbia and Croatia, as ethnic states, were the centers around which the restructuring of Yugoslavia, as a once multiethnic state, was taking place, reducing it to different ethnic identities. This logic gave rise to the construction of a new political identity, with the Serbian and Croatian leadership at its center. What they demanded was homogenization, as the crucial factor of their legitimization.

Their approach to Bosnia and Herzegovina was based on the premise that it was not viable as a stable society, because none of its nations is a homogeneous community. Its plurality had to be broken up, in order to homogenize the Serbs and the Croats. The homogeneity thus established was to have legitimized the new political identities, which meant that corresponding territorialization was necessary for the ethnic Serbs and Croats in Bosnia.

This demand is totally opposed to the nature of Bosnian identities, which are not territorial. To be a Muslim, Catholic, or Orthodox has never meant to be defined by a particular territory. Being Bosnian was the framework for the independence of individual identities from territory.[16] Identification of an ethno-nation with the state results in reducing the collective *I* to the ethnos and its territory. Since compact ethnic integrality cannot be established in any part of Bosnia, this logic produces *enclaves* of Others. The political identity that was legitimized by the pull and support from general ethno-national centers outside Bosnia led to a total demarcation from these enclaves. Others became an obstacle to the postulated ethnic and political integrality, and the next step in legitimizing the political identity was the persecution and killing of Others, who were confined and clearly defined in enclaves of ethnic territory.

This approach transformed Bosnia and Herzegovina into a stage of onto-topological strategy. The adopted and absolutized separate identities demanded, in this view, the recognition and establishment of the absolute authority of one and only one ethnos in a particular territory. As the right to respect of everyone's ethnic identity—with ethnic identity completely transferred to the area of legitimization of political identity—cannot be denied from any perspective, the question of Bosnia was drawn into a debate on "demarcation." The demand for demarcation was accompanied by an emphasis on the general right of the people to self-determination.

The blazing problem of Bosnia, which the dissolution of Yugoslavia comes down to, is thus presented to the world as an issue of demarcation between ethnic communities. The issues of the sovereign state and the aggression against it, of the citizens of that state and the genocide which was being committed against them, were in this way simply translated within the international community into a civil war and ethnic cleansing. That such interpretations were prevalent is evident in the mediation of the international community in seeking an agreement on Bosnia. All the talks—from those chaired by Jose Cutileiro in early 1992 to the Dayton Peace Accords in late 1995—regarded ethnicity as the most important criterion in the resolution of the problem as a whole, thereby confirming and legalizing the original premises of Miloševićism and Tuđmanism.

Erosion of Identity

The fact that a large number of citizens of Bosnia and Herzegovina embraced Miloševićism and Tuđmanism, and their consequent participation in the war against Bosnia, can be explained as a result of the erosion of modern identity. In Communist countries individual identity was for the most part determined by the heteronomous elements of the self—family, ethnos, confessionalism, home region—and by the Communist ideology, which overpowered the basic and given element of identity. After the collapse of the latter, its proffered replacement took the form of ethno-nationalist ideologies as new political identities. As a result, individual identity was reduced to its baser elements. What it needed in those circumstances was to be circumscribed into territory, history, organization. Since in this restructuring there also exist pluriform elements that cannot be drawn toward the new perspective, violence against them must become a factor of self-legitimization of the ethno-national programs.

The considerations outlined above demonstrate that the war against Bosnia demands a persistent and extensive examination of its different layers—from the purely exoteric to the deeper or higher, in which questions emerge of the individual self, its freedom, society, and its stability. It is likely that a normalization of the situation in Croatia and Serbia will lead to some sort of withdrawal from Bosnia. Since the suffering and destruction in this country were a result of the active presence of the programs instigated and directed by the governments of Serbia and Croatia, their mere withdrawal will not be sufficient. Their disengagement demands effective elimination of the consequences they produced. Though Bosnia in its nature is different from those two states, their insistence on differences and on the unfeasibility of territorialization of ethnic identities is a prerequisite for a future without deadly conflicts.

8

On the Self

Introduction

The deepest and most crucial layer of the Bosnian drama lies in individual selves. The discussions in these essays for the most part touch on different aspects of the outer forms of that drama. They are, however, reflections or manifestations of the inner contents. Understanding them presupposes answers to questions regarding the sources of selfhood in this part of the world and in this age, where and when a unity of differences was transformed into war. It is easier to identify and describe separate entities in a conflict than to do the same for the individuals who take part. Do they all accept the consequences of the war? How and why do they accept the killing and persecution of others? How and when do those inner contents of the self come to exist and how are they triggered? Are they a consequence of external circumstances or are they themselves shaped by those circumstances?

The search for answers to these questions also calls for consideration of the different circles of the outer world—neighboring countries, Europe, and humanity as a whole—and not only in spatial terms. Providing answers is possible if the review takes into account the full range of relationships and the interpenetration of the cosmos and the self. Here, too, eastern and western divisions and contacts manifest themselves in a multitude of different ways. But that is not all. The multiplicity and mobility of all phenomena in the cosmos cannot be understood externally to and without the self. In the process of understanding, however, selfhood is always only one of the possible narratives. For its projection in the future, it is necessary to identify both its present complexity and its temporal depth. This takes the discussion to the realms of ontology and metaphysics. Unless we enter these realms, politics, ideology and tradition alike inevitably remain obscured. The descent of humanity into murderous and destructive enterprises is far from self-explanatory. It requires a different view which is not a sketch of life seen from outside, but a crossing of the boundaries within which the self is confined. But before the discussion continues in that direction, it is worthwhile pausing to explain the concept behind the title.

The Self

There is no crime without a perpetrator; nor can there be any knowledge of a crime, other than that of the victim, without a third party coming to know of it. The selfhood of the person who comes to know of it is, therefore, the key to the answer to the question about the crime. The same applies to cosmology as a whole—the science, theory, or study of the universe as an ordered unity and of the laws governing it. The modern cosmologist endeavors to be an "objective" observer, which, as he understands it, is possible only if he as the observer becomes a disembodied spirit, existing simultaneously both in the cosmos and outside it. The nature of the subject is thus excluded from what is to be understood, which is the fundamental paradox of modern knowledge: an understanding of the object of knowledge without knowing the nature of the observer.

From the perspective of tradition, however, the knowledge of the observer is of crucial importance: a genuine knowledge of the cosmos is not accessible without a genuine knowledge of the self. What can be learned about the cosmos largely depends on the starting point. And clarification of this leads the researcher to the question: Who is the "I" who is doing the observing? The progress of learning is also affected by the procedures and devices applied. The researcher acts like a net. What will be caught by it depends on his disposition. All understanding must begin somewhere. The "where" of the beginning determines the "whither" of the journey. The fundamental questions of the philosophical limits of ethics also stem from this. Utilitarianism, too, has to resolve the issue of its "Archimedes' point." However, it does this—by adopting a universal view or simply by proceeding from the revelation and God's commandments—the self and its nature remain crucial. To produce a theory while neglecting this fact is simply to take refuge in ignorance.[1]

The idea of "objective" knowledge is one of the deepest of obfuscations. It is tenable only as dogma. The possessor of such knowledge must deny every other form of knowledge, as the latter can be only subjective. Only a subject who has no idea who he or she is can make such a claim. Hence, it follows that the question of the human self or soul is crucial to the entire enterprise of learning.[2] Answers to this question or forms of knowledge of the self— regardless of how they are expressed—always remain only approximations or indications. Lack of knowledge about oneself means to lack understanding of where one stands. This also results in lack of understanding of the general implications of what one knows. Knowledge rooted in ignorance of the subject is not real knowledge. As such, it is nevertheless susceptible to manipulation, as we see from the popularity of such knowledge in the modern age.

According to Ibn al-'Arabi, the human self is "an ocean without shore; gazing upon it has no end in this world or the next."[3] However, the self tends to lose sight of its own unboundedness and ties itself down to specific configurations within the individual limitations that it adopts as its own, which determine where it stands and what it can know. It can escape from these limitations only by means of objective standards provided by the external provider of the limitations, not by the self itself. That external provider is called by different names. For example, he can be called the "Guide." The Guide is the God Who offers paths to deliverance from the limitations that make the unbounded self perceive itself as finite and constricted. God offers these paths through certain human beings whom He chooses as His emissaries.[4]

Knowledge

The question may be asked about any form of knowledge, how did the possessor acquire it? There are three sources of knowledge: following the authority of knowledge conveyed by others, rational research, and immediate experience of the "real." Understanding these roots of knowledge, together with their order and relationship, determines the identity of the self. It should be stressed that the experience of the "real" is hampered by all the sensitivities rooted in the ignorance of the self. Tradition points to knowledge of the self as a condition for knowing God: "The Messenger of God said that there is no path to knowledge of God but knowledge of self, for he said: 'He who knows himself knows his Lord best'."[5] The God that someone worships is the configuration of the reality which determines his condition. It is not possible to know the configuration of the reality that makes a person what he is if the person does not know himself. An unlimited multitude of viewpoints can be selected as important among the infinite number of objects accessible to the experience of every individual. This offers different principles of order and arrangement, as testified by the many different views expressed by people around the world and through different histories.

This is, in the first place, an issue of identity or identities. An important determinant of every self is that it is constantly subject to change. Bosnia's future depends on the nature of those changes. But this present self will change, and it is inseparable from the entirety of the Bosnian experiences that converge in it. Providing an answer to the question of the future therefore also includes that which forms the basis of identity contained in the question: Who am I? It is not possible to answer it without knowing whence the person who asks is coming from and where he is going. Though the general content—the acceptance of life and human dignity as good—is known, the conceptions of history, nation, religion, and the different loyalties to these remain to be distinguished within the complex Bosnian identity. The answers to these questions are different for the Bosnian people who call themselves Serbs, Croats, and Muslims. (Indeed, they are different for every individual.) These differences are expressed in one language, within one and the same geopolitical territory, in one ethnogenesis. Individual and collective answers in the form of "yes or no" within those identities mainly become reduced to "no." Identity is thus reduced to knowing and feeling what the self is not. In this, the consciousness and perception of what is answered by "yes" fade into the distance. The different identities can only insist on those differences, while growing ever more distant from one another and gradually losing the awareness of everything that they have in common. As the country itself cannot be divided, this distancing produces those categories of interpretation that survive only accompanied by complex mental tensions: the total transcendent otherness disappears and the self falls towards its given contents, which exist independently of the consciousness.

The view that they "cannot and will not live together any more" can be interpreted as a corrupted state of the self, with many consequences.[6] Yet, "they" are, nevertheless, living together. The declaration of this "inability," combined with an actual unwillingness to live together, still demands a change which, in principle, can be achieved in three ways. The first way is for "them" to separate from those with whom they cannot and will not live. The second way is for "those" with whom "they" cannot and will not live to depart. As neither the former nor the latter—in the case of Bosnia there are more than two parties to the conflict—can nor will depart from their selves, or from history, or from their country, any resolution of this contradiction must result in abandoning that aspect of the self that confirms the sacredness and inviolability of human life and dignity. Further, this rejection requires taking a view of the history of the self in time that justifies this inability and unwillingness. This, in turn, opens the way to an increased corruption of the self, which means the consciousness of the good that transcends individuality will grow ever weaker. Thus, the orientation of the individual within the arena of moral issues becomes ever more intricate and insoluble.

Homogeneity

The nature of knowledge also determines the scope of discourse in a community. In any society, people maintain stability through their tenacious hold on a stronghold of security—the different elements that are regarded as unquestionable within the framework of culture and time. In tradition, these are primarily holy people and messages. They are universally accessible, and are both the first source and the crucial confirmation. God is understood as an objective reality, totally different from the subject. But herein lies the key paradox: God is the Truth; man is nothing but its manifestation. For human beings, perfection lies in being fully human. Such beings are forms of the perfect, complete whole, while others are only partly so.[7] Humanity as a whole was created in God's image: duty towards one's neighbor is thus inseparable from duty towards God. The "arena" in which God reveals himself is humanity, this individual who is our neighbor, our vis-à-vis. And thus it is with the whole of the cosmos. Both the cosmos and humanity are entire and perfect images of God. The cosmos reveals God's names and attributes infinitely dispersed through all worlds, space and time. Everything in the cosmos is thus an infinitely small part of the whole. Human beings, however, are called upon to reveal the whole of God's image. The degree to which they succeed in responding to this call establishes their value as God's servants and vicegerents, and determines their station in this and the future world. Humanity has an innate disposition to that perfection. The path towards it means bringing all the Divine attributes out of latency into manifestation. Understanding this disposition and the process of its realization requires an external authority. Instead of a genuine external authority, people may follow a false authority: their reason alone, their power alone, or their passions alone. Their "lord" is then shaped by what they follow, and from this derives their answer to the question: Who am I?

The aspiration of the self to create its own configuration always carries the danger of conditional constructions being adopted as objective reality. It is to attribute to God the conditional construction of the self that forgets its boundless nature. The self then absolutizes its image of reality as objective, and demands, as its justification, the homogeneity of individuality. This is the reciprocal support of selfhoods in the form of kin, tribe, society, religious community, or nation. Anything that is different from the established configuration is seen as wrong.

In the demand for homogeneity lie the rudiments of genocide.[8] Since this is a demand that cannot be justified by either authentic religious intellectuality or a systematic rational approach, the notion of homogeneity as the basis of genocide has recourse to poetry. Thus, a form of mediation is procured between the set goal and the sacred exemplars. This mediation is universally accessible but also transcendentally noncontingent, and is open to falsehood and to constructions based on falsehood.[9] It requires both philosophical anthropology, and absolute belief in science. The external authority is denied for the sake of the autonomy of the self and the presumed sufficiency of reason. From this result the political ideologies of the modern era as an essential component of the enterprise universally known as modernity. This enterprise is, in the first place, characterized by belief in reason, detached from any higher order, and in the possibility of social progress and of attuning every individual to take part in it on the basis of an ideology-established scale of values.

These interpretations call for a discrimination of the self in its supratemporal content and its change: "Plato's distinction stands at the head of a large family of views which see the good life as a mastery of self which consists in the dominance of reason over desire. One of the most celebrated variants in the ancient world was Stoicism. And with the development of the modern scientific world view a specifically modern variant has developed. This is the ideal of the disengaged self, capable of objectifying not only the surrounding world, but also his own emotions and inclinations, fears and compulsions, and achieving thereby a kind of distance and self-possession which allows him to act 'rationally'."[10]

In the Bosnian pluriformity, identities were determined in different ways, in terms of their general content. Asked to identify the bases of their appreciation of life, many people refer to theistic views and indicate the general position of human beings as creatures of God. Others reject this in favor of a purely secular view and refer to the dignity of a rational life. However, given these distinct elements, their definition of their identity invariably adopts the reading of history associated with it, a specific religion, and, essential to this whole discussion, different ideologies that present themselves as "taking precedence" over every other factors of identity. The ideologies of nationalism are thus of crucial importance for understanding the tensions linked to identities. If one wishes to forecast their future, this can be done only by taking a systematic cross section of their nature.

To achieve this, in turn, their genesis must be determined, regardless of the fact that at the level of discursive thought they now reject many historical dimensions. This "cult" of ethno-national ideologies resists change, because it is engrossed by the archetypal self, which it never brings into the arena of scrutiny and reexamination. But this does not mean that traditional forms are transcended. The unity of differences is an important obstacle to nationalism, for it means that different forms of partial affiliation cannot be fetishized to the point of full exclusion of the right of every individual to be different; and this exclusion, for an ethno-national ideology, is the cornerstone, the unquestionably sacrosanct. An ethno-national ideology, however, proffers evidence of its superiority through a symbiosis with a mysticized attitude towards "modernity," and the aspiration to locate its power in the sovereignty of a state based on a homogeneous ethno-nation. An ethno-national ideology usually resorts to and finds justification for its undertaking in such a nation, though "modernity" is, for such an ideology, only a complex and unintelligible myth. For such an ideology, the modern identity is something vague and distant: that totality of understanding of what should compose humanity, the feelings of interiority, freedom, individuality, and of being a part of nature, which have taken root in the modern West. From the contradictions of the modern idea of nation and the untenability of closed states emerges the theory of multiculturalism, and, linked to it, that of civilizations and their clash.

Identity

Identity is determined by loyalties or identifications that secure a framework or arena within which we try to identify, from case to case, what is good or valuable, what should be done, what should be supported or impeded. This is the arena within which the *self* is powerful enough to survive. People may see their identity as in part determined by various moral or spiritual loyalties. They may determine these loyalties within the language and the system of an inherited or adopted community, tradition, or ideology. They also determine them in part by their belonging to the nation or heritage within which they developed. Embracing those moral and spiritual views and the awareness of belonging to a setting may be more or less strong, more or less conscious, or more or less vague. However, a sense of affiliation of this kind always provides a framework within which it is possible to establish where the self stands in relation to the question of what is good, or valuable, or worthy of enthusiasm. Without this affiliation and the consequent adjustment of the framework, the self would not be able to orient itself amidst the multitude of phenomena that call for the adoption of a stance, and of the behavior consequent upon this stance. Without this, it would be impossible to determine the importance or unimportance of the phenomena the self encounters. This suggests the link between identity and a point of reference of some kind. To know the answer to the question "Who am I?" is to be able to answer the question "Where am I?" And this means to be able to orient oneself within the moral arena, where the questions of good and evil, appropriate action or inaction, significance and importance, emerge.

The markedly spatial metaphor used here is typical of any tradition. Metaphorically speaking, the world is a desert in which, somewhere, there is a "house."[11] The meaning of human knowledge and movement is the orientation towards that house. One can move around it in perfect circles and proceed towards it along a straight radius. However, every movement is multiple: neither purely circumambulating nor purely approaching, but always both—as orientation in space is always both. The signs of spatial orientation are embedded deep in the human soul. Circling is a confirmation of the center, and the approach is elevation of the meaning of life and dignity. Without this, the self descends into insecurity and "narcissistic disorder." Lack of orientation and insecurity about one's own position are reflected in the inability of the self to discern and to receive guidance. This is the link between identity and orientation. The whole of the cosmos consists of dispersed signs, which, both individually and collectively, indicate the human capacity for orientation towards good and truth. The house at the center of these scattered signs is the human self. It is the starting point, both individually and generally. Its self-knowledge is the realization: *We shall show them Our signs in the horizons and in themselves, till it is clear to them that it is the truth.*[12]

The question already raised of the inclusion or exclusion of the self from the act of cognition or awareness becomes central. There can be neither a desert nor a house therein without the self. The separation of the self from the external goal, therefore, offers itself as a duality to be resolved. Concentration on the external center, orientation towards it and circling around it must, eventually, lead to the realization of the self as the Absolute. This is the approach in which the individual self will become "the sight with which God sees."[13]

But what urges and impels the self to moral orientation in the form of the question: Who are we? From this question follows another: Have people always asked this, and in the same way? Would the modern "question of identity" also be understandable to the ancestors of the people of this age who lived in earlier centuries?

Some views of the self are undoubtedly contingent on highlighting the question of identity. For most people, the questions of identity remain determined by general notions, such as those concerning human rights to life and dignity. The difference between the people of this age and their ancestors may be in the form of these rights, a form determined, to greater or lesser extent, by changes in the framework. What determines human identities is always more complex than any framework. It is therefore necessary to understand that identities are invariably merely a kind of dynamic model through which one comes closer to "squaring the circle" of the human self. In principle, the human self is infinite, but it is expressed in derived and conditional configurations. This also resolves the question of broad affiliations, such as being Catholic, Orthodox or Muslim, as well as of specific belonging—of being Bosnian, Bosniac, Serb, Bosnian Serb, Croat, Bosnian Croat.

In principle, any individual self and the totality of all selves together are one and the same inclination towards Being and openness to perfection. The derived and conditional configurations of the individual or collective self result from the "input" of spatial and temporal finitude, family, people and nation, religion, culture, and ideology, and the like, which constitute their horizon. The ideological notion of homogeneity denies the original unity and promotes contingencies to the level of objectivity. But this is the path of desacralization: the unchangeable and the unquestionable become reduced to the changeable and the questionable, the absolute to the conditional. The pure and absolute otherness is thus replaced by an idol, false deity, or satan. Any attempt to legitimate the authority of an individual or a group in this way must produce violence. The greater the feeling of powerlessness on the part of the authority, the more passionate the resort to its disguise in religious forms. In other words, more idol worship means more violence, more cruelty.

Though identity is complex, it is often revealed only through one of these elements. But, that identity is always deeper and more multifaceted than any possible discursive shaping, any possible perception of it. In other words, human mediation exists in the space of questions, which means that discrimination, discernment, is an important aspect of both the framework and identity. Answers are provided by the frameworks of determination, which offer the arena within which we discover where we are and what the meanings of phenomena are. This arena is outlined by strict evaluations or qualitative distinctions.[14]

Direction

What we are dealing with here is the answer to the question: Who am I?—integral to which is the question of the meaning and significance of phenomena, awareness of the position from which the question is asked, and to whom it is put. This question of identity is derivable only through language. Or, to be even more specific: what is concerned here is the language of interpretation adopted by the person who is asking the question. For, according to Martin Heidegger, understanding is the way of being.[15]

To ask what a person is in the abstract, without taking account of his or her self-interpretation, means to ask a fundamentally flawed question, one to which, in principle, there can be no answer. Living, in the organic sense, does not depend either on self-interpretation or on the meaning which phenomena have for a certain person. We are a self only while we are moving within a dimension that consists of questions, while we are searching for and finding orientation towards the good. This happens in language, and not only in one language. The multiplicity of languages determines every framework of identity. Explaining oneself means interpreting the language through a language or languages. Diversity of traditions therefore enables one to recognize in each one of them, in the process of self-understanding and self-interpretation, the conditionality of the external and its incapacity to exist without the internal: *We have appointed for every nation a holy rite that they shall perform.*[16] This path, as an answer to the question "Who am I?" and "Whom am I addressing, and from where?", includes, of course, different languages. As the truth is revealed in human language, the following statements can be understood: *Each nation has its Messenger*;[17] *We have sent no Messenger save with the tongue of his people,*[18] *And of His signs is the creation of the heavens and earth and the variety of your tongues and hues.*[19] Consequently, identity in its most comprehensive and most inner content is in a relationship with the self or with the face of God. And this means that both God's revelation and God's word are "situated" within humanity and summed up in an individual. Dialogue between people is a testimony to the speech of God. Identity in its greatest potential is, therefore, relative to that transcendental otherness.

A multitude of paths leads to the language of languages, which is the essential condition for their survival. Identity without the other would not be possible. This means without the other with whom the self converses:

> *O mankind, We have created you*
> *male and female, and appointed you*
> *races and tribes, that you may know*
> *one another. Surely the noblest*
> *among you in the sight of God is*
> *the most godfearing of you.*[20]

Language exists, however, only in a linguistic community. Hence, it follows that the self is possible only among other selves. It can never be described without reference to those surrounding it. No one can be a self without this reference, and a self can therefore say: "I am a self only in relation to a specific interlocutor in a dialogue, in a way relative to the dialogue with those partners who are important for my attaining self-determination; in other words, relative to those who are important for my understanding of the language of self-understanding". Of course, it is possible for these aspects to overlap. Therefore, the self exists only within a "network of negotiators." Orientation within the dimension that consists of questions includes this network. The awareness of goodness as the goal requires a reexamination of these negotiations. They make sense if external differences are used to underline both unity and oneness: this establishes mutual support.

> *Help one another*
> *to piety and godfearing;*
> *do not help each other*
> *to sin and enmity.*
> *And fear God.*[21]

Hence follows the conclusion that the question "Who am I?" also includes the question "From what position and to whom am I speaking?" But the self is also determined by the names it calls itself and by those which others call it. In the process of identification and the acquisition of identity, the question of names is often a substitute for the named essence.

Modernity often imposes, and sometimes even resolutely demands, that the second aspect of identity be transcended—it should be noted that the first aspect is the universal aspect (life and dignity), whereas the second is the specific aspect (history, heritage, community). This means that the notion of the freedom and autonomy of the self should inspire and achieve "liberation" from the net imposed by the participants in a dialogue, linked by origin, history, heritage. Human conversation, however, is always mediated through the works of oral or written culture, sayings, holy scriptures, works of the imagination, poetry, and works of art in the most general sense. These always take part in the dialogue and are destined to be taken up, heard and read repeatedly. However, all these forms derive from previous modes of social celebration or rituals, and at times they are simply heritage. Their place and exact symbolic meaning in traditional doctrine cannot be established.[22] At the same time, without them the identity that can be used as a position from which to address them is not possible either.

The objective is, therefore, to examine the frameworks that articulate the human sense of orientation within the dimension of questions about goodness. This qualitative definition allows of an answer to the question about the sources of moral responses and judgments, because this framework lends meaning to the responses. Here, however, there are two crucial, though often opposed views. In the first, reason is the highest level of individuality: the aspects that cannot be linked to pure common sense or to the history of the world—such as, for instance, the immediate understanding of beauty, feelings of disgrace, shame, and sin, of orientation towards "the world behind the world," and similar aspects of the self—remain more or less unknown and alien to it. But it is these very expressions of intuitive intellectuality, from which immediate and immeasurable values derive, that offer those realms of the self which elude the measurable world.

Disengaged Reason

Modern identity does not resolve the dilemma of the sufficiency or insufficiency of the self to a proper orientation within the moral arena. It simply opts for the premise of sufficiency. It follows from this that it accepts reason as the highest level of human individuality, needing no higher source of knowledge. Distrust of any transmitted knowledge or received wisdom, and even the very possibility of the direct experience of reality, becomes the essential element by which ideology and the scientific mind set deflect us from a re-examination of their foundations. The perfect creation of the self and its original infinite nature become reduced to the changeability of its configuration. The self thus becomes translated into development. Force and power are proffered to its ontological frailty as the most important means by which reason introduces order into the world. As a result, matrixes or paradigms can be established that justify the use of force and power to attain a given goal. If there is no such thing as objective knowledge, those who hold the greater power have a warrant to behave towards others as if their power superseded such knowledge.

In this view, the multiplicity of languages is no longer seen as the reflection and confirmation of a transcendent unity. The diversity of individualities is thus brought into a state of irreconcilable contradiction. Since, for example, religions are thereby detached from unity as the first confirmation of the Mystery, they are merely discrete forms, and it is the quantities of force and power that pass judgment on their relationships. In the multitude of forms it is impossible to recognize the truth of what *sophia perennis* says: the perfect creation of the self corresponds with the absolute law and the revealed language, which are the elements of any tradition.[23] Although this statement too is subject to knowledge, which may be acquired in three ways—by receiving it from an external authority, by rational research, or by immediate "contact" with reality—it should be noted that it does not lead to any final or organized view. This is, in the language of Ibn al-'Arabi, the "view of no view" or the "position of no position." The objective reality, quite distinct from the subject, as such disappears in every view. It becomes the god of one view, which is different from every other. The integrity of life and dignity is entrapped in the determination of both.

The self is the full potential; otherwise, it is nothing. It is, therefore, the treasury of the full potential of being. This fullness is its incontestable right. There follows from this the duty to recognize and acknowledge the same potential for any other self. This duty, in turn, carries the corresponding right to be recognized by others. The modern ideology of liberalism sees this as the basis of humanity's infinite capacity for constructive progress. The issues of recognition and rights lie at the center of that capacity. But this fundamental right of the self, to be recognized in its full potential, becomes entangled in the human totality, where identities are derived from and subsumed into collectives. The claim for recognition of a collective, and of the self's determination by it, imposes many contradictions—these are today known as the debates on multiculturalism and on the politics of recognition.[24] However, this issue takes us back to the nature of modern knowledge and its sources. It is impossible to find answers without facing the fact of different religions, traditions, and civilizations and the modern inability to recognize diversity as the external expression of one and the same esoteric center.

Desacralization

From the perspective of the autonomous self, there is no sacred root of knowledge. The root is the self itself, with reason as the individual's highest potential. Reason (*ratio*) thus replaces intellect (*intellectus*), and perception replaces internal illumination. The concept of disengaged reason, which is the foundation of modernity, places humans in the position of an isolated individuality, which has nothing that could be the source of knowledge of a higher order relative to the knowledge resulting from the power of reason. Unlike traditional humans, who turn to intellect as the highest treasury of knowledge, modern individuals deny even the very existence of such a possibility. For traditional humans, the root of knowledge is in the sacred, and knowledge itself is therefore inseparable from sacredness. This is not so for modern humans: neither knowledge nor its root is sacred to them—everything is subject to scrutiny, everything is negotiable, for only thus can the self distinguish one good from others and determine their order from higher to lower.

From the perspective of traditional humans, *gnosis*, theology, and philosophy remain linked through that sacred root. Modern views result in the secularization of reason. Hence follows a more or less categorical separation of philosophy from theology, reason from belief, and mysticism from *gnosis*. Individualism and rationalism are the natural expressions of this trend. Descartes was the first to give shape to the reduction of knowledge to the exercise of individual reason, detached from intellect in its microcosmic and macrocosmic expression. It is this reduction that is the essence of both philosophy and modern science. Descartes addresses the individual consciousness of the thinking subject. His "I think, therefore I am" refers to the human "self," and not to the Divine Self. The illusory *self*, with its experience and consciousness of thinking, thus becomes the foundation of all epistemology and ontology, and as such, is adopted as a source of security.

The premise of an intellect that transcends every individuality leads to the premise of an authority that is not only a need of the self, but its higher potential. When reason is detached from its supra-individual and nonindividual source, both authority and transcendence become meaningless: they are left without a "link" to the Truth. Knowledge embarks on its odyssey in which desacralization and separation from the essence become the intrinsic determinants: this requires the desacralization of the world as well—one of the essential elements of the project of modernity.

In the traditional perspective, listening is the most sublime human skill: it is the orientation towards unity that confirms the ineffable. The meaning of this orientation lies, indeed, in accepting the infinity of content of any finite expression of the truth. Hence follows the acceptance of the diversity of those expressions, for, in their presence in the world, they are but manifestations of their archetype in the intellect. But if the source of all knowledge is inside every individual, then speaking and writing are his most sublime skills. While silence and learning are a confirmation of the wisdom that stems from an orientation towards discovering the perennial principles, speaking and writing are expressions typical of modern humans.

There is nothing more sublime for the traditional teacher than testimony of the mystery. There is nothing more important for modern individuals than speaking and writing. It is understandable, therefore, why the age of modernity is inseparable from the passion for individual speech and the need of every individual to present himself in writing. Given that tolerance is a derived form of listening, the feeling that in principle an individual has nothing to hear outside himself is then also the source of the manifest lack of attunement to the speech of others. Higher planes of being, just like intellect, do not exist for him. As a result, it is impossible to reveal to such a man anything other than what is inside him; he himself is the discloser of everything that can be known. By placing reason at the very root of all knowledge, with the full exclusivity of its individual nature, self-confinement in conditional space and time is misperceived as openness to development. The knowledge that results from development so conceived renders the self ever more distant from itself, and at the same time ever less able to understand its own limitations, due to the exclusion of the higher planes of being. From such a perspective, the knowledge of infinity and eternity is meaningless: they are marginalized, declared to be aberrations. Linked to this is the loss of the sense of beauty as an expression of infinity and eternity in the finite world.

One Self or Two

The act of sketching an image of the modern age raises the question of the difference between traditional and modern individuals. If the first is delineated with sufficient clarity, the distinction will be instantly visible.

Traditional humans are understood as a bridge between Heaven and Earth, or as God's vicar or vicegerent on earth.[25] They are the peripheral reflection of and have the potential to attain the center. At the center of each individual self is the Self as the source of sacred knowledge and the knowledge of the sacred. It is both the center and root of human intelligence. Knowledge of the center is thus the center of knowledge. The truth "descends" into intelligence or flows into it. Intelligence is the gift of God that shines through the curtain of phenomena. It is the ray of light that travels from the source through the curtain of cosmic existence, linking its verge, at which fallen individuals live, with the center where the Self is. Intellect belongs entirely to God, and is human only to the extent in which individuals participate in it. It is both substance, and function, and light, and vision: reason is only its reflection on the human plane. It is the root of consciousness or the soul. If the notion of "soul" is understood to mean "*anima*" or "psyche," then intellect (*intellectus*) is Spirit (*spiritus*). Their merging begets a perfect and consecrated self.

Intellect is a metacosmic principle. It is the source of both knowledge and being, of subjective consciousness and the learned objective order. In addition, it is also the source of the revelation that links man with the cosmos and all the other planes of Being, as well as with non-Being itself. *Logos*, Budhi or Aql, the names for intellect in different traditions, is the luminous center of both man and religion. It is the knowledge of the Self about the Self, the first manifestation or creation.

And since there are many worlds or planes in the manifestation, there are also different planes of consciousness and degrees of Intellect's descent through them down to individuals, in whose heart its ray still shines. Regardless of how much the ray may be obscured, every tradition insists on the nature of the Center and the Source. Through it, human beings remain open to Perfection. Their primordial nature is that Perfection: it is God's image, the point of convergence for all that is dispersed in the whole of the cosmos. The entirety of humankind's earthly presence directs them to it. Multiplicity confirms Unity; transience, Eternity; and mutability, Peace. Revelation and religion constantly impel them toward the Center and the Source, or, in other words, towards realization in the perfect individual. But their oblivion manifests itself as the state of being bound to the earth, which becomes the totality of multiplicity, time and change. Individuals are the Promethean: the earth is their house. The earth for them is not the pristine nature that mirrors paradise: it is only the building material for their "creation," through which they will strive to forget God and their inner reality. Life, for them, is a vast market-place in which they buy and sell whatever they want. Divorced from peace and constancy, they follow their baser nature, which they regard as freedom. Yet the nostalgia for peace constantly compels them to change their direction and path. This is the essence of the Hegelian turning of constancy into change.

The dialectic course not only deprives man of the concept of immutability, which is the basis of the traditional view of man: it leads to the humanization of God, which is the ultimate point of secularization in the life of modern man. Hegel "equates" the ultimate consciousness with God's infinite consciousness. From this it is an easy step to Feuerbach's view:[26] the human consciousness of infinite consciousness is nothing but the consciousness of infinity in the human consciousness of itself. This reversal, in turn, produces the view of God as an image of man and as a projection of his consciousness.

9

Whence and Whither?

Introduction

The aspiration to fulfillment can be met by building a structure that incorporates greater action or higher meaning. It can be met by linking one's life to some higher reality or narrative. It can be either belonging, in terms of tradition, to those forms of imagination that are typical of premodern times, or embracing the autonomy of the self and its freedom of choice in fostering the culture of the quotidian, or both of these. Humans are thus positioned on the axis linking the mundane, or the domain of reason, with the higher world of archetypes and the resolution of multiplicity and motion. The link between the poles of the axis may be active and conscious or forgotten and denied, or even disrupted. However, there is no phenomenon which does not contain this duality, either in confirmation or in denial. It can be resolved in two ways. The first is to regard reason as the highest plane of existence. This is the separation of reason from transcendence, thereby meeting the condition of the autonomy of the self. The second is to see reason as a "reflection" of the nonindividual and supra-individual intellect, where the archetypes abide of all that forms the images in the phenomenal world and, therefore, in reason itself. This difference between "disengaged reason" and the supra-individuality and nonindividuality of intellect explains the disjunction between modernity and tradition. This disjunction is marked by two views of the good. For tradition, the absolute and only good is God: man can be more or less open to and intimate with Him, but is in principle attuned to Him. In the modernist perspective, the supreme good is the individual, who is consequently the measure of everything else.

In the Abrahamic sacred tradition—Judaism, Christianity, and Islam—both the the cosmos in its entirety and the human self within it are but a revelation of the transcendental truth, its expression or sign. This truth is thus revealed and confirmed as absoluteness but in a contingent way: as unity in multiplicity, as stillness in motion. This form of expression does not disappear from the horizons even of those who are not consciously part of the world of tradition or religion. The phenomena of a totally secularized and even atheist world acquire meaning only when one understands their link with the traditional foundations of civilization.[1] Even the most committed leftists in political life are perceived as contributors to social transformation or to the "march" of human history towards its culmination: this is what gives a fuller and higher meaning to their lives.

It is fair to note that all of these different cases concern the "contact or connection" with the good, or the definition of a position in relation to good that overarches differences. Thus, in the religions referred to in these discussions, the "link" is always with God.[2] This link can be understood as the process of "turning" from a lower to a higher reality, from evil to good, from ignorance to knowledge, from indifference to ardor, from passivity to loving. This is the meaning of dogma, morality, and ritual alike. The existence of an "outer" and an "inner" center, to which the self is linked, is confirmed in them. Realization should, in the final analysis, merge them, making them one and the same. This definition of duality—as the outer and inner centers—leads to the yearning to create movement towards the good, which, in different forms of life, is expressed as a distancing from and avoidance of disgrace; coming closer to or acquiring fame; moving from illusion to reality, from tedious to pleasant, and the like. This is how the yearning to avoid confinement and humiliation shows itself. In the language of tradition, this movement corresponds to the stations of wisdom. All six spatial dimensions—right and left, forward and backward, upward and downward, or north-south, east-west, nadir-zenith—converge in every individuality. These dimensions correspond to will, love, and knowledge. In the domain of will, humans choose escape or attack; faced with beauty, they relax in contemplation or are drawn to it through the power of love; while knowledge includes the external world of phenomena and its transformation into the fullness of the self or "self-knowledge."[3]

The Scale of Values

The century that has just ended was characterized by ideology. The premise of the unlimited development of society can be examined on the basis of the effects of ideology in the course of the past two centuries. The conclusions of that scrutiny will, however, be essentially flawed if the question is both posited and answered within the confines of an ideological framework. In this reexamination, tradition can at least be the alternative that is required for the purposes of definition and comparison. The parable of the daughter fish asking her mother "What is water?" is instructive. Her mother said to her: "I could give you an answer only if you could first tell me about anything that is not water!"

If liberalism as the most prestigious ideology of the modern age is placed at the center of this examination, it can be asserted at the very outset that the self and its freedom are postulated as the greatest good. The world is subordinate to the free self: it is below humans in the hierarchical order, and, consequently, entirely at their disposal as the one who created it according to their own design. No heteronomous authorities, be they conceptual or institutional, can restrict or hinder individuals in this, because all of them are their work. Humans alone are able to create and deconstruct them. As postulated in this view, individuals are not the work of a higher being which bestows full purpose on them. Their condition and potential come to exist through development from a minuscule biological root. Both the overall ability to learn and all knowledge itself lie in this biological development. Individuals as the highest good project their position in the world through their rights. It should be noted that this perspective excludes the existence of any plane of existence above the plane comprised by the spatiotemporal continuum. It also requires philosophical anthropology, but it does not need either metaphysics or symbolism.

Tradition has its root in pure intellectuality, the origin of which is not human. Its highest good is the Truth. Knowledge of the Truth can depend on nothing outside the truth itself. If it were otherwise, the Truth would not be absolute. Both the self and the cosmos express this absoluteness. Man knows it directly, says Meister Eckhart, through his uncreated and uncreatable aspect.[4] Whenever absoluteness is expressed, it must assume finite and contingent forms. Those different forms provide a "link" with the Truth, but never comprise it fully. Revealed in human language, it becomes religion: dogma, morality, and ritual. Dogma is a limited derivation of pure intellectuality into formal expression, substantive or normative. The deductive application of dogma to society takes on the form of morality. A ritual is symbolic communication of an individual or a community with the Truth, which is both non-individual and supra-individual. In this view, the self has unlimited potential: to be human is to know the Truth. This is the sole human right. Everything else is duties, against which the highest is the right of the Truth, its absolute good. Unlike the perspective of liberalism, that of tradition leaves us with a duality: the self is both autonomous and heteronomous. The former is the domain of discursive reason, which is a solely human feature. Discursive reason is the refracted and mediated dispersal of the intellect oriented exclusively towards the exterior, towards motion and multiplicity. Reason believes that everything is possible to it, though it is evident to it that it can never be at peace. Intellect, as its higher principle, is the universal feature of overall manifestation, and is always the inner nature of every expression, the principle of its link with peace and unity.

The disjunction of these two perspectives, here outlined schematically and approximately, marks the beginning of modernity. The premise of the self as a separate identity which is sufficient for its own unlimited development requires and imposes a categorical rupture with continuity, which is the nature of tradition. Nor can it be a mere rupture and disjunction. It is also a persistent denial. The question "Whence and whither?", which is the essence of the confrontation with modern identity, and also the answer to it, carries at its center both disjunction and denial. That is why the question of tradition is raised ever more insistently as the denial grows stronger. Linked to this is the enigma of the scale of values, which is irresolvable in the ideological perspective. The conflict of the right of an unborn child to life and the right of its mother to take its life, on the basis of the undeniability of the freedom of choice, is only one of the examples for which there is no solution in philosophical ethics.

New Realms

Religion is an integral expression of tradition. The purport of all its essential factors—dogma, and morality, and ritual—remains a means of turning towards and forming a link with the Truth, which transcends all their forms, thus making them into symbols that tell of and lead to the Truth. It is important to note that religion has two essential realms—the exoteric and the esoteric. The exoteric can be linked with the terms "morality," "action," "merit," and "mercy." The realm of the esoteric corresponds to the terms "symbolism," "concentration," "cognition," and "oneness." A passionate human will thus draw closer to God through action supported by the moral law, while the contemplative, on the other hand, will unite with the Divine Essence through concentration supported by symbolism, without, of course, excluding the former view within the limits that suit him. Morality is a principle of action, and therefore also of merit. Symbolism is both a support to contemplation and a device of intellectuality. The goal of merit gained through action is the Grace of God. The purpose of intellectuality, if the latter can be distinguished from its goal, is unification or identification with that which never can be denied its being within the existential and intellectual "essence"; in other words, the supreme goal is that of reestablishing man's link with the Truth, the conditional with the Absolute, the finite with the Infinite. Meister Eckhart calls this undeniability of the presence of the inexpressible in the expressed, through which absoluteness is possible, the "uncreated and uncreatable."[5]

Morality as such obviously does not have any meaning outside the conditionally limited arena of action and merit, and therefore does not in any way extend to such areas as symbolism, contemplation, intellectuality, and identification through cognition.[6]

When morality is detached from its revealed universal principle and relocated within the framework of philosophy or discursive thought, in the arena of the social drama of the free and self-sufficient individual, the authority that derives from religious dogma becomes redundant, superfluous to the ordering of the world by man to the human scale of the free and independent mind. The solution to this redundancy takes the form of secularization, or the separation of individual and collective totalities into two realms—the private and the public. Religion and sentimentality, linked to religious dogma, are consigned to the private domain, which is de facto peripheral, the domain of the outsider. The mainstream of social change lies in the public domain, which is the arena of ideological thought and action. This distinction deprives ritual of its meaning and role, and the vacuum is filled by the affirmation of "ordinary life." The ramification of the awareness of and quest for rights prevails over the orientation towards and preoccupation with the Truth. In this view, humans have the highest right. All duties are directed towards them or towards the institutions, orders, and ideas which they have established.

Thus, to see, in the modern promotion and confirmation of "ordinary life," means to watch the self in motion, fostered by that life and the expansion of its horizons. This expansion is, however, taking place within the "horizontal being": there is no world outside the world known to discursive reason. The result is the reduction of knowledge to only one plane of being, declared to be the only plane. Science—by which is meant the modern natural sciences—is accepted as a reliable foothold in the human aspiration to the truth. The prevailing belief is that these sciences are capable of objective truth. However, the idea that modern science is what absolute knowledge should be can also be interpreted as a placebo. More important than this, however, is the potential to answer the question, to what extent can the concepts of objective truth be extended to social understanding.

The "yes" or "no" question relates not to how near or far people are from what they perceive as the good, but rather to the direction of their lives—whether it is oriented towards or away from the good, or the source of the human impulse towards it. Questions of this kind are clear in religious traditions: the self is allowed to ask those questions in the face of the absolute, determining the context within which the relative questions of proximity to or distance from the good are raised.[7] It is also possible to point to the secular derivations of this religious perspective. It is a matter of where people stand, on which side; and to this there are only two possible answers.

The circumstances of one's can never be exhausted by what one claims to be, because one always has the potential to change and become. In this gradual development, individuals become autonomous mediators and participants in negotiations. They thus gain their own place relative to the good, which is, however, constantly challenged by potential scrutiny and change. Therefore the question "Where are we?" alone is not sufficient for them. They also need the question "Where are we going?", which includes direction and path. The answer to it is "somewhere/nowhere." This is why an absolute question always frames relative questions. Since they cannot be answered without an orientation relative to the good, and since indifference to one's position with regard to the good is not possible, and since this place is always subject to change and becoming, the issue of the direction of our lives must arise for us. This is where the second important feature of human life sets in. In order to make even minimal sense of our lives, in order to have some identity, there must be an orientation towards the good, which means some sense of qualitative discrimination. It is evident that this sense of the good must be woven into our "understanding of life" as an unfolding story. And this defines another basic condition for making sense of ourselves: that we grasp our lives in the form of a narrative.[8] Making sense of one's life is, like orientation towards the good, not an optional extra. Only a coherent narrative can answer that our lives exist within the arena of questions. Knowing how to answer the question "Who are we?" includes knowing the answers to the questions "How did we come to exist?" and "Where are we going?" But an important difference sets in here. If human existence "grows" from the bottom upwards, from simple matter to the complex brain, the answer to the question of human orientation, as postulated by the Enlightenment, then lies only in reason. If, however, growth is from above downwards—from the ineffable to the contingent—then orientation towards the ineffable requires a resource that transcends reason: and this resource is, in the language of tradition, intellectual intuition.

Freedom

Every tradition postulates the human self as an undeniable and inviolable sanctity. There is full agreement in the Abrahamic traditions that humans are created "in the image of God." In the language of the latest revelation, the link between the outer world and our inner selves as signifiers of the Truth points to this feature of humanity.[9] The perfection of the Creator defines the fairest stature as the essence of humanity's createdness.[10] Given this full openness of the human selfhood to the truth, its individuality is not separable from either human or cosmic totality. An individual self is in principle identical to all selves combined.[11] This is the self in its primal perfection, filled with its inherent leaning towards the good.[12] This leaning turns the human self to the outer world, which is also everything that is outside it. It also directs it towards itself as everything that it is both without and within. "When we come to understand these two affairs together," explains Ibn al-'Arabi "we come to know Him and it becomes clear to us that He is the Real. Hence the signifying of God is more complete."[13]

The human being is per se potential perfection. To realize this potential is to achieve full humanity. Humans are different from other creatures because they are, as individuals, an image of the whole. Both the cosmos and humans are images of the Truth. Since the Truth is one, humanity's realization is in the understanding that selfhood incorporates and tells the whole message of the outer world as revealed through the dispersed host of signs. As long as the openness of the self to perfection is limited to some degree, irrespective of the configuration of narrative or identity, it can be called "slavery or poverty." The self is worthy only of slavery to and poverty before perfection, and freedom from everything else. As such, it is always the image of God. It may be concealed by different forms of weakness and depravity. But the self will never be left without any attribute, without its original nature, just as darkness cannot exist without any light.

The fullness of this aspect is freedom. It is not mediated by any other freedom, but is what it is, authentically and completely. However, its manner of manifestation in extension, among the totality of forms, depends on its positioning between its primal and first aspect and its final achievement. That is why its perfect interior is always accompanied by a perfect exterior. It can be observed as autonomous, yet it always has its heteronomous aspect as well. This is the polarization of the earthly and the heavenly. It represents the two extremes of the human presence—one archetypal and perfect, and the other earthly and limited by multitude and motion. Individual mediation, and, with it, the hierarchical order of society, is thus established through interpretation and establishment of the earthly order on the basis of the heavenly archetype.

The autonomous and heteronomous aspects of the self are thus transferred into individual and institutional authorities. The possible freedom of an individual is limited by the non-transcendental authority of the world in which it exists. Instead of concentrating on submission to freedom, it concentrates on the institution or individual that represents and interprets it. This therefore includes the potential for transformation of a free authority into a tyrant. One way to oppose this is to deny the heteronomous aspects of the self and turn the entire self towards autonomy.

However, this gives rise to the question of the cosmos. Is it only one level of being, since the truth transcends each of its levels? Contact with nature and the experience of relationship with it become the source of direction and the context of judgment. Humans are regarded as a sufficient source of knowledge and orientation towards the good. In this interpretation, they need neither external guides nor judges for realization. Their realization is possible in the earthly dimension, which holds and offers all that the human nature requires, and in sufficient and unlimited measure. This freedom demands a refusal to submit to any exoteric authority that is not subject to doubt and to constant reexamination in the course of public negotiation, as science is subject to scepticism. In this view, sanctity disappears, for nothing escapes scrutiny.[14] The need for an external authority also disappears, for no individual has higher innate potential than any other. Knowledge of the truth does not come from outside. It lies next to the very center of every individuality. The consciousness of universal good is transformed into a sense of the rights of the individual.

There are thus two essentially different views of freedom. In the first, freedom can be achieved in the dynamism of oppositions: nobility in submission or freedom in slavery. If freedom is the fulfillment of the self, its attainment is then possible only through submission and slavery to freedom alone. However, such a path requires the transcendence of every individual form through its symbolic position relative to the first and the last. In this view, being has many planes or manifestations. They all have their roots in unity as the first confirmation of the ineffable. In other words, this is the revelation of freedom. On the earthly plane, this revelation is possible only through humans: it is the manifestation of the highest human potential. This is why their poverty relative to transcendence is their most sublime expression. The names of that manifestation can be submission, slavery, humility, and the like; the messenger of the revelation of freedom, however, speaks the language of people. As that language is meaningful only in the community of those who use it, every instance of its conveyance is always concentrated on an interpretation that is linked to the absolute, but is never the absolute itself. This confirms the ontological weakness of the human being with regard to its potential for perfection. Along with the "fairest stature," timidity and weakness were conferred upon humanity.[15] This maintains and strengthens the potential for perfection, as the absoluteness of the good and of freedom can come out of nothing but themselves.

In the different view which has emerged as the foundation of modernity—and which may also be called a "response to the reductive interpretations of freedom in submission"—freedom becomes the name for human independence from external rules and systems offered on the basis of unquestionability and authority. In this view, the achievement of a "happy life" depends on the human spirit of enterprise. Reason is a sufficient lamp to light the way towards the end of history. The question of *now* and *the moment of death* is pushed aside. The space and time of the earth between them, with all of their contingencies and mutabilities, are adopted as the only arena of the human drama: the only world is this measurable world. Timidity and weakness as ontological manifestations of an individual's orientation towards absoluteness become either denied or neglected. This altered view of the cosmos and the self—in which frailty is replaced with stability and weakness with strength—requires an exclusive ideology: in it, *now* and *the moment of death* are overarched by the design of an earthly order in which exclusivity and arrogance prevail. From the adoption of the premise that the self is determined by social circumstances, the conclusion is drawn that it can be altered by influencing those circumstances.

The Self in the Triptych of Modernity

The basis of this view is the premise that there are no limits to progress and transformation. Its application always includes two possibilities. The first is for this unlimited progress and transformation to be understood as the "creation of new man." Elites, ideologies, and their organizations, which are the subject of progress and transformation, are then promoted to the level of a god, with full rights in relation to the world and humanity. Fascism, Nazism, Communism, and the different forms derived from them are examples of this. The second application of the premise is summarized by Jürgen Habermas as follows: "This should transform arbitrary will into reason, a reason which through the open competition of particular arguments establishes a consensus over what is practically necessary to realise the general interest."[16]

However, the self is not a neutral bullet point. It is an arena of questions, with constituent concerns and preoccupations. The questions or concerns touch on the nature of the good that orients the self toward the path it follows with regard to the good. The nature of its question is determined by the nature of the person as a whole. It is not an arbitrary determination, but can be understood as comprising the past and the future. Or, as Heidegger says, in its past and future "*ekstaseis.*" It is not possible to answer the question "Where am I?" without also answering the question "Where did I come from?" The sense of the self includes a being that comes into existence and grows, which requires time. It is an open process of externalization, objectification and internalization. The human nature becomes changed in this process. In the course of becoming and growing, the person thus gets to know himself through a history of maturations and regressions, victories and defeats. The self, therefore, has a necessary depth. It also incorporates narratives. In contrast to it is the totality of manifestation. Wherever this development may begin and wherever it may reach, the manifest is comprised by the non-manifest, which is, therefore, in the temporal sense, the first and the last; and in the spiritual sense, the inner and the outer. The modern image of the world, which takes the form of a triptych—the philosophical idea of progress and reason; the political understanding of republican governance; and the notion of a civil society that can *realize* progress and enlightenment, which mark the modern era—excludes these questions from its framework. The ineffable, as the essence that assumes form in the unity of being, is in this world view beyond the reach of reason: it cannot, therefore, be the goal of human orientation. The ineffable thus becomes reduced to superstition, while intuition is excluded.

These premises once again lead us back to the question of freedom. "As well as the affirmation of ordinary life, there is the modern notion of freedom. The ancient notion of the good, either in the Platonic mode, as the key to cosmic order, or in the form of the good life *à la* Aristotle, sets a standard for us in nature, independent of our will. The modern notion of freedom which develops in the seventeenth century portrays this as the independence of the subject, his determining of his own purposes without interference from external authority. The second came to be considered as incompatible with the first. The conflict was originally conceived in theological terms. Late medieval nominalism defended the sovereignty of God as incompatible with there being an order in nature which by itself defined good and bad. For that would be to tie God's hands, to infringe on his sovereign right of decision about what was good. This line of thought even contributed in the end to the rise of mechanism: the ideal universe from this viewpoint is a mechanical one, without intrinsic purpose. But with the modern era, something analogous begins to be transferred onto humans. Normative orders must originate in the will. This is most evident in the seventeenth-century political theory of legitimacy through contract. As against earlier contract theories, the one we find with Hugo Grotius and John Locke starts from the individual . . ."17

This mixture of Kantian and naturalistic notions has yielded the picture of the human agent so familiar in much contemporary moral philosophy. Iris Murdoch captures it in a memorable description: "How recognizable, how familiar to us is the man so beautifully portrayed in the *Grundlegung*, who confronted even with Christ turns away to consider the judgement of his own conscience and to hear the voice of his own reason. Stripped of the metaphysical background which Kant was prepared to allow him, this man is with us still, free, independent, lonely, powerful, rational, responsible, brave, the hero of so many novels and books of moral philosophy."[18]

Authority

This division of the self into two aspects, one composed of reason and what is below it, and the other which is above reason, can be resolved through two perspectives. In the first, the self is autonomous and self-sufficient. In the latter, it is neither autonomous nor self-sufficient, and can exist as such only if its heteronomous nature is also accepted. This means that orientation towards the good within the space filled by questions is possible only if an external authority is embraced. It is always the perfect man, whether he manifests himself as the totality of existence in which all aspects of humanity as "the image of God" converge, or as the historical presence of a person through whom transcendence speaks: which, in the language of the Abrahamic traditions, may be "the Anointed" (*Hristos*) or "the Praised" (*Muhammad*). Their nature of being anointed or praised signifies full "contact" with transcendence. Thus, they become authorities who enable the self to achieve fulfillment. However, their historical extension in the temporal course of tradition is also an *authority*. Regardless of how feeble and obscure is the modern consciousness of morality's root in the "realm" beyond negotiation and change, it can nevertheless be claimed that all forms of authority surpass, in terms of their choice, the world of contingency. Three sources of authority can be identified. The first is determined by modern, liberal, and civic references; the second is shaped by the givens of identity (origin, race, ethnicity, nationality, etc.); the third is created and determined by transcendent commandments. As the "*loci*" of authority, each determines a different meaning of the sacred. Hence follows a different definition of the self, too, both as individual and as collective. We have, therefore, three sources of moral authority. Their forms are linked with the attributes of the self: one cannot be understood without the other.

Qualitative distinctions, as definitions of the good, offer reasons in this sense, so that their presentation is the articulation of what underlies ethical choices, leanings, intuitions. It brings into salience precisely what we dimly grasp when we see that A is right, or X is wrong, and that Y is valuable, worth preserving. "It is," as Charles Taylor notes, "to articulate the moral point of our actions. That is why it is so different from offering an external reason. I can only convince you by my description of the good if I speak for you, either by articulating what underlies your existing moral intuitions or perhaps by my description moving you to the point of making it your own. And that is also why it cannot be assimilated to giving a basic reason. Relative to the most basic action-description, we can still strive to make clear just what is important, valuable, or what commands our allegiance, as with the above example of respecting human rights. This isn't a step to a more basic level, because there is no asymmetry. But we can see how articulating the good may help further definitions of what is basic."[19] Here, too, one should note the importance of the distinction between the sources of selves and the corresponding authorities. Emile Durkheim postulates the individual as the source of moral authority and *locus* of the sacred in modern society. This takes one back to the civic humanism of the Renaissance city-states, and resonates with the claim "that modernity rests on a wager that the terms of collective meaning, those of liberal individualism, can be maintained autonomously at the center of the civic polity, without the need for either the armature of a transcendent Deity or the referents of a primordial collectivity."[20] However, this idea of civic humanism and pure civic values is denied by the experience of the twentieth century.

In modernity, the absence of authority in the broadest sense of the term is most frequently replaced by naturalism, "the belief that we ought to understand human beings in terms continuous with the sciences of extra-human nature."[21] This view, together with the experience of the twentieth century, points to the question of the absent structure of transcendence, without which, judging by current experience, it is not possible to institutionalize the idea of republicanism. The idea of transcendence secures the *locus* of moral authority and the self. This is foreign to modern perception, but the sum of human circumstances and knowledge at the turn of the millennium offers only this conclusion. Thus, it is possible to provide for what is missing in a purely autonomously conceived model of the self, without falling back on ascriptively defined and primordial categories of selfhood.[22] "However paradoxical it may seem to us," notes Adam B. Seligman, with transcendence in mind, "its very authority calls the self into being as moral evaluator, as agentic in a sense other than power."[23]

Transcendence

The question of transcendence is untenable outside the metaphysical context. Existence in its entirety is manifest as multiplicity and motion. Yet, as such, it is the confirmation of unity and stillness, thus revealing the unity of Being. But it also leads us to ask what confirms the unity of Being. If it requires manifestation in motion and multiplicity, is it possible to determine what it is merely the requirement of? For this is the greatest metaphysical mystery. Unity is expressible, but its metaphysical zero is not. The expressible thus leads to the inexpressible, without which no meaning is possible. In other words, the in-expressible is revealed in the unity of Being, which is in itself not possible without multiplicity and motion. Looking back, which is the same as looking ahead, the first and last meaning of every individuality transcends its form. This means that it transcends its own limits. The revelation of both unity and ineffability takes place in each individual. Consequently, the human self carries within itself the fullness of multiplicity and unity, but also the inexpressibility confirmed by them. Hence, it follows that this individuality must have two aspects—one that is its own and another that transcends it, but from which it is nevertheless inseparable. This is the question of reason as the manifestation of intellect in individuality. Modernity as the idea of the secular nature of human individuality—which means that rational individuality is detached from every nonindividuality and supraindividuality—effects the transformation of the self as the individuality which is absolute. The self is thus introduced into a world in which transcendence is denied in different ways, and the cosmos is reduced to a passive and undirected framework of the human centrality.

This position of human individuality does not require a definition of the good outside humankind itself, because there is nothing that can be revealed to individuals from outside, nor anything that can judge them in their openness to the world. In this view, individuals are no one's image, but are their own absolute. Though it is not their own choice to be such as they are, they grant themselves freedom of choice in all things. And this means that their will and reason are the highest plane of his selfhood. This is the perspective that perceives authoritarianism as authority, transcendence as enchantment of the world, freedom as submission to what cannot be free in and of itself, and religion as a reflection of the past inability of human beings to solve the ontological mystery. That is why, in the project of modernity, there is a denial of authority, a withdrawal from transcendence as enchantment and deliverance as a retreat from authority external to the autonomy of the self.

This view also requires a new anthropology. It does not start either in ineffability or in silence, because, in that case, the initial state would be the perfect unity, which receives multiplicity and motion in expression. It must start from some insufficiently shaped state and keep moving towards its own perfection. This course requires clear and full tracks in the measurable world, not outside it. To reason, the measurable world is the only world that exists. What does not exist in relation to another has no existence. This view denies dissimilarity and incomparability, because as such they stand outside the potential of reason. And as reason is individual, therefore neither nonindividuality nor supraindividuality are possible.

Thus, humans are reduced to a horizontality that corresponds to their plane of existence. Evolution operates within it. Its image is the philosophical and then the scientific substitution of the theistic or revealed anthropology according to which individuals are "the fairest stature" and "the image of God." Since what lies beyond the measurable world is not accessible to reason, it therefore has to be declared as non-Being. There can, therefore, be no source of knowledge beyond reason. The revelation of transcendence thus comes to be denied and ascribed to a "lower level" of the human development. From these two perspectives there derive different answers to the question of human relationships. If there is no God, which is the essential perspective of elevating discursive reason to the highest plane, relations among people are then unmediated, and reduced to the mere potential of the autonomy of their selves. But if this is not the case, then reaching out to the Supreme Being is the source and essence of relationships among people. From their orientation towards the Supreme Being and faith in Him stems mutual trust. These are two perspectives of "morality."

The self and authority, as two aspects of one and the same phenomenon, are therefore determined by three essential elements: the basic (origin, family, race, nation, etc.), the exoteric (with reason as the highest principle of individual and collective assessment, negotiation, and action), and the transcendent content (in which the self has a comprehensive and present perspective, which it can always identify with, but which can never identify with the self). Modernity, as a civilizational project, is postulated on the wager that transcendence can represent nothing more than transcendent reason, yet it nevertheless maintains its authoritative nature and sacred crown: Immanuel Kant's "the starry skies above us and the moral law within us" is the emblem of that wager. It seems that an answer to the question of the present circumstances of humankind and the world may be sought in this deliberate separation of the self and authority from transcendence.

Morality

"Morality" can be, and often is, simply defined in terms of recognizing others. It is believed that the category of morality includes obligations towards others. However, if this definition is adopted, then one must allow that there are also other issues outside morality that are of central importance to understanding the identity of the individual and society. The idea of an autonomous self and the sufficiency of individual reason separates morality from the supraindividual source. Its definition becomes exclusively bound to *cogito ergo sum*. The desirability and usefulness of social values are so obvious that, in this view, the religious roots of ethics easily vanish from the horizon. But as soon as morality is detached from its religious and metaphysical bases, it inevitably becomes subordinate to lower purposes: the source of moral authority is shifted from transcendent otherness to the interiority of the individual self. The need for a restoration of the ethics of vocation becomes the central issue of the society—the "calling" which is that state of life with which God is satisfied, rather than a "job," to which one is driven by personal ambitions, through which both morality and authority are almost as an invariable rule reduced to power.

"In general, one might try to single out three axes of what can be called, in the most general sense, 'moral thinking.' As well as the two just mentioned—our sense of respect for and obligations to others, and our understandings of what makes a full life—there is also the range of notions concerned with dignity. By this I mean the characteristics by which we think of ourselves as commanding (or failing to command) the respect of those around us."[24]

It should be noted that morality in this case, as in other references to it in these discussions, is not without value. But this only concerns its insufficiency. "The purity of morality itself represents a value. It expresses an ideal, presented by Kant, once again, in a form that is the most unqualified and also one of the most moving: the ideal that human existence can be ultimately just. Most advantages and admired characteristics are distributed in ways that, if not unjust, are at any rate not just, and some people are simply luckier than others. The ideal of morality is a value, moral value, that transcends luck. It must therefore lie beyond any empirical determination. It must lie not only in trying rather than succeeding, since success depends partly on luck, but in a kind of trying that lies beyond the level at which the capacity to try can itself be a matter of luck. The value must, further, be supreme. It will be no good if moral value is merely a consolation prize you get if you are not in worldly terms happy or talented or good-humored or loved. It has to be what ultimately matters."[25]

Even those who are not committed in such a single-minded way recognize higher goods. That is, they acknowledge second-order qualitative distinctions that define higher goods, on the basis of which they discriminate among other goods, attribute differential worth or importance to them, or determine when and if to follow them. Those can be called "higher-order goods," "hypergoods." Those are the goods which not only are incomparably more important than others, but also provide the standpoint from which these must be weighed, judged, and decided about. This is the concept according to which the judgment of the highest good is assigned entirely to the self, which is capable of assessment, choice, and decision. Both sanctity and authority are, consequently, alien and repellent to it. Sanctity, because for it there is nothing "set aside" that would be the unquestionable measure of the highest good. Authority, because moral judgment, given this autonomy of the self, does not need external interference. This means that the self itself has become the only *locus* of sanctity.

In our day, Habermas identifies a set of issues that have to do with universal justice and hence with the universal acceptability of norms, which are the domain of a discursive ethics; and he accords this superior status to issues concerning the best or most satisfactory life.[26] In modern culture, many accept as their highest good (or perhaps we could say at this stage, principle of right) a notion of universal justice and/or benevolence, in which all human beings are to be treated equally with respect, regardless of race, class, sex, culture, religion.[27]

"Morality is perceived purely as a guide to *action*. It is thought to be concerned purely with what it is right to do rather than with what it is good to be. In a related way the task of moral theory is identified as defining the content of obligation rather than the nature of the good life."[28] But optimistic thinking requires more than this. It is not possible without belief in the truth, love of the truth, and the meaning of individual life. The difference between this belief, based on the project of modernity, and the belief emerging from the heart of tradition, may be the crucial measure of the contemporary identity and an indication of its future changes.

The disillusionments resulting from the experience of the last century—Fascism, Nazism and Communism, together with the killings associated with them—encourage a deconstructionist denial of God, the self, order, and integral knowledge on the one hand, and the constructionist search for a traditional evaluation of the experience of the century of modernity on the other. The former offers a descent of dogmatic rationalism into total relativism and agnosticism, in which consciousness and concern about militarism disappear. The latter heralds a redemptive synthesis through which it would be possible to pause and redirect those elements of "development" that manifest themselves as the steady increase in the number of those persecuted and killed over the last few centuries.

But we should turn from this experience once again to the question of the identity of the self. The Kantian premise of its sufficiency as moral judge was demonstrated in all the cruelty of the twentieth century. The obscure universal individual, who declared the sufficiency of his selfhood as moral evaluator and judge, is thus often precipitated into those elements of individuality according to which it is impossible to distinguish him in any age. The question of rethinking identity takes us back—which in this case, nevertheless, means to move forward—to those elements that have been denied by modernity: the need for the pure transcendent otherness that teaches and instructs us how the self can be opened to its primal and ultimate purpose.

Idolatry

Doubts about duties and rights can be found in the idea of the autonomy of the self, as a feature of modernity. To dispel those doubts, one should address another issue that accompanies them—that of submission and freedom. If I can say that I have the right to some good, this is then an obligation of the possessor of this good. I demand that the possessor ensure this right of mine. I am thus in the position of someone who expects or demands a right. It is much the same with the modern idea of freedom, which is the denial of the individual's link with an external authority in the broadest sense of this term, because, otherwise, the ability of the self of its own accord to discriminate, evaluate, and choose among goods would be denied. This is the premise of the sufficiency of the self. With it, an individual has everything he needs for a full relationship with himself, others, and the world: and that is his position of rejecting the external for his own sake. The unquestionable source of authority is, consequently, totally internalized.

External authority and sanctity are features of tradition that are in opposition to the premises of modernity. The supposed ability of an individual self to be an autonomous moral evaluator and judge means that the absolute transcendence of moral authority is also shifted to the individual self, which is the potential for absoluteness, but not absoluteness itself. If an autonomous self evaluates and chooses among different goods, its decision and its will are then simultaneous. The means of this will is power. The will for power therefore becomes the crucial element in the expression of this self. Expressed in the language of economics, this is maximization of gains, and their acquisition in the most efficient possible way. But as morality, according to this essay's definition, is outside power and gain, it is a willful submission to a moral authority that surpasses any quantitative power.

The perspective can also be reversed. If humans have the right to absoluteness, then only absoluteness can grant that right to them, which is its duty. The identity of an individual can strive towards absoluteness only if determined by absolute and unquestionable transcendence. But this means that humans themselves, as an individuality in a multitude, can confirm this right by many duties discharged within the world of their contingency. Otherwise, the right to absoluteness would not make sense. Humankind's duties thus transform them into an active factor in the realization of their right. The secular notion of freedom then also receives a different meaning. Absoluteness is freedom. Submission to it from the perspective of contingency means detachment from the non-absolute and orientation towards the absolute.

This, too, places the individual in a working relationship with freedom, which thus ceases to be dissociation from the absolute. On the contrary, such a perspective of freedom means that man is "dissociating" himself from the contingent and "associating" with the absolute, as the pure transcendental otherness. But this requires both the nonindividual and the supra-individual reality of reason. The perfect potential of individuals then become the supreme good, and every manifestation of theirs in the world is arranged in the derived order of goods: existence is in a descending causality, from values to matter, from the truth to the sign, from stillness to motion, from absoluteness to contingency.

The self does have the possibility to choose, but the question remains of its ability to decide on its own, without the aid of an external authority, which of the available options is the best. According to the modern view, human action and mediation are determined by the ability to assess desires in qualitative terms. If this assessment can be encompassed by science, the self whose identity is determined by transcendence then must be sacrificed.[29] This sacrifice produces destructive effects in the whole edifice of modernity, in which the understanding of society is based on power, force, and the calculation of strategic action. And this, in turn, means that the identity of the self is determined, in the final sense, by an unclear conditionality, which can justifiably be called "idolatry."

From its beginnings, modernity has offered, as should again be noted, the wager that the self and moral responsibility are based on individual moral autonomy. The experience of violence in the twentieth century requires a categorical reconsideration of this wager. The moral autonomy of will is not, as is confirmed by that experience, a sufficient foundation either for personality or for civic life. Despite references to the abstract universal individual, that possessor of the universal right, the history of killing, persecution, and destruction in the twentieth century indicates the readiness with which the identity of the autonomous self is reduced to familial, racial, ethnic, territorial, and other similar aspects. This is the descent of the autonomous self towards its baser elements. In this case, authority is neither transcendent nor transcendental, but merely immanent. The adoption of the immanent as the authoritative is, in the language of tradition, idolatry. This justifies looseness of morals, or, in view of the current circumstances of humanity, to a blurring of the boundaries of social order, authority, and self-imposed morality. The self established in this way is untenable without violence. As the given features of the individual and his relevant community are absolutized, the reality of their immanence requires a denial of the Other.

10

The Decline of Modernity

Introduction

The human self and the cosmos are two aspects of a single revelation—of the sovereignty of God. The revelation they offer is in no way conditional upon the capacity of the individual to receive and reflect this sovereignty. The causality of this chain of revelation descends from the highest link to the lowest: pure and absolute knowledge, the ineffable, is the alpha and omega of creation, the supreme origin of all, revealed and made manifest throughout the universe. The perfect guide, the Prophet of God, was not man's choice, although it was ordained that his nature, in its entirety, should be matched by the teaching he passes on to us. The prophets, with their immediate disciples, have all departed from physical presence in this world; yet their nature and teaching are part of a living flow of tradition, lasting through generations. Each is evidence of the full meaning of the self and the cosmos as the speech of the "real," and every individual can access their teaching through three methods of discovery: acceptance of traditional teaching, individual rational enquiry, and direct experience of the "real." It is not in dispute that the individual's choice in this regard should be free. Nevertheless, there remains the question of the legitimization of society and government within this context. For it is not easy to verify claims of a close relationship to the sacred archetype and its application in different political structures., and it is hard to prevent these claims being abused at the expense of the life and dignity of the individual.[1] There have been many attempts to resolve this issue: the project of modernity is perhaps at once the most resolute and the most bizarre of these attempts.

The French Revolution, as well as the American, promulgated a new theory of political legitimacy: government is legitimate only in so far as it derives its authority directly from the people. This was the foundation for the construction of a new world order, with humanity as the ultimate measure and standard. It finds expression in the radically different world view that the

chain of causality begins with the lowest link, and that humanity is its ultimate and most perfect attainment. Thus, the source of all authority lies in national sovereignty. The fundamental question, however, is what form this
national sovereignty takes. There is a danger of new parties emerging that
speak the language of democratic politics, but use the powers ostensibly
granted them by the people for their own ends—overriding, if necessary, the
will of the people.

The politics of modernity offered or envisioned the replacement of the
old structures by political communities, civic associations, republics, or "nationalized nations" nation-states as the setting for democratic government.
The transformation of society as unlimited progress, and the knowledge on
which this advance is based, were thus emptied of all sacred content. Thus,
the whole of creation is relocated to the world of the material, relative, finite,
and temporal. The absolute freedom of the individual, on the one hand, and
the ever-accelerating progress of society as a whole on the other, form the
enigma that modern ideologies contend with. Yet between these two extremes
lies an endless spectrum of relationships. At present, the most readily recognizable links in that spectrum are liberalism, socialism, conservatism, and nationalism. Each is rooted in the concept of a rational political order that not
only guarantees the basic and universal rights of the individual, but also at the
same time restricts them to the social or ideological structure through which
the putative progress is to be achieved. This is the concept of a political system
that guarantees the basic goal of "national sovereignty" or "government by the
people," and goes hand in hand with building a "democratic nation," always
seen as a unified nation of self-governing citizens. However, every unity may
become opposed to diversity and to plurality. Again we are left with a question: if the modern political system of democracy is based on the will of the
people, then why should the state, which is the visible manifestation of this
will, be in any way restricted or controlled? Effective government always carries the danger that the "will of the people" will be used as the justification for
criminal acts by the "elected." We are forcibly reminded of this possibility by
the powers that tore Bosnia and its society apart: they were nurtured and supported by Bosnia's neighbor states, and arguably possessed all the democratic
legitimacy that free and fair elections can bestow.

Discernment

The concept of an eternal hierarchy, which extends from the supreme good to
its multitude of manifestations in the contingent world, calls for incessant
discernment. In this order, reason has a guiding star by which it steers. The

conflict of different goods, unresolvable in the modern liberal world view, finds its answer in this hierarchy. Every phenomenon of the created, contingent world has, in addition to its likenesses and equalities, an ultimate with which it cannot be compared. To discern between similar and equal phenomena means, in this context, the acceptance of the "real" as the root of everything in creation, which in itself both is and is not the real. It is, because its nature points towards the real and is not, since without transcendence, its finite nature has no unconditional reality. Thus, the deeds of humanity are placed in two perspectives: their relative nature is matched to the conditionality of every moral judgment; and yet, through the acceptance of the transcendent character of contingent phenomena, their very concept embodies their ultimate potential.

Down through the centuries, these two aspects have been divided into two opposing and seemingly irreconcilable world views: the traditional and the ideological. Both seek to resolve the dualities presented to them: the contingent versus the absolute; the temporal versus the eternal; the spatial versus the infinite. At different levels, each corresponds with the aspiration to construct unity from diversity. The ideologies of modernity are inseparable from this aspiration, although they believe it will be achieved through science, rooted in natural philosophy. The traditional world view has its counterpart in religion, a view that does not regard rational knowledge as the only knowledge, but sees humanity as having innate intuitive links with the higher levels of being, and the highest forms of knowledge as originating in direct intuitive contact with these levels.

Science and religion are the most important elements of the conflict between the opposing world views of the modern era that find their expression in ideology and religion respectively. It is true to say that in modernity, science has come to dominate religion. Secular power, as a result, has shifted from religious to ideological institutions and organizations. However, this has not resolved the conflict, and many feel indeed that we have not even begun to answer the fundamental questions that confront humanity. This until recently unchallenged victory over religion becomes all the more questionable, therefore, and for many is no more than an illusion in the anomalous period of human history known as modernity. Exploration of the two potentials, the ideological and the traditional, is therefore essential to our understanding of the human condition as the product of misguided desires, and consequently of the possibility that these desires may be changed. This demands a critical examination of all elements of our world view, which in turn will help recall us from our oblivion to human nature which, it seems, is never changed by circumstances, although they force it to forget the truth of that very nature.

The invulnerability of the human personality involves the relationship with the primordial infinitude and the framework within which it is manifest. This is a matter of the legitimacy of individual and social structures; to quote Charles Taylor:

> I want to defend the strong thesis that doing without frameworks is utterly impossible for us; otherwise put, that the horizons within which we live our lives and which make sense of them have to include these strong qualitative discriminations. Moreover, this is not meant just as a contingently true psychological fact about human beings, which could perhaps turn out one day not to hold for some exceptional individual or new type, some superman or disengaged objectification. Rather, the claim is that living within such strongly qualified horizons is constitutive of human agency, that stepping outside these limits would be tantamount to stepping outside what we would recognise as integral, that is, undamaged human personhood.[2]

The unity of a society based on ideological foundations takes the freedom of the individual as its source and support. This freedom, however, also means the full right to individual differences, whether they are inherited or arise from the attitude of the individual to his surroundings. Although the reconciliation of these two extremes is the goal of building a stable society, such reconciliation is impossible without compromising either the freedom of the individual or the effective unification of society. There is no measure of equilibrium accessible to reason in the pull between these two extremes. The world drama is evidence of the sensitive and complex nature of the search for such a balance. The savage forces that assault the various inhabitants of a region where there are aspirations to create a nation-state regularly seek justification in the will for and interests of national unity. "For instance," Charles Taylor notes:

> [I]n Habermas's case, the boundary between questions of ethics, which have to do with interpersonal justice, and those of the good life is supremely important, because it is the boundary between demands of truly universal validity and goods which will differ from culture to culture. This distinction is the only bulwark, in Habermas's eyes, against chauvinistic and ethnocentric aggression in the name of one's way of life, or tradition, or culture. It is thus crucial to maintain it.[3]

Differences are an essential part of identity. But how are we to confirm and strengthen, in that which defines their difference, in that which is delineated by the borderlines of otherness, the element that imposes obligations towards others as a prerequisite for respect of oneself? This awareness of the Other enables the individual self to emerge from the cocoon that offers and maintains an illusory sense of sufficiency. But if exoteric religious differences are almost always understood as a reason for the demarcation of identity, then the lack of respect for the other, regardless of whether that other differs scarcely at all or very greatly, means at one and the same time the simultaneous reduction of religion to something relative, temporal, spatial, material. And thus religion ceases to be what it originally was, and becomes an element that is either wholly redundant in the ideological picture of the world and its established order, or compliant to the service of ideological, nonreligious goals.

Knowledge and the Sacred

The self is divided between being and knowledge. Its being may or may not accord with its knowledge. If knowledge forms the bridge between the self that learns and what it learns, the learner and the learned fact, the self and its knowledge define what is learned. Within religious tradition, what is learned is the Truth, at every present moment equally as at the beginning. What is learned is sacred: the source and content of each being which, through contact with it, becomes what is known. Through knowledge, whatever now manifests itself as a symbol, becomes one with what it signifies. Unification is made possible through the intellect which as a single and eternal light shines in the center of every created individual, in everything temporal and finite. Reason is its expanded, refracted, and scattered reflection at the level of human individuality. But it was only with the disengagement of reason from the intellect and its newfound status as a sufficient source of knowledge that there came about the desanctification of knowledge: the source and purpose of knowledge are no longer the sacred.

Humans and the cosmos have become the subject of knowledge; multiplicity and the temporal have become the highest goals; Being has become ever more separate from knowledge. The self can achieve knowledge and yet remain unchanged by it; moreover, Being and knowledge can become wholly conflicting elements of one and the same self. As a result, humans can be defined as "rational animals," guides sufficient unto themselves. But humans can also be defined as beings gifted with intelligence, beings focused on perfection and created to know perfection. To be human is to know and transcend the self. "To know means therefore ultimately to know the Supreme Substance which is at once the source of all that comprises the objective world, and the Supreme Self which shines at the center of human consciousness and which is related to intelligence as the sun is related to its rays."[4]

The "rational" concept, and the project based on this concept, which can be roughly described by the term "modernity," lie on the trajectory of this division. The path they take is development, but the question remains whether this distancing from principle will lead to the final destruction of humanity. Before an answer can be found, before alternative possibilities can be sought, this trajectory should first be traveled and mapped. The lost knowledge of the sacred can be rediscovered through an understanding of the sacred nature of principled knowledge, the need for which never leaves us. It remains the unexamined element of the isness of the self, regardless of the extent to which the intellectual capacity has been obscured by the reduction of the self to its merely rational capabilities. It would again be possible to establish a relationship with the source of all wisdom, the source of every religion. But this would first mean returning the intellect to its central role, that of joining us to the real.

Although the concept of the sacred is controversial, and often rebarbative even, to modern language, shedding light on it in the language of modernity through opposing perspectives can make an important contribution to resolving the question of identity in this age, distinguished as it is by the collapse of faith in the all-sufficiency of individual reason. As far as the sacred is concerned, the issue of changing perspective is increasingly urgent. A form of consensus exists that there are numerous levels of being, but there is no consensus on the causal hierarchy of these levels. In the evolutionary picture, the first is the lowest. With such a root, even humanity, as the final fruit of this growth, can in no way be seen to have a changeless core, beyond these roots, beyond time. But from a creative perspective, of the revelation of Truth through all the levels of Being, the root is the absolute, the inexpressible, the ineffable.

This root, therefore, is the sacred: undefinable, intangible, set apart. But in each of its manifestations, from the unity of being to the ultimate limits of its physical manifestations, this sacredness is both present and absent. Its orientation towards a truth that transcends the knowledge derived from the limited experiments of modernity, suggests an entirely different form of quest, as opposed to the scientific quest endorsed by modernity. All phenomena, in the traditional view, are subordinate to the higher: the more a phenomenon is subject to greater influences and change, the lower its position in the chain of being. However, it never loses touch with the ineffable and intangible. The world is thus made sacred and filled with purpose. (Modernity takes the opposite view: its nature lies in its absolute freedom from a sense of either sacredness or awe.)

"Good" and "Right"

When the "good" means the primary goal of a consequentialist theory, and what is "right" is decided purely on the basis of its instrumental significance for this goal, we need to strive to ensure that the right comes before the good. However, wherever we use "good" in the sense of this discussion, where the good means everything that is discerned as superior by a process of qualitative discernment, then we could say that the reverse pertains—that, in some sense, the good must always precede the right. So the good is that which gives articulation to the laws that define what is right.

According to Charles Taylor:

> This is what has been suppressed by these strange cramped theories of modern moral philosophy, which have the paradoxical effect of making us inarticulate on some of the most important issues of morality. Impelled by the strongest metaphysical, epistemological, and moral ideas of the modern age, these theories narrow our focus to the determinants of action, and then restrict our understanding of these determinants still further by defining practical reason as exclusively procedural. They utterly mystify the priority of the moral by identifying it not with substance but with a form of reasoning, around which they draw a firm boundary. They then are led to defend this boundary all the more fiercely in that it is their only way of doing justice to the hypergoods which move them although they cannot acknowledge them.[5]

In the debate between the advocates of "returning" to primordial tradition and those who propound new syntheses for the experience of modernity with its perennial values, the question of rights remains central: but a differing interpretation is placed on it by these two opposite perspectives. This is in explicit relationship with the hierarchy previously referred to—that of the causality behind the levels of being. If God is the root of all being, then God is the greatest and highest good; thus God's right must be the alpha and omega. It can be realized from an ascending perspective, from the lowest levels of being towards the Most High, and solely through duty. If causality is perceived as flowing in the opposite direction, from matter towards consciousness, humanity itself must appear as the supreme good, and thus as bearer of the supreme right. There is a relationship between this and the metamorphosis of trust, as a relationship between individuals mediated by a common faith in God, to a form of reliance, in which the relationship between participants is defined by direct negotiations leading to or accepting a "social contract."

Modern political ideology is inseparable from the means used to achieve its goals. Nation and state are its highest goal. The unity of the nation and the effectiveness of the state require that both should be "homogeneous." This demand leads to a paradoxical relationship between universal rights and the sovereign state. The result is tensions between the postulated national unity and the rights of the individual, group, and community to maintain their differences. The nature of the established political order is justified by will and "the common interest." Difference is no more than a right that is maintained on the basis of political realism, pushed to the social margin, or sharply divided from both public and private life. Difference is tolerated on the basis of political realism, since the ruling majority view this as a lesser evil, the time for its elimination or resolution not yet come. Similarly, we have the relegation of "minorities" to a position outside the social mainstream, where they are forced to accept and endure the standards imposed by the ruling system.

In the third case, the freedom of the individual is an accepted and protected principle. The ruling ideology defines, however, the boundary between the public sphere, where values and laws are general, and the private, in which individuals and groups have the right to differences in so far as these have little influence on the political order as a whole. A scale of values is created: the highest level is the ruling ideology, while the right to differences is secondary. The state cannot and does not remain neutral with regard to this issue. This is encapsulated in the familiar dilemma of modernity as seen by liberal philosophy: How can every individual be included in the entirety of equal rights and opportunities? We are left with the question of the general good and the goods that form part of the right to differences.

Charles Taylor explains:

> The rather different understandings of the good which we see in different cultures, are the correlative of the different languages which have evolved in those cultures. A vision of the good becomes available for the people of a given culture through being given expression in some manner. The God of Abraham exists for us (that is, belief in him is a possibility) because he has been talked about, primarily in the narrative of the Bible, but also in countless other ways from theology to devotional literature. And also because he has been talked *to* in all the different manners of liturgy and prayer. Universal rights of mankind exist for us because they have been promulgated, because philosophers have theorized about them, because revolutions have been fought in their name, and so on. In neither case, of course, are these articulations a sufficient condition of belief. There are atheists in our civilization, nourished by the Bible, and racists in the modern liberal West. But articulation is a necessary condition of adhesion; without it, these goods are not even options.[6]

History

In history constructive, integrative trends are at war, in an infinite number of ways, with those of destruction and disintegration. But will the vital needs of responsibility and the potential of the human individual, or the general character of the quality of life, be totally metamorphosed in the course of this battle? After all, it is impossible to state with certainty whether the forward march of history is the genuine existence of nature and humanity, or just a human illusion. Although hope is necessary to life, only the most uncompromising proponents of naturalism feel the need to confine hope to the horizontal plane of history. It is true that historical hope can stimulate and strengthen. But this has its dark side too: many use it to escape their present difficulties, sketching imaginary divides across the current of time. Modernity could almost be defined as the transference of faith from God to historical progress, and postmodernity as the collapse of this faith, as the experience of the twentieth century suggests.

In the context of the project of modernity history is seen as a major refuge.

> The articulation of modern understandings of the good has to be a historical enterprise; and this not just for the usual reasons valid for any such enterprise, *viz,* that our present positions are always defined in relation to past ones, taking them either as models or as foils. There is ample evidence of both in the modern world—from the civic humanist tradition, which has defined itself in relation to the paradigm models of the ancient republic and *polis,* to the philosophy of the Enlightenment, which defines itself in opposition to a past dominated by religion and tradition. The very fact of this self-definition in relation to the past induces us to re-examine this past and the way it has been assimilated or repudiated. Very often, understanding how this has in fact come about gives us insight into contemporary views which would not be otherwise available. In understanding our differences from the ancients, we have a better idea what our assimilation of their paradigms of self-rule actually amount to for us; and in looking more closely at the 'traditions' which our Enlightenment thought supposedly repudiated, and at the forms that repudiation took, we may come to see the difference between the two opposed terms in a new light; and consequently to take a new view of contemporary philosophy.[7]

Given the experience with the faith in historical progress, to take this view is to pose the fundamental question about the relationship between the modern world view and human suffering in wars and revolutions, and the emergent structures of suffering and death. The modern equating of knowledge with modern science, excluding the metaphysical, and reducing premodern world views to cosmology and social philosophy, imposes the feeling that humanity has no way out from its present state. Since cosmology and social philosophy are preoccupied with contingency, they cannot escape constant change. If modern science is accorded a monopoly over truth, then humanity is doomed to suffer purposeless torment. In this light, there exists no perennial knowledge, nor any road to it. The experience of modernity demands, however, a totally different view. Humanity is not the final product of development from the depths upward, from the inchoate via the primitive to "civilized society," but one of the levels of manifestation deriving from perfection.

And there is, of course, the spiral chart of history, from innocence to conflict, then to greater harmony, a picture borrowed initially from Judeo-Christian history and the Millennial movement, but, secularized by Marxism and a host of other theories, exceptionally powerful in its influence upon modern thought and feeling. With these forms of narrative comes the new concept of society and the forms of communal life. Corresponding to the free, disengaged subject is the view of society as something built with the consensus of free individuals, and, linked with this, we have the concept of society as something built by the holders of individual rights. This is, probably, one of the most deeply entrenched views of society that modern civilization has yet developed. It has its roots in the seventeenth century, in the theory of the social contract, but has developed and changed in countless ways, surfacing today in a debased form at the interpersonal level, in the contemporary concept of a love "relationship" between two absolutely independent beings. The concepts of self-expression and self-exploration closely match the picture of society as a nation, and are linked to similar expressive roots, which, given that they claim to define our common human potential, demand our full loyalty. Modern nationalism has on the other hand developed its own form of historical narrative, as Benedict Anderson has demonstrated.[8] These multiple connections have been blocked from view by those contemporary modes of thought which have no place for the good. They are quite unaware of the way in which our modern sense of the self is bound up with and depends on what one might call a "moral topography." They tend to think that we have selves the way we have hearts and livers, as an interpretation-free given. And, of course, they have no sense at all of the inverse relation.

Once these connections are drawn, it may not be so easy to repudiate certain moral visions. That is, their repudiation, while one still defines oneself as a certain kind of agent, may turn out to be a sham; one still goes on living by them.[9]

If the Bosnian drama is pigeonholed in the category of opposed and conflicting identities, it can be also be said that it was a matter of the "space of questions," which covers a far wider area. Bosnia is merely the place where the conflict happened: the centers and sources of the conflict lay outside the country itself. The identities can be given as Serb, Croat, and Bosniac, if we look at the opposing elements. (Of course, we can also employ the terms Yugoslav, European, Catholic, Orthodox, Muslim, and so on, if we study their transnational elements.) In this hierarchy, the Serb identity provided the initial stimulus; the others shaped themselves largely in response. The Serb identity is profoundly opposed to all things Turkish and bases its claim to relations with the European powers on this. The Turkish Empire is freely blamed as directly responsible for the ancient collapse of the Serb state, and the symbol of this is the Kosovo conflict: the defenders on one side, the aggressors on the other. The defenders sacrifice themselves for what is good and right, and therefore are destined to rise again in the future to destroy the aggressors and lay waste to all their works—an uprising that leads to the reestablishment of the fallen state. Thus, the embodiment of the "good" is integral to the historic narrative of the destroyed state, which is predestined for resurrection, and anything contrary to this is the embodiment of evil. When this concept is transformed into a national project, those who oppose the project, consciously or unconsciously, must be considered "evil" by the renascent state. Their slaughter or expulsion is, therefore, justified by the narrative that is a vital component of the identity.[10]

However, the modern concept of the nation-state also resolves the issue of the confinement of a homogeneous nation within its own borders, by raising the right to difference higher up the scale of values. Thus, the nation-state in its homogenized form is opposed to the world's unity of differences.

"Leveling"

The role of history in the project of modernity adumbrates the entire nature of the sea change that started with the Renaissance quest for identity. It includes all the depth of penetration into the self, but not only, as it is often thought, the transmutation of rational models of the perfect outcome of the human adventure through the stimulation and definition of decisive historical changes. This profound penetration of the self can be termed a changed understanding of time and the events that take place in it. Phenomena in space and time have ceased to be a reflection of their heavenly archetypes. The questions of creation *ex nihilo* or the time-space revelation, of eternal potential in a hidden treasury, are reduced to the level of motion and the measurable. In this perspective, forms hold no imprint of their transcendent archetypes. Their changes do not reveal the realization of perfect potential in eternity: they are examples of linear development from the lower towards the higher.

The concept of the "first coming" of Christ, and the Christian belief in redemption and the second coming, reinforce this linear view of time. When the sacred knowledge of Christ as the Logos, through whom every moment in the current of time represents the touch of the temporal upon the eternal, and the transcendence of every phenomenon towards its archetype, is weakened, history itself takes on the role of God, for it has the power to direct and shape the whole of time and space. Treating the abundance of the world as history or a historical trend is the obverse of the desanctification of the Christian world. The secularization of this linear current of time encourages the growth of historicism and denial of the transcendence of truth. This can be singled out as the most important element of modern thought. The flow of history is transformed into a god in secular terms. The cause of this lies, as some traditional writers maintain, in oblivion to metaphysical teaching, closely linked to the desanctification of knowledge and the universe.[11]

In Western Christianity, history is treated with complete seriousness. Its notion of irreversibility, together with the power to introduce novelties that alter the order of phenomena, the decisive role certain of its events are seen as playing, and the potential of individuals and institutions to influence them, have all become vital elements of the thinking and behavior of a Promethean, forward-looking human. How the future of the individual is to be defined depends, therefore, on the individual's freedom to influence the future. The individual thus takes charge of destiny. From such a secularized Christian concept of history, together with messianism, have emerged materialistic and secularized philosophies, which adopt the view that the historical flow is real in itself, and that humans can achieve, via material advance, the perfection that tradition describes as the state of paradise. The adoption of history as God has become so powerful as wholly to replace religion in the minds of many people. The result is an explicit or implicit denial of the original Christian view of the influence of a reality that transcends space and time, and without which the mysteries of time and space can never be resolved.

Modern humans are thus left without the necessary intelligence to resist the dubious impulses induced by contact with facts which, although natural, lie outside ordinary experience. Linking what springs from ordinary experience with those facts that lie outside ordinary experience is impossible on the basis of disengaged reason alone. History then comes to resemble a dough from which bread can be kneaded and baked without one seeing in it anything of what should be sought from God.

Ascribing Divine attributes to history can be linked with mistaking the "enthusiasm" of phenomena—remembering that in its original meaning, enthusiasm is infusion with the divine spirit—for their "propulsion." The *Anima Mundi* or the *Weltgeist* become Hegel's *Zeitgeist*. Since the mover is not outside the changes, but is coequal with them, permanency is thus a priori negated. This is evidenced by events in religion itself, which is more and more influenced by the *Zeitgeist* than the *Heilige Geist*. Tradition tells us that "God will judge;" now we say that "History will judge," although it is clear to all that both the guilty and their tools, the perpetrators, can readily evade this court.

Nationalism and Tradition

Nationalism, unlike other ideologies of the modern age, can be said to have a dual nature, a Janus-like perspective[12] on both the past and the future, which brings it into context with with vital traditional interpretations of the perennial nature of wisdom.[13] Although this comparison is essentially flawed, its superficial image does remind us of the need for profounder research into the paradoxes of nationalism.

Liberalism and socialism are definable and clear manifestations of the project of modernity. The ideologies at their center are based on "disengaged reason," based on the perception that there is a set of rational principles necessary for the construction of a new social order—principles on which general consensus can be reached through social agreement. This opens up the possibility of unlimited transformation and progress, for both individuals and society, in attaining the consensual goal of general well-being. No external knowledge, or external guide, are necessary for this emancipation and progress. Supra-conscious and supra-individual elements of the self are, given such a view, denied or even overturned: the subconscious is substituted for the supra-conscious, and the subhuman for the supra-individual. Tradition and traditional structures are seen as belonging to a less developed era; progress therefore demands a fundamental break with this past.

The two ideological systems, liberalism and socialism, differ only in their view of the means by which they propose to arrive at their goal. The first holds that individual freedom and rights, together with national sovereignty, are the basis of progress. The second holds that it is the social structure—in its original sense, with the working class as the mover and beneficiary of this progress—that enables these same goals to be achieved. Conservatism, too, is an ideology that has developed within the context of the modernity project. Integral to conservatism is resistance to the radical concepts of a rational shaping of society and the denial of its organic integrality, as established throughout a long period of historical development. But conservatism also embraces the effort to obtain the fruits promised by the project of modernity. This consensus, shared by nationalism, can be summarized as follows:

- There is a set of basic and coherent principles upon which every society should be founded, and it is possible for rational and enlightened citizens to reach a consensus on these principles.
- There are no insurmountable obstacles to the transformation and reconstruction of society on the basis of these principles.
- There exists an agency—a force or set of forces, a subject—that is adequate to the task of social transformation, and hence this task is a practicable one.[14]

It can be claimed that liberalism and socialism are both firmly opposed to the concept of the self as an unbounded sea of potential, containing a reflection of the whole of creation, but at the same time dependent on the guide that transcends it.

Conservatism resists the concept of the autonomous self as the unquestioned foundation of the evolution of the individual and society based on reason. However, nationalism accepts the promises made by modernity of the unlimited potential for emancipation and progress, of reason as the unchallenged guide of the self, of the inexhaustibility of natural resources. However, the elements of the self that it addresses are those that manifest themselves in tradition, attempting to interpret them and subvert them to its own ideological outlook. The nation, in this ideology, is the moving force, which is realized in the nation-state through a synthesis of traditional elements and the projected modernist progress. Thus, tradition is placed in a subordinate relationship to the ideological plan. Here lies perhaps the most dangerous of all ways in which fissures can open up in the self. If traditional wisdom tries to maintain a clear relationship with the rational systems of modernity, which in turn deny its existence, and with conservatism, which wavers in its interpretation and defense of such wisdom, the result is often that the traditional forms, reduced to emotionalism and morality, are accepted by nationalism—rationally desacralized but rhetorically maintained in their original expression.

Thus, the call of nationalism uses the resources of modernity, but supplements them with the sentiments and morality of the bemused majority to which a carefully constructed past, complete with ready-made enemies and defenders of the nation, is offered, as the motive for absolute loyalty to the nations, elites, ideologies, and structures that propose to implement the nationalist project. This state of affairs expresses itself in an increasing desacralization of traditional structures, which are exploited to the full by nationalism. Ignorance of tradition, together with mass sentimentalism and morality, provide an essential prop for the unification of the majority around their leader, state, and party. Nationalism succeeds in absorbing into its own matrix what other ideologies dismiss as the nonrational needs of the individual—customary and communal sentiments, cultural differences and so on. They are tied in with the antitraditional design of absolute power on the part of the nationalist leaders, and, in truncated form, are presented to the majority as their "sacred heritage" and affirmation of the defenders of national sovereignty.

National unity is seen as the prerequisite of efficiency in achieving the social goals. Its basis is a group identity, sharing a communality of history, language, religion, or state. Since this is a rational construct, unity can be achieved only if the whole consists exclusively of those elements that can be readily assimilated into this national homogeneity. Nationalism is, therefore, by its very nature opposed to the freedom and rationality of the self, as the subject for which the goals of modernity are to be won. Moreover, it is opposed to every form of class, religious, linguistic, or other identity that in any way challenges this national homogeneity.

Thus, the axiology of nationalism cannot be general. What is of value for the loyal members of the majority nation cannot be so for the Other. Thus, nationalism, as a matter of principle, is reduced to a form of homogeneity that excludes all possibility of pluriformity—in other words, to the tyranny of the majority. The most effective nationalist campaigns are those that rest on ethnicity. This is, inevitably, opposed to the traditional view, in which every individual is sacred in his/her authenticity and potential to achieve perfection, every language fundamentally related to transcendence and capable of achieving it, and every individual the affirmation of unity.

The very term "tradition" is given its own interpretation in the project of modernity, and therefore, given as much significance as this project is prepared to allocate to it. It is reduced to those elements exploited by the ideology of nationalism to achieve its antitraditional designs. The prevailing tensions and not infrequent conflicts between differing nationalisms are projected onto the differing traditional forms, although these by nature cannot conflict with each other, since all teach the fulfillment of a transcendent unity—a unity which, if realized, is the strongest opponent of nationalism. The latter cannot eliminate it totally: it can only debase it to meet its own needs. The current national ideologies, or rather their external forms, are always an aggregate of ideological and traditional elements.

This view inclines to the adoption of highly exclusive elements—those that do not belong to the posited nation by birth, history, or inheritance are outsiders, Others. They must therefore be excluded from the national society. These extreme forms of nationalism manifest themselves in outworn states whose governing structures are no longer effective; the divided, disoriented, and dissatisfied majority must choose where to put their loyalties—in powerful social movements that threaten suicidal disorder, but they do not in fact have the strength to bring about real change, or in nationalist sentiments. Thus, the presumed autonomy of the self, the basis for the right to freedom of choice, is forced into conflict with the concept of national homogeneity.

Deconstructivism

The modernist premises that humanity has the ability to arrive independently at a full understanding and knowledge of the laws of nature and history, and on this foundation to build a world view through which it defines its ultimate purpose, can be assessed on the basis of the experience of history. Every world view contains a cosmology, a social philosophy, and metaphysics. The first two elements of the modern world view have been shaped into forms significantly different from all their forerunners. They are founded on the postulates of the autonomy of the self and of the evolution of science as the only source of knowledge. This has its corresponding anthropological philosophy: humanity's roots lie in the most basic material particles, not in any form of transcendent absolute. Metaphysics, in the modern view, has lost all its former significance: the placing of the totality of human potential in a fully sufficient self leads to the denial and exclusion of the sacred, of authority—authority in its sense of accepted higher values.

The autonomy of the self requires that everything, without exception, be negotiated. Only open dialogue, in which the participants are individuals reliant on the sufficiency of reason and freedom of choice, promises and guarantees progress. The exclusivity of "scientism" as the basic element of modernity is a threat to establishing the clear relationship between the modern world view and the persistent increase in killing and destruction. Scientism advances the data and knowledge of modern natural science as the only possible components for the construction of a superior, triumphant world view—and with it individualism, economism, consumerism, militarism, and nationalism. One of the by-products is the denial of any need for a differing worldview. Neither God, nor the self, nor purpose, significance, the real world, nor the truth can stand without fundamental reexamination: in the view of the advocates of this thinking, everything must be subjected to deconstruction or elimination.[15]

Although this attitude is inspired by ethical concerns regarding totalitarian systems, this form of postmodern thinking leads to relativism, even to nihilism. It could be called "ultramodernism," since it is the end result of taking modern postulates to their logical conclusion. It proves that the self cannot find direction, no matter how much it opens itself. For no direction can be "rooted" in the lowest forms of matter, whence it evolved—and above and behind the self is nothing. The process of reexamination is one of desecration: the sacred which can be negotiated is no longer sacred. Thus, the autonomous self merely sabotages the self. This may explain the increasingly urgent human need to seek, against the background of modernity's decline, other props for the self, resulting in the often hasty and dubious adoption of what turns out to be merely another form of identity. Given these efforts, even the perception of democracy is changing. "A society is democratic, not insofar as it postulates the validity of a certain type of social organization and of certain values vis-à-vis others, but insofar as it refuses to give its own organization and its own values the status of a *fundamentum inconcussum.*"[16]

The project of modernity, in the full meaning of the notions on which it is founded, is inextricably tied to the "world of multiplicity and motion," in the forlorn hope that an inner unity might thus become known and confirmed. This goal is epistemologically defined. In as much as it is "grounded" in contingency, the drama of history must lead deeper into the abyss of relativism and nihilism. This is the case since the self becomes ever more distanced from its inherent unity, which is primarily ontological, then epistemological. Amid disintegration and collapse, the self will seize upon an escapist fantasy of what was, or what could be. But an underlying awareness that the fantasy will never be fulfilled shatters the dream, and destruction thus becomes the most important element of the newly evolved world view.

Constructivism

Identity incorporates the knowledge of the past that is contained in the full present of every individual, and is also an awareness of the future. Individuals are engaged in a series of mutual relationships, which form different groups of identities. When individuals' visions of the future are different and confused, they resort to "constructing" reasons for this difference in their narrative of the past. The result is either the exclusion of some in regard to others, or the association of one with another. Since the right to dignity and the right to life have their foundations in the authentic nature of humanity, which can be distorted or falsified in many different ways, public negotiation aimed at overcoming egomaniac chaos requires that recognition should take place outside the frame of given institutional norms. This means that the identity of modernity can escape its otherwise inevitable end in relativism and nihilism, but only if its foundations themselves are reexamined, and not merely the manifestations visible in its world view and the established social order.

This process of reexamination is already offered to us by perennial wisdom, or primordial tradition. One and the same nucleus of knowledge exists, according to tradition, in all ages and among all peoples. It is always transcendent, but is expressed in the different languages of different times and places. Only with it and through it can the self be known and guided. But modern humans know far less about their own selfhood than about the world around them. The reversal of this state of affairs can save humans from ending in nihilism. The name for this reversal, remote as it is to modern humans, is often a return to primordial tradition, a new finding of the self in the self. "Our hope lies," writes Huston Smith, "in returning to an outlook which in its broad outlines is carried in the bloodstream of the human race."[17]

This offer does not deny the picture of the world as it is. It aims at a resurrection of the primordial world view, as the reverse of modernity and the only form of salvation from the disastrous state in which the twentieth century has most explicitly shown us to be. In this view, modernity is, in sum, a pernicious anomaly, which it is impossible to alter.

There are other ways of viewing the possible reorientation of modernity. Process theology offers a "harmonization" of modernity and a renewed return to the unity that pervades and embraces all phenomena, all different levels of being. This would allow all levels of being to be interpreted in terms of a single set of principles. The totality of existence would be revealed in the unity of these principles, for which both philosophy and science are still searching. For this the criterion of the primordial truth is necessary. And the best criterion consists, according to David Ray Griffin, of "ideas which are inevitably presupposed in practice and have therefore been at least implicitly affirmed by human beings of all times and places."[18]

As soon as this criterion is known and accepted, he insists, it would open the way to an exciting postmodern cosmology, in which the primordial truths would be gathered from the different traditions, including modernity, and reconciled, as they would with the greatest achievements of modern science. This would presume the existence of an objective and universally accepted court of appeal that could judge between world views, identifying them as true or false. It would consist of reason, which would act as the stable nucleus of commonsense ideas or the clear facts of direct experience.

But modernity, as this word is generally used in philosophy, refers to the collapse of faith in the power of reason to hold such sway.[19] Thus, the question of the criteria that could be used to discriminate between different world views remains at the center of human needs. One answer is that there is no criterion capable of clear formulation independent of the data from which it was deduced.

It is therefore worth turning to the intellect, in the belief that the self or soul will thus be directed and led towards the truth.

11

Changing the State of Knowledge

Introduction

The future of Bosnia and Herzegovina is being defined by the currents of European unification. It has no option but to take part in this process, whether through *force majeure* or its own free will. Fighting against the currents that are irresistibly linking Europe into a single economic, monetary, political, and cultural community will only increase the need for solutions to be imposed from outside, with a concomitent warping of people's minds and behavior. This will merely prolong the unnatural condition caused first by ethno-national utopian totalitarianism and then by Communism, which so distorted politics, culture, and the economy that people were reduced almost entirely to the self-centered need to rationalize their grasping pursuit of material goods and their efforts to dominate others. This process reached its logical climax in the war against Bosnia and Herzegovina.

If politics, economy, and culture are to evolve from their current status, moulded by totalitarian ideologies and the habits they generate, into a framework that would enable humankind to distinguish the common weal from sheer self-interest, the rights of the individual from naked greed, they need a blueprint to guide them; a blueprint moreover that would allow the inclusion of Bosnia and Herzegovina in the unstoppable currents of harmonization within Europe and the wider world to change from an externally imposed process into a movement based on free will, one in which the whole of human nature might find expression.

This is not a simple change of direction, and it calls for capacities possessed by no recognizable force on Bosnia's contemporary political stage. This is because the issue of Bosnia and Herzegovina's future requires two crucial factors to be taken into consideration. The first is liberalism as a key determinant of the contemporary understanding of the world. The second is tradition, the nexus where individuals and the totality of their world find their ultimate meaning. These two factors give rise to two languages, which tend to be mutually incomprehensible.

In seeking an overall understanding of Bosnia and Herzegovina's future, an appropriate way of finding out how the country reflects this duality would be to examine its social system in its entirety. But the very concept of "social system" is obfuscated or contested nowadays. So many prejudices and misinterpretations are bound up with the term that it is viewed by many with hostility, and avoided by others; it is, however, an issue that must be confronted head-on if we are to understand and work towards the future. The models currently prevalent embrace neither the individuality nor the universality of the Bosnian-Herzegovinian experience—an experience that remains largely misunderstood, even by its own people, when studied exclusively from one viewpoint, be it liberal or traditional.

The Illusion of Multiculturalism

As the Bosnian question is generally addressed by reducing it to its military, humanitarian, political, and economic aspects, it is worth looking to culture for a way out of the current impasse, which prevents us from moving towards a sustainable and harmonious social system. Bosnia is often cited as an example of "multiculturalism," but no other approach to the Bosnian enigma arouses as many prejudiced and uninformed responses. It is the key to the ideological extremes that have robbed Bosnian society of both its reality and its potential. If culture may be defined as a set of meanings expressed through ideas and symbols, the central intellectual challenge in examining the blinkered assumptions underlying "Bosnian multiculturalism" is to disentangle the variety of meanings, ideas, and symbols implied by the "cultures" in the Bosnian space. From this understanding of "complexity" to a demand for the "territorialization" of ethnic identities and their cultural correlates there is but one step: the inevitable construction of political identities, for which history, culture, and ethnicity are only masks, and violence against the Other the only way to impose their authority and win the loyalty of their subjects. The examination of this matrix is the central challenge and main task of any intellectual effort. This, though, is not yet being done in Bosnia itself,[1] which hinders the possibility of systematic collaboration among those forces in the world order that have not been able to remain indifferent to the slaughter, destruction, and mistrust within Bosnia.

Since every social system operates according to a wide variety of norms and values, any serious examination of these norms and values will be a long, slow process of validation and elimination, with the aim of preserving their true content while stripping them of everything that stands in the way of arriving at the goal defined by tradition as the "common weal," and by liberalism as the "rights of the individual." But achieving such an end would aid today's political processes, organizations, and decisions. We urgently need a better understanding of the multitude of ideas and symbols that form the essence of Bosnia's culture. What we know about ideology must be radically revised if we are to prevent the structures of Communism or any other totalitarian world view from continuing to operate in a superficially altered guise.

Meanings, ideas, and symbols, as the key elements of culture, are crucial factors in any social system. Culture is structured in terms of ideas and symbols—language, law, science, religion, ideology, values, literature, music, art, architecture, drama, philosophy, mathematics. If we use this model of culture to examine Bosnia's "multiculturalism," it can be shown simply and convincingly from a sociological viewpoint that Bosnian culture is essentially a single culture, not an agglomeration of several cultures. What we have is a complex of different elements which comprise the selfsame culture, with the differences between the majority of the elements often so slight as to be barely perceptible even to the most eagle-eyed observer, though there are greater differences between religious forms and ideologies. One cannot talk of three cultures in Bosnian society. There are three ideologies and three religions, defining the triple background against which Bosnia's complex drama unfolds.[2]

An Ideological Model of Culture

Bosnia was fated by history to be a country in which different *Christologies* would converge. The concept of the *Messiah* or *Hristos* as the model of individual salvation is at the center of every tradition as the revelation of the path between transcendence and the world as its confirmation, with man at its center. This concept is expressed through different ideas and symbols, yet it always remains one and the same. In Bosnia's historical experience, these ideas and symbols have manifested themselves as the Bosnian Church, Catholicism, Orthodoxy, Islam, Judaism. Though the external forms of these ideas and symbols are utterly exclusive, they can only survive amidst the tides of life, where the individual and the community are constantly faced with the possibility of choice based on values and norms, if there is a prevailing awareness of the purpose they serve. Therefore, if ethno-national collectivism departs from this purpose, the members of such a community are then denied the choice between freedom and the "common weal" towards which those ideas and concepts direct them. When this purpose is forgotten, traditional ideas and symbols turn into closed and dead forms that do not serve life but rather demand that life serve them: they thus become a host of cultures. To operate in this way and to secure their own promotion, these ideas and symbols need a totalitarian ideology that raises its proponents to the absolutized position of legislators, judges, and executors.

The prevalent image of Bosnia and its culture today is the construct of ideologies whose model of culture is a deeply anticultural one. Because Bosnia's complex, pluralistic cultural matrix refutes the concept of the "nation-state" as an historical goal, supporters of the latter must deny culture's universality, its underlying essence, and construct in its place a reductive image based on differences alone.[3]

The Politics of Collectivism

The reduction of culture to ideas and symbols alienated from their original meaning and purpose is a key demand of political movements that find their place in collectivism. Moreover, universal norms and values have to be whittled down to fit a blinkered field of vision based on differences between "us" and "them." It then follows that "our" aims cannot be reconciled with "theirs" within the same social system.[4] In such a case, the ideological aspiration for politics to pervade the whole of the social order demands that the universality of culture be denied, both in general terms and as an arena for action. This artificial division between cultures, between "conflicting" political interests, becomes a touchstone for political decisions. Concepts of "the common weal" and "individual rights" are pushed aside and are no longer allowed a central role in discussions about how universal norms and values might guide our choices and decision-making processes.

This gives politics the power to destroy society itself. Mutually hostile, irreconcilable cultural and political blocs are formed. The community, incited by the politics of separation, demands the wherewithal for its own political movement to build its own separate "reality." Political dialogue becomes reduced to a squabble for material interests, driven by people's need to rationalize their own acquisitive desires.

Tradition and the Language of Politics

The fact that no language can be alienated from its symbolic aspects is in direct conflict with the "rule of quantity." Language testifies that human nature cannot be divorced from values, meanings, and purpose—those manifestations of being that lie outside the reach of science. Language cannot be reduced to quantity and numbers, and that is why modern ideologies find it difficult to adjust their stance towards tradition. The language of politics reflects the ideological reduction of language to a changed pattern, which seeks to free itself from elements related to myth and symbol.

From the perspective of modernity, technology is perceived as the power of influencing historical progress. This perspective focuses on society rather than on the individual; it debates, highlights and promises what society can offer the individual. But this is always projected into the future; it speaks of what society can provide the individual with tomorrow, but not today. The full human potential is thus deferred into the future, and the language of the past is rendered inadequate to encompass and express what humankind is focused on.

Politics is, therefore, always a promise of the element that is promoted as the central and paramount value in the construction of identity. Its advocates and proponents address a group as the architects, implementers, and defenders of the project designed to achieve their goal. They make a promise, assuring their audience that the goal cannot be achieved now, which is the cause of their current difficulties and suffering, yet at the same time claiming that their advocacy and action is a guarantee that the situation will change in the future. Thus, the language of politics becomes a reflection of the ideology of progress. Lies, and the rhetoric that makes them so persuasive, demand ideology and politics, whose primary foothold is scientism, and its secondary a suitable—which invariably means distorted—interpretation of tradition.

Since evidence of Bosnia's unity can be found in language, given that there are no obstacles to communication in the culture as a whole, the insistence of political elites that there are different Bosnian, Croatian, and Serb languages, each with its own particular characteristics, within that same culture is invariably part of the effort to mark out the area of loyalty to their authorities. These elites focus on linguistic and religious differences because their separate political identities can be proven as reasonable only when viewed from the superficial perspective of those differences. And superficiality is a prerequisite for the imposition of political will and to facilitate the management of people's current misfortune by making illusory promises for the future. As soon as the issue of language is subjected to serious discussion, where its unity, as that of religious forms, is recognized, the political elites qualify it as "going beyond" the limits of "political reality," because what they need is superficiality and simple exploitation.

Culture and Economy

The reduction of all social action to the selfishly rationalized acquisition of goods on the one hand and an obsession with differences between "us" and "them" on the other, both of which stem from an ideologically distorted perception of culture, results in a desire to see culture as merely a function of economics. In this approach, culture tends to be reduced to the level of historical heritage.

This in turn leads to an ideologized reading of history, in which any "irrational content"—the usual term for any reference to a nonindividual, supraindividual Being—is accepted only insofar as it supports popular confidence as a means of improving economic output. The vital elements of culture—the meanings revealed through its ideas and symbols—are marginalized on the pretext that they have little to do with the aim of establishing an efficient economic system. One of the clearest examples of this approach is the malignant attitude of Communist ideology towards religion. Thus, an essential element of human individuality is denied: that the human aspiration to perfection is innate, and that without this they would not be what they are.

The idea that transition from a Communist, state-owned economy is sufficient to ensure the survival of Bosnia's unity in diversity may become just another utopian dream. Though it is a necessary condition, it is not a sufficient one. If Bosnian culture is seen purely in market terms, then, instead of creating a space for self-fulfillment, it will merely stumble on in the same benighted fashion as before. It is precisely the qualitatively different presence of culture within the social system—whether as barely existent or vital element—that makes possible the building and strengthening of confidence, which is a prerequisite for social virtue and progress.

Four Ideologies

The tensions and destruction in Bosnian society can be said to have produced four projects, reflecting four ideologies. Understanding these ideologies and dealing with them effectively is a prerequisite for the success of any intellectual effort to seek solutions for the future. Three of these four ideologies will be presented here according to their relationship of cause and effect, as well as to their organizational and material power in achieving the goal they sought to justify.

The goal of three of the four ideologies is defined with fair accuracy by the term "nation-state." For the Serbian ethno-national project, it is a state that would include all Serbs; for the Croatian project, a state that would include all Croats. In response to this historically recognizable aspiration there emerged a similar Bosniac project. As such, these projects are irreconcilable with the existence of the state of Bosnia and Herzegovina, since the creation of the postulated new "nation-states" is possible only with the concomitant destruction of the plural Bosnian state, the very nature of which is an obstacle to achieving this goal. For these ideologies, then, its culture must be reduced to "cultures," to be achieved by singling out differences in the structure of culture and appealing to emotions to make them appear mutually antagonistic and irreconcilable. The result is a mental blindness to the prevailing common elements of the culture.

These ideologies offer constructions and distorted readings of history, deny the essential elements of unity and prevent their systematic examination and presentation, exaggerate the elements of mistrust, and support all divisive tendencies. Religious differences are brought into central salience, while the nationalization of religion means that it is reduced to ideas and symbols, and its ultimate purpose, the very essence of religion, is neglected, since this ultimate purpose cannot be addressed within the framework of a national project.[5] The universal character of religion is thus replaced by its "Serb," "Croat," or "Bosniac" character, which results in the loss of the meaning of diversity as a requirement of unity, of man as the image of God, and of salvation as the potential of every individual and the purpose of all religious forms and rites.

The fourth ideology seeks to justify the existence of Bosnia and Herzegovina and oppose its denial. All its endeavors are defensive, and they are never shaped into a comprehensive and credible program that would gather the forces needed to bridge the gap between the traditional nature of the inherited culture and the call to adjust it to the liberal picture of the world, which might result in an all-embracing theory of the social system.

The Need for a Social Science

Ideology can be viewed from the perspective of its two common manifestations—the first of which is usually linked to its negative role in supporting Communist totalitarianism, and the second to critical examination of phenomena within the social system.

In the context of Bosnia's future, ideology as the intellectual analysis of the relationships of other elements of the social system with culture must become a decisive factor in a reexamination of the politics based on inherited fetishizing of values and norms. What is needed is the creation and promotion of the role of social science, which can hardly be said to exist today.[6] The forms being proffered as components of this science are actually only remnants of the Communist ideological system, dressed up as science. They are offered as a prop to *politics*, as a means of fending off reappraisal and reference to values and norms through which the "common good" and the indisputable "rights of the individual" are realized.

More than economics, Bosnia today needs the greatest achievements of social science from the developed world, though it does also need a higher level of economic assistance than what it is currently receiving. The transition of knowledge relating to the social system and the ways in which it may be advanced is considerably more difficult than the transition involving changes in company management and property ownership.

Transition

The current situation in Bosnian society is characterized by calls for transition in all spheres of life and at all levels: from a postwar situation to a peacetime social system; from a Communist system of governance to one that is based on the rule of law, the enjoyment of human rights, and the democratic legitimization of politics; from social or state ownership to private ownership; from a command economy to a liberalized one. It is accepted as dogma that these changes are necessary. No one dares oppose it in any way—there is complete consensus on the issue of transition. However, this consensus is not coupled with a corresponding intellectual enterprise to transform dogma into the prevalent mode of thought, constantly renewed in a critical reappraisal of the possibilities offered by every decision and in raising awareness of the values and norms that transcend particular interests.

The absence of such intellectual efforts in the context of economic transition perpetuates the lingering habits that usually remain present in the wake of a bureaucratic totalitarian system. This results in a more urgent need for tutelage instead of cooperation. In the absence of this new intellectual dynamic, the dominant status of Communist bureaucracy is replaced by the need for an international arbiter, which is a reflection of the forms of reduction of every element of the social system already referred to, and underpins the "necessity" of different "ideologies," "politics," and the like.

Conflicting Political Identities

Politics as a key component of the social structure is given as much power to act within the social system as corresponds to its role elsewhere in the social structure—in socialization, education, the economy, kinship, formal and informal networks and organizations, status and class, communications, gender, and hierarchies of power—and in the structure of the individual—perception, attention, memory, understanding, and adaptation. Only through coherence within and between these structures is it possible to act purposefully and for the longer term.[7]

When the social system is represented as an artefact that can be dismantled or demolished, which is how the three anti-Bosnian ideologies see it, then politics becomes a plural rather than a singular noun, the property of wholly separate nation-states. This fragmentation is made possible only by fostering collectivism, that is, "community"-based sectarianism, which calls for the construction of a collectivist pyramid, topped by a single leader who embodies either "national unity," or the confluence of his personal charisma with the pattern of existing social interests. The result is an extremely simplified polarization between "us," the righteous, the misunderstood, and the threatened, and "them," the unrighteous, the privileged, and the favored. Any opinion differing from that of the leader is seized upon as treachery if it comes from within the "community," and as hostility if it stems from the Other in the immediate neighborhood. Friends are to be found only in far-off lands and among far-off individuals and societies, who fervently sympathize with and support the messianic leader as the personification of the group's eternal struggle against its neighbors.

Political institutions, decisions, and policies are reduced to a duet between the leader and his community choirs, which is how his ethno-national factions usually function in the parliaments founded according to the same logic. The final decision is always in the hands of individuals, of those leaders without whom ethno-national totalitarianism cannot function, or of close-knit groups outside the legislative body, for the survival of individuals within the pyramidal hierarchy is dependent on their loyalty to their leader. This becomes a substitute for knowledge of the social system, and no longer depends on the principles embodied in the common weal and the rights of the individual. The norms and values deriving from these principles, which should normally be central to the decision-making process, are denied or ignored, and "sacred forms" become both a pretext and a justification for rabble-rousing and emotional outbursts.

This acts as a smoke screen for a lucrative collusion of interests between social arch-conservatism, various forms of egomania, mental imbalance, and the heedless pursuit of personal and group interests. Hoodwinking others becomes the essence of politics, so that the individual has no principles to rely on, and is unable to escape subservience to this retarded system eating away like a canker at the heart of society. The concept of the social system as an organic whole is seen as utopian and meaningless, mere mumbo jumbo. Criticism of political decisions on the basis of universal norms and values is replaced by public denunciations, falsehoods, frauds, and smears built up with the help of individually minor but pervasive and cumulatively convincing lies and tricks.

Change

Neither today's prevailing reductionism, nor those elements that might contribute to an integrated concept of Bosnian politics—one which is so sorely needed—can linger at the crossroads where they now stand. Politics, in the current climate of divisiveness based on a reductionist model of society, must either move towards further fragmentation or free itself from its existing frame of reference. The former would run counter to prevailing world trends. But the latter would not mean denying individual elements of culture the opportunity to thrive and develop—on the contrary. Only in an environment where politics and political decision making is based on an awareness of shared norms and values can the present siege mentality in the social system be overcome—together with the resulting mistrust, tension, and need for tutelage, without which the factions would be free to expend their energies on killing and destruction.

The logic of economics is crucial, yet this, too, is only sustainable on the basis of shared norms and values, which must be given a central role in decision making, that is, in the process of choosing the best possible outcomes. This is the political environment needed for economic development, but it is hard to see how it can thrive in today's collectivist climate.

The defense of ideas and symbols severed from their true meaning cannot ensure the openness of tradition. Yet it is here that the opportunity for sensible dialogue and cooperation lies—between liberalism, which forms the basis of the world political and economic order, and tradition, which points to the essential content of culture in all its complexity. Bosnian politics must transform itself by means of changes in knowledge and culture, and by giving the social sciences an increased presence and role. This should be tied to the measures and actions demanded by economic theory, whose only reality is the measurable world. But the political models of today are marked by their avoidance of the world of measurability and responsibility.

A Pattern of Transition

Given the fact that, as Adam Smith tells us, economics accounts for 80 percent of human needs, and that the question of culture is complex, unexplored, and awash with mutually opposed and tortuous ideological models, it might appear that any intellectual enterprise in Bosnia and Herzegovina should have an almost exclusively economic slant. However, one must question whether such an assumption is, more often than not, merely a way of hiding unconscious attitudes towards the social system behind a structure whose sole raison d'être is economic. The current consensus that the economic system inherited from the Communist period is irredeemable, and that a free market and private ownership must take its place, confronts all schools of thought with the same task. This consensus, however, is at odds with the nation-state ideologies. The widespread survival of Communist thought-patterns and autocratic rule in neighboring states, together with their hostility towards Bosnia and Herzegovina and their refusal to accept it as a political equal, leave this country open to all sorts of illegal profiteering and the creation of financial and economic power bases, all of which are possible only in an unregulated society. Thus, economic theory becomes just another smoke screen for self-interest, where ignorance is packaged as the last word in knowledge.

A comprehensive critical appraisal of this environment is still lacking, and crucial strategic decisions are either blocked or left to foreign arbitration. The reform of educational and research institutions to enable them to build up intellectual networks capable of partnering key foreign players in the transition process cannot take place without a social system that would enable cultural, social, and personal structures to evolve and emerge from their paralysis in face of wider European opportunities and trends, a paralysis that has led to the atrophy of the macroeconomic systems developed under Communist rule, which now lack ownership and management. In the ethno-national grand plans, these systems furnish evidence for the rationality of baseless megalomania, which means that private entrepreneurship can only be allowed a marginal social role.

A Challenging Enterprise

The transformation of Bosnia into a functioning social system seems a utopian dream today. Yet matters only appear thus if Bosnia is seen solely in terms of its present ravaged, end-of-millennium state, disheartening though this is for the majority of its people and friends. The goal is a real one not only because it is attainable, but also because any other goal would be unjust. To assume that Bosnian culture, in all its complexity, could not survive in terms of a liberal or a traditional world view, would mean that the world itself has no future. But this is not so. Any intellectual attempt to attain this goal will be worthy of its name, however, only if it is based on both a liberal and a traditional world view. This will take courage indeed—but not only courage.

The new and much-desired Bosnia may be seen as a task for future generations. In making their contribution to the strengthening of that future structure, those who are now advocating and participating in this attempt are, with good reason, focusing on the issue of education, which implies the transfer of knowledge from one individual to another, from one group to another. The entire enterprise of modern education concentrates on knowledge, almost entirely excluding ignorance and the undiscovered, though they are incomparably greater than the known and the discovered. One of the elements lying at the basis of the current tragedy of Bosnia is the insistence on the available knowledge as the full truth about this country. Political decisions and reconstruction efforts completely disregard every instance of ignorance and every undiscovered aspect of the country, and this is why they invariably include anti-Bosnian plans. From the perspective of politics, it is irrelevant whether such anti-Bosnian tendencies stem from conscious will or from oversights and omissions.

The majority of the rational and ideological models of Bosnia and its internal complexity are premised on a knowledge of humans, society, and the world which is, for the most part, going through a serious crisis, as suggested by leading philosophical discussions. A more thorough and credible elucidation of the Bosnian enigma calls for approaches that would deconstruct the most relevant knowledge down to its principles or flawed and vague foundations. Such a deconstruction may yield new and sounder foundations for understanding identity, violence and justice in this country, which peace agreements have left at a crossroads with every road leading to a dead end. This crossroads is not in itself anti-Bosnian. However, the tensions have not yet been eliminated that stemmed from the failure to understand the deeper layers of the self torn between modern ideologies and their traditional foundation in the infinity of both the internal and the external. This new education for the generations that will build Bosnia calls for the ignorance of the extent and meaning of the Bosnian challenge to be identified.

"Post" Period

The last century of the second Christian millennium was concluded in southeastern Europe with three "posts."

The end of World War I marked the beginning of the first "post" period that was to last until World War II broke out. During this period, the centuries-old ideological aspirations toward unification of the southern Slavs were realized in the form of a state. Individualism and liberalism were perceived as the basis of a new world to be built as an alternative to traditionalism. But this structure imploded as a result of the desire to use irreconcilable ideologies as its connective tissue. Despite initial enthusiasm, and the belief that this period was to see the end of the possibility of general wars, the project collapsed in despair and the denial of most of the human desires incorporated in the ideological views of the world.

The second period denoted as "post" began towards the end of World War II. Its outset was less buoyant, yet it brought the feeling that the wars of the past would never be repeated. In this period, a firm, iron curtain division was established between two ideological world views—the Communist, in the countries east of the "curtain," and the capitalist, to the west. This division was ended when Western liberal capitalism prevailed. The greatest ideological world view, conceived and developed as a response to all the betrayals of the "words of God" and presented as a struggle for the liberation of the oppressed, collapsed, cruelly betraying even its own words.

The feeling that religions were retreating in the face of contemporary ideological campaigns subsided when it became obvious that tradition was reemerging on the horizon of human needs as the turn of the millennium approached. The strengthening of modernity did not, as was expected, lead to a weakening of religious sentiment. The prevalent matrix presented the multitude of languages and meanings that form a link with fundamental human needs as "numerous civilizations." Their ideological aspects are expressed in quantitative terms.

In this ideological perspective, quantitative comparisons become a "clash of civilizations." Individualism and liberalism, as the ideological foundations of the modern era, are associated with the largest power—embodied in the United States of America and its allies. The greatest achievement of "civilizational development" is thus associated with the greatest military, political, and economic power, and the plurality of civilizations continues to be judged in terms of power measurable by numbers. It was in these circumstances that the war against Bosnia took place. ("The war against Bosnia" is the real name for the disintegration of Yugoslavia in its entirety. The conviction that Bosnia is not viable because it is a complex community guided the elites in their criminal campaigns that swept over much of southeastern Europe.) The crimes against Bosnia and Kosovo are new entries in the chronicle of evil in Europe. Though evil is always the same in that it departs from principles, it assumed a range of new forms at the end of the century.

While the war was still going on, leaving behind the charred remains of houses and graves, the question arose of what the third "post" period would be.

The Enigma of Five Countries

The experience of the twentieth century inspires fear of the future. Can the future be looked forward to without fear if we turn to the past?

The most common answers to this question include the prevalent betrayals of "the divine languages." They rarely include, however, assessments that go beyond the shallow naiveté of unconvincing optimism or the grim concern of rational relativism. The widespread anaemia is framed by two radical approaches—naive rationalist relativism, on the one hand, and rigid religious fundamentalism, on the other. They create the potential for future totalitarian systems, of a kind that will be readily imposed throughout computerized areas.

The five countries of southeastern Europe—Croatia, Bosnia and Herzegovina, Montenegro, Serbia, and Albania—as a geopolitical region with different cross-border religious and national identities, are in need of understanding and action to overcome their own internal antagonisms. The ruling nation-state ideologies in Croatia and Serbia have destructive effects in Bosnia and Herzegovina. These baneful effects are not exhausted even once their destructive goals are achieved. The same principle that informs them also threatens a new "post" period in the future that might result from another war. The devastating fire that is currently smouldering cannot be abstracted as either a danger or a solution. It is thus precisely this challenge of resolving the problem of these five countries that is the crucial test of the concepts of a European Union based on economic, monetary, and political links between European countries. The challenge comprises almost every potential facet of the contemporary world. But challenge may turn into naiveté unless one recognizes the new dangers it brings. It does offer a means of overcoming the cruel and evil-consumed god of the nation-state. But does this superiority imply the continued negation and vulnerability of the human self, which has almost entirely disappeared as the sacred source of dignity and authority?

In this small territory, different and mutually opposed ideologies are present today whose advocates possess structures that enable them to achieve their goals by violent means. There is a disequilibrium between these ideologies: the more powerful believe that they can and should, by force or by will, subjugate the weaker. This attitude encourages them to transform subjugation into slaughter and destruction. Their understanding of individualism and liberalism thus changes: they start ascribing "divine attributes" to themselves, since they are shaping the world according to the intention behind their ideologies.

This is the background of the current genocide, where those who bear the most responsibility for it remain leaders of peoples and owners of states. Their mind set and actions cannot just disappear as a result of some revolutionary about turn within themselves or as a result of evolution. Nor can they remain at their current level of manifestation. If they are countered by the demands of human rights and the rule of law, the only possible solution of this tragic drama of violence and genocide is one imposed by the involvement of an external force; this, in turn, means both accepting and transcending existing borders. What is needed are the strong gravitational fields of the European Union, within which these countries will be turned into free trade zones, where human rights are respected. This transformation would also operate to prevent the criminal proponents of nationalism from gaining access to weapons and uncontrolled monetary flows, which is a necessary condition if we are to avoid, in the "post" period that is just beginning, "the maximum acquisition of goods and power" which is sometimes also manifested as "maximum slaughter and destruction." However, this condition is not sufficient. What is needed is a comprehensive approach that would look several decades forward. The current "post" period may end in a new outburst of violence or a continuation of the current atrophy. This systematic approach in which all available pro-European Union forces would be engaged is the only alternative.

The "post" period in which we live brings onto the international scene a question of universal importance: What could be the sources of slaughter and destruction in the future? If the dialectic of human relationships can be illustrated by the elliptic view "There is no god but God"—God being not similar or comparable to anything—the question may be reformulated as follows: What is the god of the new age? The concept of the nation-state has been the god so far. No one can be sure that it has disappeared, though its effects have clearly demonstrated its vicious nature. The ideology of the nation-state is in decline. What is emerging is to supersede what has disappeared in blood and ashes. But is what is emerging closer to or more remote from the view *Your creation and your upraising are but as a single soul?*[8]

12

At the Turn of the Millennium

Introduction

Yugoslavia has been visibly disintegrating as a state for ten years now. In common with all such processes, it has brought to light a number of its constituent elements that were not previously evident. In addition, the changes have affected even those elements that used to be organically connected, revealing or suggesting various hidden aspects of individual and collective identities. The resulting situation is, like any other, subject to further change that will once again mask the phenomena currently visible. However, as aspects of the past these phenomena will be written into future events, for there have been no dramatic changes either in individual selves, or in human communities and societies. The whole of human experience is recorded in every component of the current world view, and will in turn, of course, be written into all that is to come as the future of the world.

The last century saw the collapse of the demarcation between Austria-Hungary and Turkey, two great supranational empires. These empires included parts of southeastern Europe, their borders slicing that geopolitical region into two, leaving on either side peoples of the same language,[1] similar ethnogenesis, and similar views of the future. Although political borders split these peoples between separate states, the links of language, religion, sensibility, and understanding of the future remained unbroken. The shifting of borders and the political reshaping of the region, together with changes in the perception of identity and adherence to ideological programs, led to different attitudes towards the elements that connect and divide.

It has never been possible to identify the "building block" of any of these component groups without taking into account at the same time their differences from those closest to them. Likewise, it has never been possible to identify a "shared universality" without at the same time neglecting the differences. None of the component groups ever managed to establish its position so as to be sufficient unto itself. This gave rise to a cyclical pattern of efforts, both individual and collective, towards cohesion and union, followed by contrary, disconnective and separative tendencies. The component groups sought to define themselves in relation to the whole that comprised and connected them, and to the Others with which they were in contact. This created forces of attraction on the basis of their common relationship with the whole, and disputes when hierarchies had to be defined within the plurality.

The question that now faces us is the nature of future forces of attraction and repulsion. Is it possible to identify the changes that lie ahead? What could be the substance of these changes, and are they manageable?

Participants

Given the geopolitical context of the changes currently taking place, the term "southeastern Europe" is more common today than the "Balkans," which was the most common term for the region in the nineteenth century. Geophysically speaking, this region is bordered by the Black Sea to the east, the Aegean Sea to the southeast, the Mediterranean Sea to the south, the Ionic Sea to the southwest, and the Adriatic Sea to the west; its northern border follows the lower courses of the Sava and Danube rivers. Politically speaking, it also includes areas north of this northern border. It consists of the following states or administrative entities: Turkey (in part), Greece, Bulgaria, Macedonia, Albania, Romania, Croatia, Montenegro, Serbia (with Vojvodina and Kosovo as administrative entities), and Bosnia and Herzegovina. It is evident that the borders of this region have a significance that greatly transcends that of mere political and administrative boundaries between states: they both divide and join central Europe and the Mediterranean, Europe and the Middle East, and Catholicism, Orthodoxy, and Islam.

Apart from Bosnia and Herzegovina, each of these states was originally conceived as a nation-state, with nation predominantly understood to mean a single ethnic group. None of these states is ethnically or religiously homogeneous, however. As a result, the population distribution of the postulated ethnicities does not correspond to the existing borders. Bulgarians see their ethnic space as extending even to the west of their current borders, as do the Greeks; the Albanian ethnic space is at least in four different states; Serbs are present in Montenegro, Bosnia and Herzegovina, and Croatia; Croats in Bosnia and Herzegovina, Serbia. The existing state and administrative entities can also be linked to the corresponding national ideologies. Members of these states, ethnic spaces, and national ideologies link their identities to different historical narratives, languages, natural rights, and religions. Ethnic ideologies, therefore, invariably encompass more than the existing states, which are just a stage on the road to achieving the set goal: a comprehensive solution to the "national question." It is fair, therefore, to speak of Albanian, Bosniac, Bulgarian, Montenegrin, Croatian, Serbian national ideologies, which are in a state of mutual tension due to their failure to achieve the set goals.

The view expressed by Veselin Đuretić in 1993 is paradigmatic, applicable to each of these national ideologies; all that is needed is to substitute the relevant names:

> In the course of the formation of the new Yugoslav state, the Serbs subordinated not only their national goals, but also their social and state organization, to supranational goals. Carried away by their enthusiasm, they were unable to complete what they should have as a people, a nation: they failed even to homogenize the part of their ethnic space that was liberated during the anti-Turkish and anti-German wars. Entire areas that were not affected by Karađorđe's uprising, as well as those that were untouched by the uprisings in Montenegro, Herzegovina, Bosnia, remained nationally noncoherent. They remained grey ethnic zones where social experiments of a different nature would later be made.[2]

The global age of ideology has reflected differently in the various identities of the geopolitical region of southeastern Europe as a whole. It is, nevertheless, worth noting that the fundamental element of ideological identity in this region is nationalism, which shows that the region has been extensively affected by modernity. However, the ways in which the content of modernity has been adopted and applied in this region remain substantially different from those in other parts of Europe.

These specificities cannot be understood without taking into account the very nature of nationalism. Given its two faces—one turned to the past and the other to the future—nationalism is essentially both a modern and an antimodern ideology. Modern, because it has adopted the notion that there are, potentially at least, no limits to progress. In this context, this notion refers above all to the postulated national unity, for which the state is the key instrument in solving the "national question." It is antimodern, because to justify itself, it resorts to "tradition" as a major argument for the legitimization of its goal and the exclusion of the Other. Depending on its needs, this nationalism questions the liberal and social aspects of the project of modernity. It does this in all the cases where its own structure is exposed to reappraisal from the perspective of these two ideologies of modernity.

Projects

The concept of the national state as an important element of the project of modernity gave rise to national movements in southeastern Europe. From a Western perspective, they were instrumental in bringing to an end the presence of the theocratic Ottoman Empire in Europe. These movements were perceived by many in the West as a process of historical response to the question of how to eliminate the Turkish and Muslim presence in Europe. Any opinion or action that facilitated this process was met with support, but always insofar as it served partial interests in expanding or suppressing the political clout of European powers.

The region's pluriformity meant that it became a chessboard with several players on different sides making their moves. Each participant in this political, religious, and ethnic mosaic was assigned the desired role in this geostrategic game. A number of national projects were thus created, which established, each in their different ways, their internal structure—their elite, ideology, and organization. In response to these, other projects were created on the basis of the same principles but with different formal manifestations. The proposal was thus that individual ethnic groups should have their own ethno-national state that would include all the members of that nation: Greater Serbia, Greater Croatia, Greater Bulgaria, Greater Albania. Each of them sought and found close and distant allies, for it was possible to reach their goals only by breaking the resistance of those who were present in the same space but whose loyalties were different. A complex tension throughout the geopolitical region was thereby encouraged, increased, and directed, which was reflected in the shaping of different Balkan identities.

What is worth emphasizing here, given its long-term implications, is the concept and project to form a confederation of Balkan states.[3] Several more or less unprincipled alliances of Balkan movements and states from the second half of the nineteenth century until the mid-twentieth century were connected with this. The notion of a confederation itself arose at the beginning of the twentieth century within the circle of European social-democratic movements. It was clear to the advocates of this project that the remaining presence of two empires would be succeeded by a new geopolitical architecture. However, the drawing of ethno-national borders demonstrated that no process of separation was possible without a simultaneous process of connection. Every accepted border of the new states was bound to become the front line of potential conflicts unless it was transcended by a clear project of stability and cooperation.

The original concept of confederation was obstructed by the elites of nationalist programs, which believed that new opportunities for expansion had opened up after World War I: expansion under the guise of new integrations that served them alone. Such interpretations and actions reflected the conflicting presences of external European powers, with their different interests and allies among the Balkan countries. The establishment of Yugoslavia, as well as the European situation between the two world wars, together with the rise of Nazism and the subsequent European catastrophe, which brought about a sharp bipolar military and ideological division of the whole continent—all these pushed to the background, and indeed almost completely into oblivion, this idea of a Balkan confederation. The Communist intention to reconstruct it after World War II as a federation of Communist republics was made impossible from the very beginning, because the United States opposed it as a way of Communist expansion, and the Soviet Union as a way of strengthening Tito's influence.

The first integral vision of such a future is incorporated in the Stability Pact signed in the summer of 1999.[4] Although this political document reflects the will of its signatories to make the development of this whole region part of European processes, it does not specify what form this integration should take, as did previous proposals and attempts. It is a call to change the existing situation that does not insist on old and worn-out formulations.

However, the framework of ideas for the economic, monetary, and political unification of Europe and the development of common security structures was significantly altered after the collapse of the Warsaw Pact. The third European peninsula in the south is thus becoming for the first time open to political and strategic transformation without a sharp ideological and military division. The national programs present on the peninsula cannot, by their very nature, achieve peaceful coexistence. They are essentially irreconcilable, for each of them trespasses on the geopolitical space of the other. Furthermore, they are by nature exclusionary: their postulation of the truth of the "national good" means the absolutization of knowledge. If left to themselves, they will generate the kind of behavior that in principle poses a threat to the whole of Europe. The consensus reached between the key factors of the geostrategic world order is thus negated by the views and actions of small, yet essentially dangerous, Balkan ethno-national imperialisms. European tutelage in the development of an integral vision of the future for this part of the continent is, therefore, an inevitable requirement, which concerns the future of Europe and the world as a whole.

Since ruling perceptions of the Balkan region were formed in periods of complex conflicts between European powers, where different and conflicting models were used, a new and integral vision of the Balkan future presupposes a thorough reappraisal of these perceptions. This region, as an integral part of

Europe, calls for the application of knowledge and relationships that spring from the most recent views of modernity, tradition, and tolerance, with a different attitude towards ethnic and religious differences from those that characterized the ideological models of the previous period.

An Ideological Archipelago

In the light of all this, one might say that there is an archipelago of ethno-nationalisms in southeastern Europe. These are primarily ideologies that affirm or negate differences and similarities in accordance with their goals. Everything that is opposed to this in a particular ethnic space is defined as a "grey zone": an obstacle to homogeneity tolerated solely on the basis of political realism, permitted to subsist only because it cannot yet be eliminated. As soon as it can be done away with, the space it occupied is to be merged with the homogeneous entity. If the existing organizational core—the state in which "national sovereignty" has been partly achieved—is capable of it, if the "national interest" so allows or requires, it can open the doors to both liberalism and socialism, but they can never be set above the "national interest." The process of ethnic homogenization is, therefore, a continuous historical flow which, in the terms of this ideology, the state must serve. Everything that buttresses this service is to be absolutized, and whatever weakens and obstructs it is to be relativized. The rise and fall of the two Yugoslavias cannot be understood unless the irreconcilable natures of ethno-nationalisms are taken into account.[5]

The Parts and the Whole

Each of the ethno-nationalist programs is exclusionary. Their goal is "one state—one nation," but not in the sense of the "nation as civil society" at the center of which is the individual, regardless of his ethnic affiliation. The ethno-national state is closed to the Other as a matter of principle. It is not so in practice, however, since real life does not match the given ideological models. Within the relationships between the parts, there is always the more or less covert intention to weaken the differences within them and extend the presence and influence of those centers that regard that space as a "grey zone" of their projected entity.

For such ideologies, the state is invariably homologous with the ethno-national program as a whole, and its present truncated form is seen as merely interim, a stage on the way to full realization. While this same elite does not consider itself subject to any higher standards and procedures, it can guarantee rights to the Other only if they are loyal to it, loyalty being measured by standards and procedures determined by the elite. As the elite is ideologically exclusionary, loyalty means giving up "difference" in favor of the sought-after homogeneity. Human rights in such states are, by definition, contrary to the very nature of the state. States of this kind, therefore, always put themselves forward as key advocates of the rights of their ideological and ethnic kin in another state or area of the same geopolitical region, while at the same time denying these rights on the territory over which it regards itself as enjoying full jurisdiction. As a result, apparent equilibrium is achieved in relation to the principled obstruction of these same rights within the ethno-national body, which is perceived as the core of an expanding homogenization.

Since ethno-national programs define themselves as holistic, they need to be simultaneously both closed and open. Their scales of moral values cannot be universal. The national interest overrules the individual—which is why the loyalty of every member of the ethno-national community is a prerequisite for the exercise of individual rights. Those who are not loyal cannot exercise their rights. On the other hand, economic progress, as a condition of national emancipation, requires support and cooperation outside the ethno-national space and the established state structure, which implies the acceptance of rules that are supranational. This is one of the many paradoxes of the ideology of nationalism. This split can be justified through a hybridization of the autonomous and the heteronomous self. Where necessary this and other paradoxes that invariably manifest themselves when the "national interest" is absolutized, are justified by resorting to tradition and religion.

Nation-States

Nowhere in the geopolitical area of southeastern Europe is there ethnic or religious homogeneity; nor is there a single recognizable ethno-nationalist ideology that does not aim to achieve such homogeneity. Although the concept of the nation-state originally arose as the need to enlarge an entity that could be instrumental to the envisaged development, the premise of the nation-state can become a reality in southeastern Europe only through full-scale conflict with the Other.

The other face of what Đuretić sees as the liberation of certain areas during the "anti-Turkish and anti-German wars" was a genocide of major proportions, committed against those who did not fit the model of homogenization. Given that the world was ready to turn a blind eye, and given too that the genocide was not wholly carried through, there remains the implicit possibility that it will be revived once again, as an intrinsic element of collective identity, and transformed into a history that becomes our contemporary reality. No system that defines itself in relation to its environment can be a sufficient framework for such a project. What is needed is a state of disorder and chaos, because only in such conditions are acts of fraud, looting, forced expulsions and killing encouraged and exalted to the level of heroism. Since the establishment of the "nation-state" is the supreme value, each and every individual and the nation as a whole are called upon to fulfill their duty by being merciless towards everyone and everything on the way to that goal.

Patterns

Every national program is set up as a model with three functionally interconnected components—elite, ideology, and organization. Its principal and irrevocable goal is the creation of the national state. This goal is justified by ideology and implemented through appropriate organizations, which finally become an integral part of the state itself. The basic premise of such a program is national sovereignty as realized in the national state. Acquiring and maintaining sovereignty and the state call for national unity based on a clear and decisive differentiation from the Other. The very existence of the Other jeopardizes the unity sought, and the objective demands that attention should be continually drawn to their presence.

The identification of the Other further requires the establishment of an unchallengeable national elite, personified by the national leader. Since the leader himself becomes a self-explanatory rule, he, and not a comprehensive vision of change, must inescapably become the focus of the whole project of establishing national sovereignty, building the national state, and ensuring the conditions for their development. In this way the position of the leader is established: loyalty to him is equivalent to the affirmation of national sovereignty and the national state.

With proximity to the leader as focal point as the criterion, an unprincipled and lucrative social structure is built, in which two types of enemies are always present. The first is the world order, which calls into question the absoluteness of national sovereignty and the national state. Every call for the status of nation and state to be subject to supranational standards is interpreted as a threat to sovereignty conceived as absolute. The second type of enemy are internal enemies, who jeopardize the absolutized values of state sovereignty and unity by falling short of complete loyalty, by questioning the ruling regime, and by their inability to fit into the ethno-national model. The existence of such individuals and groups in ethno-national models is not merely desirable: it is essential, and as such should be encouraged and emphasized. In the ideological understanding of those who rule or advocate the nation-state and absolute sovereignty, any social and political setbacks that the regime experiences are the consequence of these two hostile tendencies.

Confused and scared, the majority is called upon to show increased loyalty and support for the existing system, for the alternative is the collapse of the national state, the eruption of subversive discontent, the defeat of the national welfare, and the like. The dominant element of the political discourse is to highlight the presence of external and internal conspiracies and the aspirations of individuals and groups to take over all the productive and financial elements of national governance. The entire domain of the media is controlled, as well as Mafia networks, intelligence services, monetary institutions and organizations. The state is ceremonially presented as a sophisticated social structure, while behind the scenes it functions as a structure for the organized promotion of all forms of illegal activity for lucrative ends.

Crime

The "national interest" transcends all other values. The activities of the national oligarchy, which is legitimized by the general will of the nation, are not subject to any restriction in drawing the entire nation into the scope of national authority. This outlook cannot solve in any principled way the issue of the relationship and conflict with others, who appear as obstacles to the process of including the whole nation within a single framework. As a result, with the collapse of institutional and other forms of surveillance and the prevention of crime, there is no impediment to the use of mass crime, made possible by the confluence of the will of the ethno-national elite with the generally accepted ethno-national ideology and the availability of ethno-national organizations. In such circumstances it is not difficult to find as many perpetrators of genocide as may be necessary: people who, convinced that they are backed by the concerns of national integrity, are willing to destroy all the obstacles—human, cultural or any other—that are identified as standing in the way of achieving the postulated national goal.

Once the process is under way of indictment and conduct of judicial proceedings against the perpetrators, elites, ideologies, and organizations without which genocide is not possible, the perpetrators for the most part remain beyond the reach of justice. Focusing the proceedings on individual guilt not infrequently allows for the crucial framework within which, and on the basis of which, the crime was committed to be disregarded. This leaves the elites, ideologies, and organizations as potential sources of the same phenomena in the future.

There has been a series of instances of genocide in the Balkans during the past century, of which only a few have been analyzed without ideological obfuscation. Since atrocities have been committed on all sides, the insistence solely on the crimes committed by the Other serves the interests of national homogenization and the reinforcement of those aspects of the national program that will be rechanneled into conflict. The objective analysis of all ethno-national programs that could result in genocidal campaigns appears to be a difficult and complex process. However, turning one's back on the issue, and taking the line of least resistance by avoiding conflict with latent criminals, contribute only to an accumulation of negative energy out of which evil may erupt anew.

Compromises with the elites, ideologies, organizations, and perpetrators of genocidal projects are interpreted as a justification of the acts committed. New generations are raised in this ambience, generations to whom the crimes are presented as the heroism and honor of their resolute ancestors in founding and developing the nation. In this context, the determination to indict and punish those who committed the crimes is explained as the result of an "external conspiracy" and exploited in furtherance of the isolation and internal criminalization of society.

Ideological Tutelage

It is impossible to comprehend the nature of Balkan particularism, as outlined here, without reference to the most significant elements of the contemporary critique of the ideological age. The liberal and democratic societies of the West are pluriform: none of them can be said to be homogeneous. In these societies the idea of nation is largely understood as the intended unity of civil society, operating within a framework of democratic institutions. These institutions embody a transfer to popular sovereignty, albeit one that is subject to control, in that there are constraints on the use of power by both individuals and groups. The key question for these societies is the question of tolerance: How can the diversity within society be reconciled with the enjoyment of equal rights by all.

Modernity offers several possible answers to this question, but these answers are for the most part founded on the undeniable premise that every individual is born free, and that life itself is the warrant for this human right. This is the concept of the autonomous self. When enlightened by reason, the autonomous self can identify its highest good, harmonize its relations with other free and enlightened individuals through a process of negotiation, and build a stable and progressive society in which optimal opportunities are ensured for everyone. This is the key element of the ideology of liberalism, in which society has no essential historical continuity, and there is no heritage from the past of the sacrosanct, that would oblige the individual to limit his right to constructive transformation of the world. The self as so conceived, and the social system based on it, need no heteronomous guide; there is no revealed knowledge that could serve as the foundation of a social system.

Socialism, which is also an integral part of the project of modernity, has adopted the view that the enlightened and liberated individual can be created only through a change in social conditions. The fundamental force of such social change is the organized subject of transformation—formerly the working class, now something new and undefined—which equally needs no heteronomous guide. In this view too, there is no reason or need for traditionalist knowledge, that which was revealed to people as the definition of the highest good.

Formally speaking, nationalism is compatible with both of these perspectives, the difference being that it justifies and strengthens its particularism by invoking tradition. However, nationalism does not accept either tradition's *scientia sacra* nor the order implicit in the link with transcendence and the authority recognized by transcendence. It needs the institutions of the inherited traditional order, in the shape of the authority of those organizations and their members, for an effective implementation of the entire project. The program and its state, in turn, offer tutelage and protection to those organizations. This symbiotic relationship provides an explanation for the more or less explicit subordination of almost every religious organization in the Balkans to the correlative ethno-national program.[6]

A careful analysis of the relationships between ethno-national programs in southeastern Europe clearly suggests that at no time in the twentieth century has been an intellectual dialogue between representatives of different religious traditions. The dialogue has always been mediated by the ideologies of nationalism, and has served only those ideologies. As a result, it was in the interests of those ideologies to strengthen the existing religious organizations in their capacity as the sole guardians and interpreters of the religious truth. Contacts between representatives of different religious organizations were always of a merely cosmetic and ceremonial significance, which was a way to obscure, when required, the essence of the relationships in the structure of power distribution. Parallel to this, intolerance, mistrust, and hatred were spread among the members of individual religious communities, confused, scared, and seized by the sense of collectivism. This encouraged the feeling that full loyalty must inescapably be transferred to the national elite which has the backing of the religious structures.

By their nature, national programs needed to create the perception that there were irreconcilable differences between religious forms. From this perspective, the members of different religions, too, are irreconcilably opposed to one another. It could then be claimed that maintaining an equilibrium in the form of tolerance was necessary as a matter of political realism and the "good will" of the ruling elites to create a system characterized by peace and stability.

Tolerance: Rediscovery of the Principle

Wherever there are "grey zones" in the Balkan region, they are a result of tolerance that is not founded on principle. A sufficient proof of this is the gradual erosion throughout the region of the presence of others.

It can be confidently asserted that the process of homogenization continued throughout the twentieth century. In the period of the ideological state, established as a Communist system after World War II, tolerance was promoted not only on the basis of political realism, but also on the basis of the need for indifference towards such loyalties, one's own and others', as lay outside the ideological model. Given the general negative attitude towards liberalism in this system, tolerance based on the autonomy of the self, which can at least be said to be close to the principled reason for tolerance, was completely excluded. There was thus an absolutized ideological vision of social change in which all other elements were excluded with scorn and left to "die off" during the triumphal advance of the planned change. In this view, religious heritage had nothing to offer to political systems.

The elimination of the forcibly maintained ideological framework increased the sense of disorientation among both individuals and groups. The proffered nationalism, one that was understood in an utterly reductionist way, was adopted as the means of legitimizing the new elites and finding an individual and collective identity for the disinformed and scared majority. In such circumstances, the relationships with the Other had no principled foothold. The shift towards the values and ideologies that lie at the very foundation of Western democracies, invoking human rights, the rule of law, and democracy, was largely rhetorical and used as a cover for the worst forms of criminal behavior and atrocities.

Two important aspects of the Balkan labyrinth are thus converging at the turn of the millennium. The first is the lack of experience of direct and non-stereotypical understandings of dialogue between the adherents of different traditions. The second is the increased distance from any principled reason for tolerance between the existing different ethnic and religious groups. The entire region has thus become one of the global issues awaiting resolution. The age of humanity now setting in, which many denote as postmodernity, is characterized, among other things, by anxiety over the possibility of finding a prompt and clear answer to both of these questions.

The common perception of the Balkans as a region where Eastern Christianity, Western Christianity, Islam, and Judaism meet and clash in a nexus of hatred and conflict is tenable only from the perspective of the ideologies that lie at the heart of the project of modernity. However, this perspective is dangerous, because it implies that the solution lies only in recourse to the available ideologies, which are, as their most prominent thinkers admit, themselves undergoing fundamental crisis. In addition, this view still further reduces tradition to the elements of the antitraditional interpretation created under the auspices of ideologies that are in crisis and decline. The experience of the turn of the millennium indicates the pitfalls of any form of absolutization of knowledge. As many contemporary thinkers note, this experience implies the need to accept an epistemological humility in which rationalism would coin fideism and vice versa.[7] This leads us to the question: Is it possible to find reasons for principled tolerance in Christianity, Islam, and Judaism, as forms of tradition with one and the same root?

The question is pertinent to the entire world, but nowhere is the need for it so salient as in the Balkans, that part of the European continent with ramifications towards Central Asia, Palestine, and North Africa.

Relativism and Fundamentalism

The future of the world as a unity of differences depends on the answer to these two questions. The failure of ideological projects—one of which is unquestionably the fate of the Communist Empire—will produce two extremes in their absolutized belief in unbounded emancipation and progress: one relativist, and the other fundamentalist. The first will lead to disillusion with the postulated values and promises, which will ultimately result in a weakening of human resistance to the tyranny of leaders, oligarchies, and institutions. This will be neither a denial nor a transformation of consciousness or modes of action.

The second response to the absolutized vision of ideological projects and their promises will produce fundamentalist anger, the proponents and followers of which will blindly and indiscriminately deny everything that is incompatible with their absolutized interpretation of traditional heritage. They will act as the absolute masters of knowledge and the fate of the world, embracing by such behavior the most pernicious kind of distortion of tradition. To use the language of tradition, it could be said that their words and deeds will be as those of "false prophets," completely convinced of their messianic role. As they grow stronger, religious institutions and organizations will also gain strength.

But contemporary fundamentalism is in fact a modern component that arises as a simple response to arrogance and the absolutist denial of all values outside the ideological framework. This response will give rise to two parallel processes in religious organizations: their strengthening in terms of organization and membership, accompanied by a weakening of tradition, its resulting deficiencies supplemented by secular ideology disguised as religious rhetoric.

Modernity and Tradition

This whole discussion can be called into question if the terms "modernity" and "tradition" are understood in the usual meaning accorded them in everyday contemporary speech. In order to avoid such intentional or unintentional misunderstanding, a brief look at the content of these terms may be helpful.

The project of modernity can be both presented and appraised through its three basic components.

The first premise can be summed up as follows: There is a set of basic and coherent principles upon which society should be constructed, and in principle it is possible for rational and enlightened citizens to reach a consensus on these principles. This has been the prevalent view in Europe for at least three centuries, and is part of the modern outlook. But is it confirmed by the current situation of the world, societies, and individuals?

The second premise can be outlined by the following statement: There are no insurmountable obstacles to the transformation and reconstruction of society on the basis of these principles. The advancing and triumphant expansion of power and administration with which obstacles were overcome has brought humans to a position where they are standing against the whole world. If humans are mere substance—as seen by naturalism, evolutionism, and progressivism, the key components of the modern world view—can they survive this antagonism between their correlative quantities and those of the cosmos?

The third premise can be expressed as follows: There exists an agency— a force or set of forces, a subject—that is adequate to the task of social transformation, and hence this task is a practicable one. The actions of this subject instituted the course of the *advance* of power and administration based on the world view of which this premise is an essential element. Behind the current fragility of societies, the weakness of the individual, and the insecurity of almost everything related to the project of modernity lies the inheritance of countless wars, the Holocaust, Communist camps and murders, and a host of unresolved issues, which may precipitate humanity into new campaigns of slaughter and destruction.

From the philosophical viewpoint, at the very basis of the project of modernity lie the anthropology characteristic of the Enlightenment, scientism, and economic development. None of these principles of the unlimited course of emancipation and progress has been revealed from without; the source of each is in the autonomous and rationally enlightened self. Tradition, in this interpretation, is just a lower-order element of human history and experience, which has been overcome by the development that has superseded it. Its remnants have survived only thanks to a concatenation of circumstances, and above all because of under-development, but they are surely doomed to disappear.

The traditionalist perspective on the human condition, however, is substantively different. The human self is unbounded in principle, or, to put it differently, "a shoreless ocean." It mirrors the totality of the whole created world. But it cannot itself define its supreme good. Its ultimate potential is perfection, but achieving it presupposes following the path revealed by the one and only reality. Knowledge is, therefore, a faculty of the self, but is, in its essence, supra-individual and nonindividual. It is the one and the same in principle, although it can be revealed in countless variations. The forms of its manifestation are, therefore, different, but it is always the one and only truth, at once present and absent in every form. It includes in itself the path towards oneself that embraces and elevates the nature of form. It also includes the path towards oneself that embraces and elevates the nature of the human self and the outer world. Reason is, thus, an extraordinary value of human existence, but it is not the most extraordinary, since it has been derived from a higher plane of being. Reason can discard that plane, but it does not become more powerful or more effective by doing so—rather, it reduces the infinity of the self to that which the self itself construes as its identity. Thus, reason leaves the self without an interest in transcendence and without responsibility towards the authority of the supreme good. In this perspective, metaphysics is either excluded or reduced to a subordinate element of philosophy.[8]

The Self, Transcendence, and Authority

The answer to the two key questions of this discussion calls for a reappraisal of the concepts of the self, transcendence, and authority from the perspectives of both modernity and tradition. Whether the tensions that are present in the world of today will be eased or exacerbated depends on whether essential differences in the understanding of these concepts can be transcended in the process of negotiation, and if not, will the two viewpoints become even more intransigent in their mutual exclusivity.

If the existing differences are reductively expressed in purely quantitative terms, which is what the scientific world view essentially demands, as such they are irreconcilable. The subsequent process of quantitative domination, the greater over the smaller, can be nothing other than a "clash of civilizations." This is a not improbable outcome of the current understanding of global differences.

However, the understanding of such an outcome as an essential betrayal of the original human potential is not far from the human horizon either. The various forms of the world, including those which are known as civilizations, cannot but reflect one and the same transcendental truth, nor can any human self be but attuned to receive this reflection. The sole purpose of diversity is to confirm the transcendental unity. But if this unity is excluded from the horizon of human knowledge, then its acceptance is actually tolerance in the widest sense, an attitude towards the world that is accepted as an inevitability. In this view, the sacredness of the diversity that confirms the transcendental unity is lost. The fact that diversity so obviously exists demands an answer, and the answer—in the language of modernity—is tolerance in all the various forms it has taken from the age of religious wars to the present day.

It is unquestionable that the awareness of the undeniability of the autonomous self, manifested in the call to acknowledge the right of every individual to life, dignity, and freedom of choice, is one that cannot be abandoned, whatever change or turn of events may come about. In this there is full agreement between liberalism and tradition: every individual has the unbounded potential to attain perfection. This is the original nature of every human self. Although this is a single truth, it manifests itself differently in the languages of modernity and tradition. The failure to recognize that these are different manifestations of one and the same essence gives rise to many tensions and conflicts. A consensus in this regard can be reached on the basis of the acceptance that none of the two sides holds undisputed sway over the truth, and that negotiation "in the fairest way" is both the right and the duty of each side. If the right to freedom of choice is linked to this complete openness and perfect potential of the human self, then consensus can be reached in this regard as well.

As clearly demonstrated by Georg Jellinek in his analysis of the fundamental documents underpinning the most significant social achievements of the project of modernity, the postulated right of every individual, as his natural or God-given right, leads to the recognition that this fundamental right is, nevertheless, given, and that it cannot depend on any measurable aspect of the world.[9] And it is precisely here that the need for resolution of the paradox of modernity meets with the basic view of tradition. The way out of the current situation, the actions needed to change decline into ascent, calls for continual debate on the issue. Tolerance between these two views of human destiny is a prerequisite for the realization of what can be identified as the most important aspect of the language, or of most of the language, of both sides that are actors in the human drama of the world.

The political stage of the Balkans today is dominated by the most pernicious forms of authoritarianism, the unprincipled exploitation of individual or group dominance over the majority as the source of legitimacy. Authoritarianism is repugnant to human nature, but it is rarely distinguishable from authority. Given the openness of every individual to his own perfection, it is fair to speak of different degrees of proximity to the goal towards which the self is directed. Individuals and groups at higher levels are never fully independent from the perfect goal towards which they are moving, yet they can act as support and authority to those at lower levels. The issue of authority is one of the contradictions of the modern age. In this regard, there is as yet no answer to the question how to give support to principled authority through which morality is enhanced, yet at the same time prevent its abuse in the form of public fraud and tyranny.

The overall situation in the Balkans demands a resolute attitude towards this question, which has manifests itself differently in moral, religious, political, and economic discourse.

Confidence and Trust

The terms "confidence" and "trust" are frequently used in the context of the Balkan drama, though their real meaning is rarely considered in the proffered interpretations. These interpretations are merely a derived or secondary element of the dominant preoccupation with the establishment of a framework described as the protection of human rights, the rule of law, and democracy. The creation of this framework, which is possible only through the involvement of an external factor, is a necessary first step, yet not sufficient in itself. The question of confidence and trust remains an essential internal aspect of the establishment of civil society.[10]

In the traditional perspective, links between people in the Abrahamic community of religions are created on the basis of a relationship with transcendence or God which is both common to all and expressed in the same language. This means that the vertical link of every individual with the Truth determines the horizontal links of direct human interaction. (And not only this, for such is also the nature of humankind's relationship with everything that constitutes the cosmos or "all of the worlds," of which they, too, are of course part.) Life in its entirety is, therefore, connected to the law which, in the final instance, is God-given. People are individually connected with the Truth, and through the Truth they are also interconnected one with another. Their tradition, as a specific derivation from the universal tradition, has its own historical, geographical, linguistic, ritual, artistic, scientific, and other manifestations. This is the frame or the horizon of a particular culture as "an historically transmitted pattern of meanings embodied in symbols, a system of inherited conceptions expressed in symbolic forms by means of which humans communicate, perpetuate, and develop their knowledge about and attitudes toward life."[11] (Culture in this sense is limited to meanings, symbols, values, and ideas, and includes phenomena such as religion and ideology.)

People's adherence to this relationship with the Truth or God, designated and framed by the relevant culture, builds confidence, specifically between the members of that tradition, through appropriate rituals, institutions, organizations. Once the awareness of God and one's duty towards Him no longer forms part of this relationship, it is reduced to nonobjectified identities and passionate adherence to non-enlightened collectivism. When this awareness of the Truth is present in any orthodox tradition (which is not possible without accepting the sacredness of every individual), it goes beyond the confines of the community of a particular culture, to include in itself the responsibility toward others as well, in principle towards every individual, but also towards the cosmos as a whole. Confidence is, therefore, in its full manifestation a transcendence-mediated relationship between people.

Given that the philosophy of the Enlightenment and the project of modernity based on this philosophy link the envisaged emancipation of the individual and overall social progress to the individual as such, independent from a heteronomous authority, confidence as a form of links between people becomes disputable. In this view, one has no need to form any relationships with others except in the direct act of negotiation. In that case these relationships are dependent on the degree to which each self involved in the process of negotiation is enlightened by the light of reason. It is assumed that the principle informing these relationships will be the same focus on the good, or rather the same recognition of equal rights for every individual. This is to abandon that part of the self that is dependent on the other to the assumed "normal response" by that other. Unlike confidence, in which the behavior of the other is prescribed from outside, the relationship of trust always includes only the assumption of knowledge or the probability of the expected response. (Such relationships between individuals are mediated at different levels of society as a whole by institutions, organizations, collective affiliations, and the like. Thus, there is confidence and trust with respect to those more or less abstract social derivations.)

In the case of the ideologies of nationalism, the original content of confidence is unacceptable. The identified national collective, in its advance toward the national goal, finds support and a foothold in tradition, as is frequently emphasized by proponents of national ideologies. But what is referred to as tradition in this context does not correspond to the traditional interpretation of tradition. In the interpretation of tradition from the perspective of national ideologies, the truth is not one. It may be an absolute value, yet it does not embrace the supreme values of all people and all nations. This view can be encapsulated as follows: "Our god is ours alone, and is different from the gods of all other nations." The original traditionalist viewpoint is, however, quite the opposite: "Our God and your God is one!" What is necessary in the current situation of division and conflicts among people is a reappraisal and more thorough understanding of these two concepts.

Nationalism tends to interpret authority as an indisputable requirement of the postulated national unity. Confidence between members of the national collective is then mediated by the "leader," who is the sublimation or embodiment of unity, sovereignty, and the state. In such societies "trust" cannot be built, because trust presupposes liberalism, and is a manifestation of disregard for the heteronomous aspects of the human self. But the ultimate consequence of this is evident: nationalist societies are seemingly linked to tradition, but are essentially both antitraditional and antiliberal.

Sovereignty Without an Army

Every national project is totalitarian in essence. It has a clear and unquestionable goal with three important manifestations—homogeneity, sovereignty, and the state. Since this goal can never be accomplished without subjugating or eliminating those who do not accept either the envisaged homogeneity or the presumptive sovereignty, or the state established on those premises, a national program always includes internal tensions in relation to those who constitute "grey zones," as well as external tensions in relation to those with whom borders have to be demarcated.

Homogeneity, sovereignty, and the state can, therefore, be achieved and preserved only on the basis of autonomy in military, security, monetary, economic, scientific, and other terms. Whenever any of these autonomies is established, its most important role is to be exploited for the sake of the establishment and preservation of homogeneity, sovereignty, and the state, which means against the Other. The extent to which the means of power can be exploited determines success in relation to the Other: the greater the power, quantitatively, in comparison to the corresponding power of others, the greater its effectiveness in subjugating them and bringing about the expansion of homogeneity, sovereignty, and the state. This is an important aspect of thought and action in the politics of current Balkan national programs. They cannot survive if they accept the principles that transcend this collective autonomy. A peaceful and stable future for this part of the world depends, therefore, precisely on preventing the autonomous use of military, security, monetary, economic, and other means against the Other. The problem of Serbia, as the paradigm of the greatest power in this part of the world, lies in the fact that behind the identification of the state with the ethno-national program is its reliance on the military, the police, monetary politics.[12]

The disaster experienced by Europe in World War II led to the experiment that found expression in the project of integration, known today as the European Union. This project sprang from the very conclusion that it was impossible to maintain a state of equilibrium between the autonomy of military powers, monetary systems, economies, security organizations, and the like. Closed national states cannot accept the fact that their jurisdiction runs no further than the border with their neighbors. Since they generally think in terms of numbers, they will apply the same logic in their attitude toward others. Nor are close links with neighbors possible, for that would constitute an imbalance of a higher order.

The countries of Europe initiated the process of integration in the most sensitive sectors of their societies—coal and steel, economy, atomic energy, monetary politics, security—as a necessity. Their borders remain where they are, and all their differences remained unaltered too, but the currents of every form of individual and social energy have thereby gained a considerably wider area to shape and control. In the Balkans, the same experiment is the only remedy for current tensions and the devastation they have produced. In physical terms, the logic of integration currently abuts on the Balkan archipelago of nationalisms. It cannot be halted at these borders, whether in the light of its own needs or of the situation of the people, nations, and countries of the Balkan region.

The future of the Balkans is therefore one of the most important issues of the European project. This issue is being resolved in the Balkans in its paradigmatic entirety: the advocates and combatants of the nationalist programs emphasize that the region's religious, ethnic and, as they like to say, civilizational differences are irreconcilable. But if such views are consistently applied, the European project itself—which includes ethnic, religious, and "civilizational" differences between its components—is untenable.

A Supranational Order

These considerations lead to a new question: Is peace and stability in the wider region possible without supranational military, security, economic, and political structures. If the assumtion is that they are not, then a further question follows: What is the future of the present nations in this supranational order.

The current world order has several pivotal elements. It is impossible to anticipate future developments without taking into consideration some important aspects of this situation. The leading military, economic, and political power in the world is the United States of America, whose future is inseparable from that of Europe. Twice in the twentieth century Europe has found itself in the midst of disasters that were halted only after the decisive military, economic, and political involvement of the Americans. The internal elements of the European structure that led to disaster have not been eliminated. The American presence is thus understood as a counterbalance to the possibility of new disasters.

Thus, the stability of Europe is a vital American strategic interest. Related to this is the current and future position of Russia, which is faced with complex changes in the process of transformation into a stable society and a democratic state. Establishing a geostrategic distribution in Europe that would reflect this European-American interconnectedness has to be viewed in the context of the American military presence in southeastern Asia, as well as the complex and potentially unstable situation in central and South Asia. Future developments will be determined by the potential for coordination of the American presence on the "grand chessboard of Eurasia" and the resistances to the moves that will result from such a coordination. This is the process of establishing an all-embracing world order according to the American vision and on the basis of military and economic supremacy.

History has shown, however, that no system of power in the world is stable, and that all are eroded and transformed by time, regardless of how they appear both to themselves and to others at their zenith. But it can also be said that it is impossible to establish such a system of power without assuming that it will be both stable and lasting. The effectiveness with which it expands and the length of time it lasts depend on its adaptability to the inevitable pluriformity of the world and its ability to govern its flows and relationships.[13]

In this global perspective, the Balkans is just one of many regions whose position in respect to the whole will be redefined. It is not important in terms of the size of its population, economy, resources; yet the further course of geostrategic redistribution calls for the pacification and stabilization of the Balkan patchwork. The same demand has been made many times before. Now, however, for the first time, the Balkans is the object of joint efforts on the part of European powers that have already to a considerable degree agreed and adopted common criteria in the processes of European integration.

Europe is now, more or less, a comprehensive military, economic, monetary, and political structure. This situation has resulted in the need for the dangerous autonomies of nationalist programs to be placed under unified supervision, which means that the current military, economic, monetary, and political autonomies will be drawn into a wider process. These autonomies can, but do not have to, recognize their own motivations in this process. Like it or not, they will not be able either to eliminate or to dominate the process, which will take place externally to them and which concerns the future of Europe and the world as a whole. This means that their view of the self, the nation, and the state will founder in the current of history, as a feature of an era that will be regarded as an abortive human attempt.

In the Language of Economics

A sequence of economic, monetary, and political projects is correlative to the consensus reached on the understanding of Europe's future. Although these three fields are inseparable, innate to the ideological nature of our time are numerous misunderstandings, which are more obvious, and often almost irresolvable, if the future of the world is viewed in the context of an inverse sequence. That a European project cannot be developed without a vision going far beyond the existing borders is evident in the areas in the immediate neighborhood of the European Union. Among these, the most urgently needed projects are those for the Balkans, central Europe, and the Middle East. This is not simply because of the situation in which the people in these regions live, but because they are the benchmark for the future of the current power centers of the world order. These centers will never be able to see and understand their own character in the fullness of their aspects and potentials if they turn solely to themselves. Their real image is the situation and the flow of changes in these and other parts of the world. And not only that. Their ability to increase the absorptive and dialogical potential in their language in the contact and reconciliation of differences within the postulated unity also determines their future.

The language of economics is approximates most closely to contemporary logic in the observation and modeling of the wider constellations of these assumed relationships, in their preoccupation with a constructive vision. However, since the tree of economic growth, as Adam Smith notes, can grow only within culture[14]—meaning with the essential link between ideologies and traditions—every economic discourse includes in itself the remaining elements of the postulated sequence, and, indeed, much more than that. One can think, using the categories of neoclassical economics, which are, say, 80 percent correct: it has uncovered important truths about the nature of money and markets, because its fundamental model of rational, self-interested human behavior, preoccupied with its own efficiency in achieving various material ends, is correct about 80 percent of the time. But there is a missing 20 percent of human behavior about which neoclassical economy can give only a poor account. Economic activity is deeply embedded in social life and cannot be understood apart from the customs, morals, and habits of the society in which it occurs. In short, it cannot be divorced from culture.[15]

Taking as a starting point the potential of economic models to provide an understanding of the connection between the future of Europe as a whole and the Balkans as part of Europe, a comprehensive vision and a sequence of changes in this region have recently been suggested. This includes nine elements:

The first element is initiating and planning the process of accession of five Balkan countries to the European Union (Albania, Bosnia and Herzegovina, Croatia, Montenegro—Yugoslavia, and Macedonia), with the usual requirements of democracy, human and minority rights, and with the suspension clause.

The second element is setting up an appropriate market regime: multilateral, pan-European, tariff free trade, and compensation to the state budgets of the newly affiliated members for the loss of customs revenues. In addition, all tariffs on industrial products will be cancelled in the process of full accession to the customs union of the European Union and its single market.

The third element is setting in motion the process of a wider introduction of the Euro—both as a currency and as a symbol of accession to modern Europe. This implies the establishment of currencies based on the Euro, with eventual full introduction of the Euro, and compensation to state budgets for the resulting loss of revenue.

The fourth element of this project is a comprehensive program of reconstruction and investment. This project would be implemented through a new Agency for Reconstruction and Investment in southeastern Europe as a replacement for the European Investment Bank. This agency would have ownership rights over the invested infrastructure.

The fifth element is the further development of civil society. This project would be encouraged, managed, and developed through the Foundation for Democracy and the Foundation for Education in southeastern Europe.

The sixth element concerns civil security, which would be achieved by the deployment, where necessary, of European customs services and police forces in order to monitor all border crossings and ports. This would also be a requirement for affiliated membership.

The seventh element is military security. It would be accomplished through the application of a new security doctrine which includes an increased role for the European Union in peacekeeping missions.

The eighth element includes institutional integration, whose basis would be a new model for progressive accession of newly affiliated members to the institutions of the European Union.

Finally, the ninth element of this program is the creation of capacities for managerial, commanding, and supervisory activities within the Commission and within the Council for their relevant competencies, using the new agencies and foundations for decentralization and debureaucratization.[16]

Together with the Declaration of the Sarajevo Summit on the Stability Pact in southeastern Europe, this project for the first time lays the foundations of a clear vision of the future of the Balkans in the new Europe. This time the shaping of this vision has sprung from the will of Europe and, probably, an unendurable feeling of responsibility in the face of the tragedies of Bosnia and Herzegovina and Kosovo, which the world for too long observed and interpreted as events that did not, perhaps, concern it directly. From this there follows the question of intellectual responsibility in the world as a whole, but also in the Balkan region specifically. Only by raising this question is it possible to speak about the internal factors and participants in this project for building the future.

Intellectual Networks

The entire geopolitical region of southeastern Europe has been economically, culturally, and politically laid waste, hamstrung, and bureaucratized. This situation can be illustrated through the terror of elites, ideologies, and organizations, whose most visible external manifestations are corruption and crime, which are just the other side of the false messianic mission and prophetic bigotry. Models of thought and action developed over a long period of time, which are only incompletely reflected in their Communist and nationalist aspects, are relocated and deployed amid the destruction, obstruction, and bureaucratization. Almost every Balkan university, school system, and scientific and cultural structure, as well as the region's religious organizations, are participating in this today. The illusion is created that all the elements required for a constructive change are present. However, the situation is essentially completely different. The organizational forms that are present are a labyrinth skillfully concealing the elites and organizations of those ideological projects that are opposed to the goal of the Stability Pact.

The question remains how to resist a structure that has been developed and maintained for such a long time and is embedded in the models of the prevalent sentimentalism and moralism. Understanding this structure is the first prerequisite for answering this question. This structure can never and will never understand itself. It needs an alternative as a way of confrontation. This does not imply just political opposition to the ruling structures. The opposition that exists today, in all its variety, includes no major elements that could be defined other than as a nominally different response to the ruling terror, for the most part remaining in principle identical to its cause. This is why the alternative proposed, which cannot become an operative policy in changes to come in the near future, means above all a critical and sceptical reappraisal of all the circumstances of the Balkan tragedy, in order to recognize and objectively analyze those aspects that render it a universal safeguard of the possible and needed dialogue and unity of differences. The stereotypical interpretation according to which the Balkan mosaic is predestined for tensions and conflicts does not correspond either to the Truth or to this defined goal. The religious, ethnic, and cultural differences of this geopolitical region, as of any other, are not either a priori a motivation or a basis for the phenomena that today constitute the dominant experience of the Balkan people. Beyond this picture and this experience, it is possible to find genuine reasons for the harmony that is a prerequisite of the survival of the world as a whole.

Afterword

Bosnia's survival in the twentieth century vacillated between what appeared to be transient defeats and periods of consolidation. Its nature is determined by these extremes. Apparent defeats are accompanied by the repetition of killing and destruction, and reconsolidation by the rise and manifestation of the elements that humankind projects as its desired image. Thus, Bosnia becomes an issue of unity in diversity, a unity that has persisted through more than one thousand years of its history, articulated in one and the same language, and of denial to which the most appalling forms of violence bear witness. It has thus grown to be the paradigm of modern discourse about tradition and, as a result, a warning to the whole world. Though examination of this issue directly or indirectly presupposes a knowledge of its essence, the nature of the decisions derived from this knowledge, the impediments to them and the failure to act upon them, bear witness to its inadequacy. The dominant approaches and interpretations of the Bosnian conundrum do not provide a satisfactory answer.

The principal concern of individuals within Bosnia itself and abroad, and of their institutional and organizational discourse embodying their views on the tensions in Bosnia, is the possibility of creating among the participants of the country's diversity a level of tolerance sufficient to achieve the necessary political unity of a complex society. But despite its ideological clarity, this enterprise seems barely if at all feasible: as the feeling and knowledge of the distinctiveness of existing political identities grows stronger, tolerance grows weaker. The selfhood of individuals and ethnic identities are increasingly barricading themselves within their distinctiveness and separation from the Other. The creation of tolerance on the basis of indifference or political realism becomes a Sisyphean task. The same applies to the belief that tolerance would be possible on the basis of the liberal idea of the autonomous self. Principled possibilities of a "transcendent" unity of religions remain outside the arena provided by the liberal image of the world.

The prevailing modes of addressing and interpreting Bosnia that have been disseminated throughout the world comprise a body of what is perceived as knowledge of the country, but which is in fact close to being ignorance, of a kind that is incapable of recognizing itself for what it is through a reappraisal of its own premises. The logical conclusion of the interpretation proffered both to the world at large and to the people of Bosnia is that the prevalent view of identity in the nation-state, as embodied in the ideologies of the neighboring countries, should be applied to Bosnia as well: in this view, the tensions in Bosnia result from the failure to achieve the only valid matrix for "settling accounts between differences" and sharing the same space and time. This call presupposes proximity to the European sphere, because the ruling national ideologies of Serbdom and Croathood at the turn of the millennium, are inseparable in their skeletal aspects from Western thought. In the process, there are frequent attempts to portray the Bosnian unity of different planes of identity as a non-European deformity.

The accepted view of Bosnia, ensconced in habits of mind dominated by the categories of European identities linked to the enlightenment, rationalism, industrialism and revolutions fails, however, to take into account an important aspect of the relationship between the modern and traditional definition of the self. In the towns and villages of Bosnia, Orthodox Christians, Catholics, and Muslims were able to live together for centuries without feeling or imagining that they were threatened by the fact that their differences coexisted in one and the same territory. The basic features of the self, both individual and collective (origin, ethno-genesis, history, etc.), of each of those different identities had its "foothold" in the total, one and the same otherness that transcends both inherited and adopted differences. The transcendent unity of religions was confirmed through intuitive intellectuality, that direct feeling for which discursive thought had neither appreciation nor a sufficient compass. When this identity, raised to the point where it outweighed transcendent otherness, became an ideology articulated in mainly rational terms, it veered towards paganism, in which origin, ideology, and so forth, became idols that can survive only through violence.

The modern experience of the West, in which the original Christian concept of the self as the crucial arena of salvation, beyond "prophets and laws," is transformed into the drama of individual freedom in which every *I* is the discriminating and judging instance in moral action and inaction, has led to clashes with the Other, the absolutized free self being unable to accept the different nature of its fellow human. This is expressed in the endeavor to "merge" the doctrinal and organizational interpretations of universal Christology, which leads to a split in the Christian world: hence, the division between the sacral as the private and the profane as the public. The definition and acceptance of Jews and Muslims as the basic Other of Europe is inseparable from this trend. This attitude permeates the millennia-long history of a world that tries to "draw into itself" an entire theodicy. The Holocaust is its comprehensive modern expression, and the contempt and persecution of Muslims is the internal aspect of the unresolved issue of the unity of the world outside Euro-centrism. Integral to the destruction of Bosnia are both prejudice against Muslims as the Other of Europe and unconscious levels of identity in which heteronomous otherness is not a transcendent moral authority.

The transformation of the sacred spirit into the temporal "spirit of the age," which leads to the relativization of the absolute and the "sacralization" of patterns or natural laws in the history of the world, excludes many planes of being: all that is above reason, and, therefore, beyond the measurable world, is denied. It excludes the experience of intuitive intellectuality, or direct contact with "reality," and relegates it to a group of vague second-order values, defining it by the term "myth," abandoning it to the museum of eras that have fallen into obsolescence in historical progress. Exoteric differences in the world, primarily in religions, thus remain without higher meaning; they are mere relations of quantity and power, in which the smaller and weaker will be subjugated to the ultimate predominance of the frontal wave of progress in the form of the "European spirit." Judaism, Christianity, and Islam are reduced on this basis to their exoteric forms, to structures and symbols lacking any features through which they themselves could be transcended on the road to absolute otherness. In this view they are mutually irreconcilable values, and are subjugated to ideological powers. In this ideological perspective, the polyphony of Bosnia loses the transcendent silence at its source. Idolatry towards religious forms, which is expressed as a collectivism without God, seeks to find its foothold in ethno-national ideologies and the politics founded on them. Disharmonies and frictions between them are interpreted, externally, as clashes of civilizations. Religious organizations, with their secularized ideologies, are unable to find the fundamental traditional component in their transcendent unity. The old harmony in Bosnia, based on the intuitive intellectuality of that transcendent unity, remains incomprehensible in modernized religious views, as well as in secular ideologies.

This interpretation, and the demand based on it that the "tension in Bosnia" be resolved in the realization of the "full right to ethno-national separation," are presented from the perspectives of two ethno-national ideologies, Serb and Croat. This means that Serb and Croat identities in the country must be territorialized: as the ideologists of these designs stress, which territories are Serb, which Croat, and which Bosniac must be determined, and clear borders drawn between them. The distinct Bosnian identities, which are in fact non-territorial—since each of them alike is manifest in Bosnia—thus resolutely demand that the Other be defined. Whenever the affirmation of the collective *I* thus postulated is called for, this is an imposed "enclavization" of others, who have become "legalized" aliens or minorities in a nationalized territory. Essentially, this concerns the articulation of ethno-national policies. Those policies, however, cannot either establish or confirm their authority without resorting to violence. The central element of their establishment becomes onto-topology, according to which the idol of that ideology takes the form of territory to be "cleansed of others." As this is not possible in Bosnia—all of its collective identities being nonterritorial or all-territorial—war is the only way to achieve that goal. A war against Bosnia has as its goal, de facto, the total destruction of Bosnia as an identity that consists of a unity of differences.

The contemporary selfhood of the Bosnian individual can be discussed with the recognition of its two essential features. The first is the traditional element, according to which it is shaped by *my kin and my congregation*: this means that within it the given elements, to which modern sociology inappropriately ascribes the term primordial, are known, as are the elements shaped by the voluntary submission of both individual and group to a heteronomous and transcendent authority. Those identities, with their full exoteric differences, are transcended through the esoteric unity or full otherness of God. The modern component locates the fullness of human potential within the self alone, or more exactly within its rational sufficiency as that which makes choices and decisions within the moral arena. A human is thus isolated from the world as a whole and confronts it as its conqueror and tamer. But this tension, placed at the very center of the self, is easily transformed, as the European experience of the twentieth century shows, into a descent towards the earthly plane of individuality, which is in its turn dangerously susceptible to the ideological narrative that modernity calls nationalism, Nazism, or fascism.

The mystery and cruelty of the Bosnian drama are not a simple reflection of "ancient discords and conflicts between its different identities," of so-called ancient ethnic hatreds. Such interpretations are merely attempts to find, in the language of politics, a narrative to mask ignorance and evade responsibility. The destruction of Bosnia, the essence of which was a war of aggression and genocide for which the world order as a whole and all of its participants individually are responsible, cannot be understood without a response to the key issue of our times: the undeniable failure of the project of modernity, resulting in the need either to return to different premises regarding humans and the world or to advance towards realms as yet unexplored.

In the extensive and fierce debate over the failure of the entire project of modernity, in which two contradictory solutions have emerged—that of reconsidering the principle of modernity, in order to restore its "human face" in the process of reformulating it; and that which totally rejects this principle, declaring it a total anomaly, and offering a substitute for it in "returning forward" to a restored link with tradition—the Bosnian question becomes an entirely international question. It is clear that there are many Bosnias in the world, the result of differing interpretations of our global present and future. Almost every modern vision of the world has failed, and the question is whether such a vision is possible at all. Thus, the survival of humanity assumes a new and, perhaps, its most decisive expression of all recorded time. The search for Bosnia in the multitude of its visions can also be expressed in these terms.

The deconstructionist perspective of the world confirms our inability to answer the question of Bosnia through the approaches that are now prevalent. The situation that has been established as the response to a war for the reduction of identities to their exclusive territories is untenable. All the tensions that were stoked for the purpose of laying waste and dismembering Bosnia have survived. External ideologies that are irreconcilable with the distinctiveness of Bosnia's complex identity remain present. Though they present themselves as conforming to the world order, they do not actually do so. Their hostility towards Bosnia—and this is a positive aspect of the overall tension—is simultaneously directed against the possibility that the world will devise a new enterprise that will accord due value to the necessity of reversing the trend of killing and destruction which graphically shows the impact of the European passion for progress in the twentieth century. Without a shift in the knowledge of this experience, which would influence the transformation of the self, the world is bound to enter a dark era of almost unimaginable horror.

The question of Bosnia, an issue that preoccupies almost the whole world—whether under pressure or out of good will—calls for a change in the understanding of the self and authority, immanence and transcendence. If Bosnia is left to the mercy of those political identities that can prove their authority only through violence, our preoccupation with Bosnia will show that there is no way out within the realm of modern thought. Only God will then be able to save the world: salvation will be wholly beyond the power of humanity alone.

Notes

Chapter 1: The Question

1. Such a view of the world, which explains the departure from principles and reinforces the obsession with quantity as "development," is summarized in René Guénon, *The Crisis of the Modern World,* trans. Marco Pallis and Richard Nicholson (London, 1975); on the same issue, see Huston Smith, *Forgotten Truth: The Common Vision of the World's Religions* (San Francisco, 1992).

2. The books of Samuel P. Huntington, *The Clash of Civilizations and the Remaking of World Order* (New York, 1996); and Benjamin R. Barber, *Jihad vs. Mc-World* (New York, 1996) examine, albeit in different ways and with differing degrees of effectiveness, the relations between the two approaches to the world's events.

3. The name Bosnia has denoted a country, a history, and a culture for more than a thousand years. In medieval times it was ruled by *bans* and kings, then it was an administrative region of the Ottoman and Austro-Hungarian Empires, then one of Yugoslavia's federal republics, finally becoming a sovereign and independent state and a member of the United Nations. This last century, its official name was modified to that of Bosnia and Herzegovina.

4. The original Latin is: "*et nullum deinceps ex certa scientia manicheum uel alium hereticum ad habitandum nobiscum recipiendum.*" The phrase "Manichean or any other heretic" corresponds, in today's terms, to the concept of the Other. Franjo Šanjek, *Bosansko-humski krstjani i katarsko-dualistički pokret u Srednjem vijeku* [Bosnian-Hum Christians and the Cathar-Dualistic Movement in the Middle Ages] (Zagreb: Kršćanska sadašnjost, 1975).

5. Quoted in Hazim Šabanović, "Turski dokumenti u Bosni i Hercegovini iz druge polovine XV stoljeća" [Turkish documents in Bosnia-Herzegovina from the first half of the fifteenth century]. *Istorisko-pravni zbornik* 2 (1949).

6. From the Resolution of the Nationwide Anti-Fascist Council of the Popular Liberation of Bosnia-Herzegovina, adopted Nov. 27, 1943 in Mrkonjić Grad. *Prvo zasjedanje ZAVNOBIH-a* [The First Session of ZAVNOBiH], (Sarajevo: Štamparski zavod "Veselin Masleša," 1953), p. 62.

7. Adam B. Seligman, *The Problem of Trust* (New Jersey: Princeton University Press, 1997), pp. 4–5.

8. Ibid., p. 63.

9. "wrong" (*grehota*)—in the Bosnian language, the etymological root is the same as *grijeh* (sin), but *grehota* denotes the ever-present responsibility of individuals towards themselves and all other beings in the world, the violation of which cannot be justified and which is in opposition to the innermost values, inclinations, and nature of human beings.

10. According to the 1991 population census of Bosnia and Herzegovina, there was a distribution of Bosnian Serbs over 95 percent of the territory of B-H, of Bosniacs (Muslims) over 95 percent of the territory, and of Bosnian Croats over 70 percent of the territory.

11. Although the "ancient hatreds" thesis was propagated along with the pursuit of the war against Bosnia-Herzegovina, every serious study of the history of this land testifies otherwise. See, for example, Noel Malcolm, *Bosnia: A Short History*, corrected ed. (London: Macmillan, 1996); Nikola Kovač, *Bosnie: le prix de la paix* (Paris: Editions Michalon, 1995); Ivan Lovrenović, *Bosnien und Herzegowina: Eine Kulturgeschichte*, trans. Klaus Detlef Olof (Wien: Folio Werlag, 1998); Robert J. Donia and John V. A. Fine Jr., *Bosnia and Herzegovina: A Tradition Betrayed* (London: Hurst, 1994).

12. Shmuel N. Eisenstadt, "Heterodoxies and Dynamics of Civilizations," *Proceedings of the American Philosophical Society* 128, no. 2 (1984): 111.

13. Qur'an, 5:32.

14. Emile Durkheim, "Individualism and the Intellectuals," in *Emile Durkheim on Morality and Society*, ed. Robert Bellah (Chicago, 1973) p. 52.

15. For an in-depth discussion of this concept, see René Guénon, *Le Règne de la Quantité et les Signes des Temps* (Paris, 1972), especially the chapter entitled "Les postulats du rationalisme," pp. 91–96, which is a study of Western rationalism from the viewpoint of perennial wisdom (*sophia perennis*). See also Wolfgang Schluchter, *The Rise of Western Rationalism* (Berkeley, 1981).

16. *grehota*: see endnote 9.

17. In connection with understanding and belief, see Frithjof Schuon, *Logic and Transcendence*, trans. Peter N. Townsend (London, 1984), especially the chapter "Understanding and Believing," pp. 198–208.

18. On this question, an extremely useful work by Whitall N. Perry, *A Treasury of Traditional Wisdom* (Cambridge, 1991), presents a summary of various holy scriptures ordered according to "stations of wisdom."

19. Schuon, *Logic and Transcendence*, p. 206.

20. Alexis de Tocqueville. *The Old Regime and the Revolution.* Garden City: Doubleday: 1955, p. xiv.

21. Qur'an 22:18.

22. Qur'an 11:56.

23. Qur'an 3:103.

24. Qur'an 13:19–21.

25. Qur'an 33:72. The term "trust" corresponds to the original *amanah* in Arabic. A more comprehensive examination of this term in the context of different forms of Abrahamic tradition leads us, however, to the doctrine of the "covenant." We will here present some of its aspects according to Qur'an. The Arabic noun *mithak*, which derives from the verb *wathika* (to trust [smb]) or *wathuka* (to be firm), means "covenant," "contract." The terms are often used in association with *'ahd*. In some cases it denotes a political alliance. It may also denote a contract between man and wife. However, in most common usage it signifies the relationship between God and the members of humanity whom he created, the unilateral imposition of the covenant on humanity by God. There is, thus, *mithak* with the prophets; *mithak* with Muhammad when he was in Medina; *mithak* with the people of the Book, once explicitly with Christians, but most commonly with regard to God's covenant with the children of Israel on Sinai. Its counterpart in the Torah is *berit*. Important are references to God's covenant (*mithak* or *'ahd*) with believers and the covenant of the Book. Related to this are the terms "oath" (*amana*) and "promise" (*wa'd*) in the relationship between God and humanity.

26. The meaning attributed to this concept is close to the concept of "trust" and its connection with "confidence", as explained by Adam B. Seligman, *Modernity's Wager*, p. 43.

27. Qur'an, 29:46.

28. For a reading of how history, within the framework of ideology, participated in the destruction of Bosnia, see Rusmir Mahmutćehajić, *Bosnia the Good: Tolerance and Tradition* (Budapest, Cental European University Press: 2000), and Rusmir Mahmutćehajić, *The Denial of Bosnia* (University Park, PA, 2000).

29. The root of the Slavic word for "freedom" (*sloboda*) and the Latin word *slavus* (slave) are probably connected with the possessive pronoun *svoj*—meaning "one's own," which is probably connected with "self."

30. Barber, *Jihad vs. McWorld*, p. 117

31. Qur'an, 95:4–5.

32. Barber, *Jihad vs. McWorld*, p. 136

33. These three possibilities of the human self are taken from Qur'an's definition of the conflicts and their resolution within man: *Surely the soul of man incites to evil* (12:53); *the soul which is ever reproachful* (75:2); and *O soul at peace . . .* (89:27). See, for example, Abu Bakr Siraj ad-Din. Martin Lings, *Muhammad: His Life Based on the Earliest Sources* (Cambridge, 1988), p. 356. These traditional definitions can be conditionally connected with the new age interpretation of the three motivating aspects of human individuality, with reference to Plato—desire, reason, and *thymos* (or spiritedness). "Most of human behavior can be explained as a combination of the first two parts: desire and reason. Desire induces men to seek things outside themselves, while reason or calculation shows them the best way to get them. But human beings seek recognition of their own worth, or of the people, things or principles that they invest with worth." Francis Fukuyama, *The End of History and the Last Man* (London and New York: Unwin, 1998), pp. XVI–XVII.

34. For these aspects of Adam Smith's examination, see Jerry Z. Muller, *Adam Smith in His Time and Ours: Designing the Decent Society* (New York: Free Press, 1992).

35. For a traditional understanding of the concept of civilization, see Ananda K. Coomaraswamy, *What is Civilization?* (Ipswich, 1989).

36. Barber, *Jihad vs. McWorld*, p. 193.

37. See, for example, Stephen Carter, *The Culture of Disbelief: How American Law and Politics Trivialize Religious Devotion* (New York, 1993).

38. Matthew, 4:8–10

39. From Imam al-Bukhari, *Sahih al-Bukhari*, trans. Muhammad Muhsin Khan, book V (Beirut, 1985), p. 157.

40. Muslim ibn al-Hadjdjadj, *Al Jâmi' us-Sahih, (Sahih Muslim)*, trans. 'Abdul Hamid Siddiqi, book I (Riyadh, s.a.), p. 2.

41. Barber, *Jihad vs. McWorld*, p. 156.

42. From "Message," Mak Dizdar, *Kameni spavač / Stone Sleeper*, trans. Francis R. Jones, *Afterword* by Rusmir Mahmutćehajić (Sarajevo, 1999), pp. 187–189.

Chapter 2: Tolerance, Ideology, and Tradition

1. Given the multiple meanings of this term tolerance, its etymology should be considered: Latin *toleratio* from *tolerare* (to bear, to endure). It suggests that the Other is wrong but that he should be tolerated. *Tolerance* is sometimes defined as "freedom of holding religious views other than the official ones."

2. See Niklas Luhmann, *Risk: A Sociological Theory* (New York, 1993). This situation, which sums up the dramatic changes of the last few centuries, is characterized by the relationships of absoluteness and probability, and of unconditionality and decision making based on a rational choice. From this follows the important distinction between confidence and trust. Niklas Luhmann compares this distinction with that between risk and danger, between defining coincidences in life as having an internal or external nature. And while Luhmann sees this separation as linked to the progress in distinction of systems (which makes risk—as opposed to danger—a particularly modern, even early modern, phenomenon, just like trust, or rather the need for it), he makes a significant distinction between *trust* in persons and *confidence* in institutions. He says: "Trust remains vital in interpersonal relations, but participation in functional systems like the economy or politics is no longer a matter of personal relations. It requires confidence, but not trust." (Niklas Luhmann, "Familiarity, Confidence, Trust: Problems and Perspectives," in *Trust: Making and Breaking of Cooperative Relations* (Oxford, 1988), p. 102.

3. As quoted in Milorad Ekmečić, *Ratni ciljevi Srbije 1914* [Serbia's War Objectives in 1914] (Belgrade, 1973), p. 117. Since modernity places religion in a lower and subordinate position relative to ideology, dialogue between religions is almost entirely ideology-mediated. The ceremonial and cosmetic meetings of clerical leaders are mostly abortive, serving to conceal their dependence on ideology. Religious tradition

is not recognized as a possible source of tolerance. "The first step towards our national unity," wrote Jovan Skerlić at the beginning of this century, "is indifference to religion, a simultaneous universal weakening of religious feeling . . . The Yugoslav idea . . . will either be anti-clerical, or it will not come to be."

4. Marco Pallis, *The Way and the Mountain* (London, 1991), p. 223. This claim can also be illustrated by the relationship between revealed knowledge and rational knowledge. The former is of a higher order, but it takes place outside individual will. The latter concerns the potential of any individual. The messengers' mission is "closed," and all that is left to humans is to approach it through the multitude of signs in the outer world and inner selves, including the doctrinal and model messages of God's messengers. The following words of Marco Pallis point to the modern split between the former and the latter: "In facing the modern world, while trying to foster one's own spiritual aspirations, though a sound theoretical grasp of the traditional doctrine is indispensable (all the more so since it also provides many of the supports utilized in realization), this theoretical basis is not sufficient by itself, and it requires to be supplemented by other means pertaining to a different order, the reason for this being that 'theory,' as such, is the concern of the mind, of thought; and thought represents only one of the faculties of perception available to a being, being itself neither the highest, which is the true Intellect or Intelligence, nor yet the lowest or most external, like many of the bodily senses. But in any case high or low or intermediate, all must participate in realization . . ."

5. See, for example, Frithjof Schuon, *De l'unité transcendente des religions* (Paris, 1979); Frithjof Schuon, *In the Tracks of Buddhism*, trans. Marco Pallis (London, 1968); René Guénon, *Man and His Becoming According to the Vedanta*, trans. Richard C. Nicholson (New Delhi, 1981); René Guénon, *Aperçus sur l'ésotérisme islamique et le Taoisme*, (Paris, 1973).

6. See Aristotle, *Nikomachean Ethics* II:7–9; IV:3. Recognition of the self and the demand for recognition of one's value are not only the source of such noble qualities as courage, generosity, and public virtue as an incentive for resisting tyranny. They can also be expressed as a demand for recognition of one's higher value relative to other people (*megalothymia*). The opposite of this is *isothymia*, the desire for recognition of other people as equal. These two aspects of the struggle for recognition determine the historical flow towards and within modernity. One should also note Aristotle's preoccupation with *thymos*, in particular in the chapter on "greatness of soul" (*megalopsychia*), which, for him, is the chief human virtue.

7. See Georg W. F. Hegel, *Fenomenologija duha* [Phenomenology of the Spirit], trans. Nikola M. Popović, (Belgrade, 1986), pp. 105–119. This concerns the universally known and much discussed model of Hegel.

8. Arend J. Wensinck, *Concordances et indices de la tradition musulmane* (Leiden, 1936–71), 2:239. (*Bukhari*, Tawhid 55).

9. John Courtney Murray, "Arguments for the Human Right to Religious Freedom," in *Religious Liberty: Catholic Struggles with Pluralism*, ed. Leon J. Hooper

(Louisville, 1993), p. 240. This question also implies possible developments of the divisions typical of modernity—the sacral and the profane, the religious and the secular, the private and the public. In this duality, religion is tolerated in the private domain, though the boundaries of the public domain remain difficult to define. This leads the American Jesuit John Courtney Murray to conclude: "For human dignity demands that in making this fundamental religious option and in carrying it out through every type of religious action, whether private or public, in all these aspects a person should act by his own deliberation and purpose, enjoying immunity from all external coercion so that in the presence of God he takes responsibility on himself alone for his religious decisions and acts. This demand of both freedom and responsibility is the ultimate ontological ground of religious freedom as it is likewise the ground of the other human freedoms."

10. The Messiah's words in full are: "Thou shalt love the Lord thy God with all thy heart, and with all thy soul, and with all thy mind. This is the first and great commandment. And the second is like unto it: Thou shalt love thy neighbour as thyself. On these two commandments hang all the law and the prophets." (Matthew 22:37–40) These words refer us back to God's commandments in the Torah: "Thou shalt not avenge, nor bear any grudge against the children of thy people, but thou shalt love thy neighbour as thyself: I am the Lord." (Leviticus 19:18) "And if a stranger sojourn with thee in your land, ye shall not vex him. But the stranger that dwelleth with you shall be unto you as one born among your, and thou shalt love him as thyself; for ye were strangers in the land of Egypt: I am the Lord your God." (Ibid, 19:33–34)

11. See, for example, in Anne Pennington and Peter Levi, *Marko the Prince: Serbo-Croat Heroic Songs* (London, 1984), p. 166; and Timothy Judah, *The Serbs: History, Myth and the Destruction of Yugoslavia* (New Haven, 1997), p. 78. The creation of a nation-state is the highest rational objective of a national project. When it cannot be achieved without the expulsion and slaughter of the Other, justification for such extremes must be produced within the framework of ideology. However, since the justification cannot be based on any consistent discursive thought or on religion, there is a frequent resort to literature, which serves as the basis for emotional and moral reasons in a realm outside those two domains. Oral tradition, supported by literary works, thus became taken for granted as the foothold of the promotion of the Serb national program. It raised the killing of Muslims and the destruction of mosques to the level of a sacred act. This became an important element of the narrative that served to determine and justify the national identity.

12. Marco Pallis, *The Way and the Mountain*, p. 9–10. The interpretation by Marco Pallis may serve a better understanding of the term: "It will already be apparent to the reader that by tradition more is meant than just custom long established, even if current usage has tended to restrict it in this way. Here the word will always be given its transcendent, which is also its normal, connotation without any attempt being made, however, to pin it down to a particular set of concepts, if only because tradition, being formless and suprapersonal in its essence, escapes exact definition in

terms of human speech or thought. All that can usefully be said of it at the moment is that wherever a complete tradition exists this will entail the presence of four things, namely: a source of inspiration or, to use a more concrete term, of Revelation; a current of influence or Grace issuing forth from that source and transmitted without interruption through a variety of channels; a way of 'verification' which, when faithfully followed, will lead the human subject to successive positions where he is able to 'actualize' the truths that Revelation communicates; finally there is the formal embodiement of tradition in the doctrines, arts, sciences and other elements that together go to determine the character of a normal civilization."

13. From Latin *religio* (*-onis*), which corresponds to the verb *religare* (re-connect, re-unite).

14. Arend J. Wensinck, *Concordance et indices de la tradition musulmane*, (Ibn Maja, *Muqaddima* 9).

15. Muslim, *Al Jami*, p. 158.

16. Qur'an 2:256.

17. John Locke, *The Second Treatise of Government and A Letter Concerning Toleration*, ed. J. W. Gough, 3rd ed. (Oxford, 1966); translation entitled "Pismo o trpeljivosti" by Vladimir Gligorov published in the collection *O toleranciji* [On Tolerance], ed. Igor Primorac (Belgrade, 1989), pp. 73–105.

18. Arend J. Wensinck et al. (*Bukhari*, Al-Jana' from 80).

19. Qur'an 30:30.

20. Adam B. Seligman, "Tolerance and Tradition," in *Modernity's Wager* (Princeton, 2000). More systematic discussions on the context and contradictions of tolerance in the modern world are to be found in the chapter.

21. Stephen Krasner, "The Accomplishments of International Political Economy," in *International Theory: Positivism and Beyond*, ed. Steve Smith, Ken Booth, and Maryisa Zalewski (Cambridge, 1996), p. 125.

22. Seyyed Hossein Nasr, *Knowledge and the Sacred* (New York, 1989), p. 293.

23. Claude Lanzmann, *Shoah*, trans. Almasa Defterdarević-Muradbegović (Sarajevo, 1996), p. 36.

24. Slavenka Drakulić, *The Balkan Express: Fragments from the Other Side of the War* (New York, 1993), p. 143.

25. David Campbell, *National Deconstruction: Violence, Identity and Justice in Bosnia* (Minneapolis, 1998), pp. 55–78.

26. The books in question are: Christopher Bennett, *Yugoslavia's Bloody Collapse: Causes, Course and Consequences* (London, 1995); Lenard J. Cohen, *Broken Bonds: Yugoslavia's Disintegration and Balkan Politics in Transition*, 2d ed. (Boulder, CO, 1995); Mihailo Crnobrnja, *Yugoslav Drama*, 2d ed. (London, 1996); Bogdan Denitch, *Ethnic Nationalism: The Tragic Death of Yugoslavia*, rev. ed. (Minneapolis, 1996); Paul Mojzes, *Yugoslavian Inferno* (New York, 1994); Edgar O'Ballance, *Civil War in Bosnia* (London, 1995); Sabrina Petra Ramet, *Balkan Babel: The Disintegration of Yugoslavia from the Death of Tito to Ethnic War*, 2d ed. (Boulder, CO, 1996); Laura Silber and Allan Little, *The Death of Yugoslavia*, 2d rev. ed. (London, 1996); Susan L. Woodward,

Balkan Tragedy: Chaos and Dissolution after the Cold War (Washington D.C., 1995); John Zametica, *The Yugoslav Conflict* (London, 1992).

Chapter 3: Ignorance

1. Peter L. Berger and Thomas Luckmann, *The Social Construction of Reality: A Treatise in the Sociology of Knowledge* (London, 1991). Important aspects related to this claim and the bases of its elaboration can be found.

2. See endnote 9 in chapter 1.

3. Tim Judah, *The Serbs: History, Myth and the Destruction of Yugoslavia* (New Haven: Yale University Press, 2000), p. 90. It is indisputable that over a period of almost ten years there have been attempts to portray Serbia in a different light, despite the criminal alliance of Milošević and Tuđman in destroying Bosnia through slaughter, expulsions, and devastation. This attitude also meant participation in the genocide of which Sarajevo, Prijedor, Stolac, Mostar are only some of the visible signs. British policy in this tragedy remained faithful to the huge mural which dominates the Grand Staircase of the Foreign Office. The mural was painted during the First World War and portrays *Britannia Pacificatrix* and its allies. "While *Britannia* grasps the hand of America with one hand, with the other she 'encloses within the folds of her royal mantle' those whom she had hastened to protect in 1914. Here is Belgium, a 'Psyche-like figure of pure girlhood-, alongside Serbia, who in turn comforts little Montenegro."

4. Ivan Lovrenović, *Unutarnja zemlja: Kratki pregled kulturne povijesti Bosne i Hercegovine* [The Inner Land: A Short Cultural History of Bosnia and Herzegovina] (Zagreb, 1998), p. 47. Many examples of the denial of Bosnia's history could be listed, which served to create propagandistic pictures out of falsified knowledge. When the church in Mile, where the Bosnian kings were crowned and buried, was discovered in 1909, the discovery was crudely covered up, because it did not fit the interpretation needed by politics: "In any case, only the authorities could have had the means and power for such a comprehensive and effective campaign of erasing traces and *organizing* the oblivion of such a capital discovery," notes Ivan Lovrenović.

5. Robert D. Kaplan, *Balkan Ghosts: A Journey through History* (New York, 1993).

6. Rebecca West, *Black Lamb and Grey Falcon: A Journey through Yugoslavia* (New York, 1943).

7. Fitzroy Maclean, *Eastern Approaches* (London, 1991).

8. Though Serbian megalomania was at the root of the war against Bosnia, it was for the most part covered up for the sake of the old alliances of Britain, France, and Russia with that ethno-national program. The central Europe historian Edward Crankshaw, however, notes different perceptions of Serbia as well: "Serbia had been regarded generally as a thoroughgoing nuisance, a nest of violent barbarians whose megalomania would sooner or later meet the punishment it deserved. There had been several occasions when the rest of Europe fully expected to see Austria lash out and wipe Serbia off the map."

9. Carnegie Endowment for International Peace, *Report of the international commission to inquire into the causes and conduct of the Balkan wars* (Washington D.C., 1914), p. 51. Instances of genocide against European Muslims can be observed over a very long period. Ultimately, these are all manifestations of the same phenomenon from, for example, the total destruction of Muslims in Slavonia and Hungary at the beginning of the eighteenth century to that of Muslims in whole areas of Bosnia towards the end of the twentieth century. The reports on the treatment of Kosovo Muslims by the Serbian army in 1913 illustrate a pattern that can be recognized in many past and future cases: "Whole villages are reduced to ashes, unarmed and innocent populations massacred en masse, incredible acts of violence, pillage and brutality of every kind—such were the means which were employed by the Serbo-Montenegrin soldiery, with a view to the entire transformation of the ethnic character of regions inhabited exclusively by Albanians."

10. See Frithjof Schuon, *Language of the Self,* trans. Marco Pallis and Macleod Matheson (Madras, 1959), p. 7.

11. Ivo Banac, *The National Question in Yugoslavia: Origins, History, Politics* (Ithaca and London, 1984), p. 410. This is also indicated by the conclusion resulting from a systematic examination of the national relations in Yugoslavia: "The moral doctrine of modern materialism, among the South Slavs no less than elsewhere, assumes the antipopular drift of religion. Once this premise is accepted, it is only a matter of detail whether the rival churches damaged South Slavic unity by dividing the homogenous South Slavic mass into separate communities, which then evolved into separate nationalities, or by preventing the symbiosis of separate religions, which could have evolved into a uninational community. In either case, the preoccupation with the religious roots of Yugoslavia's national question is typical of unitaristic attitudes and tends to exaggerate the admittedly harmful effects of religious bigotry. The truth is that, except for the clash of Christianity and Islam, and then in an attenuated form, South Slavic interconfessional relations never occasioned religious wars on the scale of those fought in Western Europe after the Reformation."

12. Georg W. F. Hegel, *Philosophy of Right,* trans. Samuel W. Dyde (1996), p. 134. With this question, we should remember that Hegel designates the traits of modernity with the view that "man must be accounted a universal being, not because he is a Jew, Catholic, Protestant, German, or Italian, but because he is a man." It is evident that this view of Hegel's is in line with Paul's emphasis on a shift from collectiveness to individuality and from the law to faith, as is stressed in particular in his messages to the Corinthians and Romans. This view justifies emphasizing again the "important link" of modern liberalism and tradition. The essence of man is his a priori given disposition for perfection (*fitrah*), of which the Qur'an says (30:30): "So set thy face to the religion, a man of pure faith—God's original upon which He originated mankind." Related to this is the Prophet's well-known statement: "Every child is born according to *fitrah*. Then its parents make it a Jew, a Christian, or a Sabaean." This amazing modern parallel is nothing but the new universalism of the individual as a moral entity replacing the former Christian idea.

13. Al-Amaali, *The Dictations of Sheikh al-Mufid*, trans. Mulla Asgharali M. M. Jaffer (Middlesex, 1998), p. 115. The intention of this reference to the self is to indicate the intransient and supra-individual aspect of humanity as an extension of eternity in the finite world. All phenomena serve to this aspect and it serves nothing. Its purpose is perfection. The words of the eminent 'Ali, son of Husain, are the common traditional expression of this view: "O son of Adam, you will always be on the right path as long as you have an admonisher from your inner self; and as long as you remain concerned about taking your own account; and as long as the fear of Allah and the repentance remain your apparel. . . ." Emile Durkheim, "Individualism and the Intellectuals," p. 46. The same meaning is expressed by the words of Emile Durkheim, chosen here as a complement to those of tradition: "Since each of us incarnates something of humanity, each individual consciousness contains something divine and thus finds itself marked with a character which renders it sacred and inviolable to others."

14. Adam B. Seligman, *Problem of Trust*, pp. 171–172. At the very end of the twentieth Christian century, changes are taking place that defy the understanding of their living witnesses. Their underlying aspect can be outlined by quoting the words of Adam B. Seligman: " . . . as Western societies are approaching the closing decade of the twentieth century, they are also, perhaps, increasingly losing their ability to establish trust as a mode of social interaction. Trust then would seem to be a decidedly modern phenomenon, emerging from the changing terms of role behavior in the early modern period and, just possibly, declining with the changes that have accompanied the late- or post-modern world. Perhaps indeed, the idea of the individual as unconditionality or, *pace* Durkheim, as precontractual principle of social solidarity was too demanding a principle, one that carried too much baggage, to which, ultimately, there adhered too much risk to be maintained. To put the matter somewhat differently: as role segmentation progresses exponentially and the limits on systematically based expectations increase at the same rate, it becomes less and less possible to assume shared strong evaluations with others and less and less possible (perhaps plausible) to constitute a moral community on the basis of the idea of the individual precisely because that familiarity upon which community and hence self must be based is increasingly eroded."

15. Ibid.

16. Hegel, *Philosophy of Right*, p. 178. What is missing is the environment in which the individual can exist and be recognized, and the inner established self cannot be recognized as such because recognition can occur only within a shared and common framework. And this is undermined by the development which leaves us in the situation in which "every individual is a small world." This "small world" remains separated from the cosmos as its extension, and thus incomprehensible in the Sufi view: "The cosmos is a vast man and man a small cosmos." On this traditional link between the totality of existence and man, see the discussions of Ibn al-'Arabi, for example, William C. Chittick, *The Sufi Path of Knowledge: Ibn al-'Arabi's Metaphysics of Imagination* (New York, 1989); William C. Chittick, *The Self-Disclosure of God: Principles of Ibn al-'Arabi's Cosmology* (New York, 1998).

17. Whitall N. Perry, *A Treasury of Traditional Wisdom* (Cambridge, 1991).

Chapter 4: Paradigm

1. See Franjo Šanjek, *Bosansko-humski krstjani i katarsko dualistički pokret u srednjem vijeku*, p. 135. Knowing and affirming their position between the schismatic elements of the Christian world, Bosnians in the early Middle Ages denied their dependence on external canonical establishments of churches and their monopolization of interpretation of the Truth of the Anointed and the Good Tidings. Recognizing them as the truth open for all people, they could say that "the only true church of Christ is the Bosnian Church." They considered themselves as "successors of the apostles"and their bishop (*djed* or *did*, literally, grandfather) "the only true vicegerent of Christ on earth," and "the only true successor to Peter." See Alija Isaković, *Bosnia and the Bosnian Muslims: the Bosnian Language* (Sarajevo, 1991), and Mustafa Imamović, *Historija Bošnjaka* (Sarajevo, 1998), pp. 165–166. Their entire teachings and religious life were, therefore, based and developed in their own language, in a dynamic relationship of autonomous and heteronomous acceptance and application of submission and freedom in relation to the Absolute. This bond with the universal, independent of externally imposed systems, reinforced their expectation of confirmation in the form of the arrival of the announced Paraclete. In this, one can recognize their consent and ability to become involved in the leadership of the state and in the Ottoman Empire. Part of this was also their attachment to the Bosnian language.

2. Pallis, *The Way and the Mountain*, p. 10. Revelation of the Truth, the sequence of its transmittance through different mediators, the dependability of what is received in the states reached through the transmitted rites, and the civilizational norms that derive from this—all this constitutes "tradition" (Latin *traditio* from *tradere*: to transfer, to deliver), which, depending on how the transmission was mediated, manifests itself in a multitude of *traditions*. "Quite evidently, the first two of these four elements lie outside any possibility of corruption; the third element, though likewise incorruptible in its principle, can yet be lost from view through human neglect of the opportunities and means it provides; as for the fourth element, traditional form, this will necessarily be exposed to the vicissitudes affecting all forms as such, since who says manifestation in form also says limited and conditioned, and this in its turn spells subjection to the triple fatality of changefulness, decrepitude and eventual death. Only the divine Suchness is unborn and therefore also undying, limitless and therefore not limiting, free and therefore the seat of Deliverance. The voice of tradition is the invitation to that freedom whispered in the ear of existential bondage; whatever echoes that message in any degree or at any remove may properly be called 'traditional;' anything that fails to do so, on the other hand, is untraditional and humanistic, and this reproach will apply whatever may be the nature of the apparent achievements, within the world, to which that thing has given impetus."

3. This is an ayat from the Qur'an (5:48): "To every one of you We have appointed a right way and an open road. If God had willed, He would have made you one nation; but that He may try you in what has come to you. So be forward in your

good works; unto God shall you return, all together; and He will tell you of that whereon you were at variance."

4. Though religious diversity is the essence of Bosnian history, the conclusion resulting from a systematic examination of trends of thought in this country and its environment over the last century sounds paraodoxical: the modernity project has prevented a direct dialogue between religious communities. They are assigned a lower and subordinated position on the ideological scale in relation to the idea of creation of a nation-state, and the relations among them are mediated through national ideologies. Cosmetic and ceremonial meetings of religious prelates have merely served as a justification of this situation.

5. Banac, *The National Question in Yugoslavia*, p. 413. This objective becomes the ideological center, and the Orthodox religion its essential aspect. From this follows negation of the other elements of the unity in diversity. "Catholicism and Islam were opposed not because they were more obscurantist than Orthodoxy, but because they were not the spiritual homes of the Serbs. This being the situation, it is hardly surprising that relations between the churches deteriorated after the unification. But that is not the same as defining a general disposition from goaded responses. The failure of unitarism called for *un bouc émissaire.* . . ."

6. *The First Session of the Nation-Wide Anti-Fascist Council of People's Liberation of Bosnia and Herzegovina, 25 and 26 November 1943* (Sarajevo, 1953), p. 9. Two irreconcilable ideas converge in this issue—the idea of state-nation, as the only possibility for Bosnia's survival, and that of the nation-state as a total denial of the possibility of Bosnia's unity in diversity. This is why Bosnia is odious and monstrous to all advocates of ethno-national homogeneity: its organic complexity conflicts with simplistic ideological models. Analyzing conflicts and dissolutions, Josip Vidmar in 1943 recognized this crucial and paradigmatic dimension: "Bosnia is a country in which people of three religions: Catholic, Muslim, and Orthodox, live. It is the most complicated country in Europe, and if brotherhood of Serbs, Croats and Muslims is achieved there, it will then not be difficult to achieve it among Serbs, Croats, Slovenes, Macedonians, and even Bulgarians."

7. Banac, *The National Question in Yugoslavia*, p. 186. The national ideologies of Serbs and Croats postulate the national state as the highest value and the paramount objective. Speaking of Milorad Drašković, the minister of internal affairs of the Kingdom of Serbs, Croats, and Slovenes, Svetozar Pribičević, an advocate of Yugoslav unitarianism, wrote in 1924: "He loved and respected liberty, but was deeply convinced that full, real, and lasting liberty could be granted only by an organized and universally respected state." The creation of a national state, as discussed here, is feasible by nationalization through assimilation, or by destruction of the Other. This is confirmed by the overall Yugoslav experience.

8. Paul Mojzes, *Yugoslavian Inferno* (New York, 1994) p. 153.

9. Banac, *The National Question in Yugoslavia*, p. 13. The tensions and conflicts among southern Slav peoples cannot be explained either by religious plurality or by "rivalries over distribution of wealth." "On the contrary, mutually exclusive national

ideologies have been most responsible," as Ivo Banac noted in 1983: "for the tensions between particular nationalities, contributing more to these tensions than the attempts by various of Yugoslavia's political groups to encourage and perpetuate particular forms of national inequality."

10. Peter L. Berger, *The Sacred Canopy: Elements of a Sociological Theory of Religion* (New York, 1990), p. 110. This approach is almost invariably accompanied by advocacy of idealized secularism. The premodern sacral culture is seen as an obstacle to modernization, and secularism is offered as a simple way to overcome it. This gives rise to numerous oversimplifications in the understanding and interpretation of the complexity of Bosnia's culture, to which the theory of secularism cannot be applied in the same way as in the West. This conclusion corresponds to the general statement of Peter L. Berger: "It should also be clear that any demonstration of the secularizing consequences of the Western religious tradition tells us nothing about the intentions of those who shaped and carried on this tradition."

11. See Mahmutćehajić, *The Denial of Bosnia*, pp. 45–55.

12. Berger, *The Sacred Canopy*, p. 51. In this context, religious organizations are mainly at the service of ethno-national ideologies. This is why they lay the emphasis on construing the chaos of the past and the possibility of its recurrence at any time. This perpetuates separation and ethno-religious homogenization. In order to understand this ideological dynamics, one should turn to the sociological definition of religion: "The establishment, through human activity, of an all-embracing sacred order, that is, of a sacred cosmos that will be capable of maintaining itself in the ever-present face of chaos." The danger of chaos lies with the Other, and the "sacred order" within the nascent ethno-religious community.

13. Banac, *The National Question in Yugoslavia*, p. 30–31. These are the national programs and their elites, of which Ivo Banac says: "[The elites] prefer to deal with the uncertainties inherent in maintaining the troubled status quo. When the national movements of constituent nationalities (regardless of whether they develop among large nations or among small minorities) succeed in upsetting state integrity, the dominant political forces manifest an inclination toward authoritarianism."

Chapter 5: Europe's "Others"

1. See Branimir Anzulović, *Heavenly Serbia: From Myth to Genocide* (New York, 1999), p. 52. These two events—the Holocaust and the genocide in Bosnia—are linked here in order to draw conclusions about their essential aspects. *Holocaust* (Greek *holokauston*, from *holos* [whole] and *kaustos* [burnt]) is the term used to denote the systematic destruction of more than six million European Jews, conducted by the Nazis before and during World War II. "Genocide in Bosnia" is here used to denote the systematic elimination of Bosnian Muslims and all their cultural elements, conducted by Serb nationalists from the beginning of 1992 until the end of 1995. This campaign has been most commonly referred to as "ethnic cleansing." "Cleansing" was also used to describe earlier campaigns against Muslims in Serbia and Montenegro.

2. Clifford Geertz, *The Interpretation of Cultures* (New York, 1973), p. 89. As defined by Clifford Geertz, culture is "an historically transmitted pattern of meanings embodied in symbols, a system of inherited conceptions expressed in symbolic forms by means of which men communicate, perpetuate, and develop their knowledge about and attitudes toward life."

3. Arthur J. Evans, *Through Bosnia and the Herzegovina on Foot during the Insurrection, August and September 1875* (London, 1877), introduction, p. xcvii. The destruction of this unity was never justifiable from the viewpoint of different sacred traditions. Different national identities were shaped in such a way that religious differences were subordinated to putative ethnic identities. They then reflected hatred and fanaticism, through which sentimentalism and moralism were expressed. Observing this trend in the uprising of 1875, Arthur J. Evans concluded that "discordant as are the political materials in Bosnia, fanatic as are the Christians as well as the Mahometans, I feel convinced that there exist elements of union in that unhappy country which might be moulded together by wise hands."

4. Berger, *The Sacred Canopy*, pp. 22–23. The constitution of social reality resulting from this is conditional on two crucial elements: the marginal situations in the life of an individual and his suspicions. "The sheltering quality of social order becomes especially evident if one looks at the marginal situations in the life of the individual, that is, at situations in which he is driven close to or beyond the boundaries of the order that determines his routine, everyday existence. Such marginal situations commonly occur in dreams and fantasy. They may appear on the horizon of consciousness as haunting suspicions that the world may have another aspect than its 'normal' one, that is, that the previously accepted definitions of reality may be fragile or even fraudulent. Such suspicions extend to the identity of both self and others, positing the possibility of shattering metamorphoses. When these suspicions invade the central areas of consciousness they take on, of course, the constellations that modern psychiatry would call neurotic or psychotic."

5. Elie Wiesel, "The Question of Genocide," *Newsweek*, 12 (April 1999). Evil is in principle always one and the same. It never reappears in the forms it has once appeared in. Opposing evil demands the ability to recognize its one and the same essence in many forms. The destruction of Muslims in Bosnia is genocide. It is in principle the same phenomenon as the Holocaust, though the formal differences between the two are enormous. The genocide in Bosnia was committed with the intention to eliminate the political and cultural presence of Muslims in this country once and for all, specifically those of its dimensions which posed an obstacle to the territorialization and delineation of the Serb and Croat political entities. Muslims were being killed and persecuted because of this, and all that was associated with their historical presence was being destroyed. In connection with this, it is important thoroughly to examine and explain Elie Wiesel's remark: "As early as 1992, media coverage of the war in Bosnia mistakenly compared Serbian 'ethnic cleansing' to the Holocaust. The Holocaust was conceived to annihilate the last Jew on the planet. Does anyone believe that Milošević and his accomplices seriously planned to exter-

minate all the Bosnians, all the Albanians, all the Muslims in the world? Some reports referred to 'Auschwitz' in Bosnia. I saw the prison camps in Banja Luka; the conditions were deplorable and the prisoners terrified. But it was not Auschwitz. Auschwitz was an extermination camp, a black hole in history. Victims were taken there to be turned into ashes." The Nazis dedicated immense resources and energy to committing their atrocities. The extent of their criminal objectives was determined by their power. Milošević and his partners had incomparably less power in the case of the destruction of Muslims in Bosnia. That is why their method had to be different, but their motives and goals were the same.

6. The objection to this view may be that the extremists, militants, terrorists, and fundamentalists discussed here define themselves as "Islamic," unlike the perpetrators of the same actions in parts of the world with a Christian majority, who do not define themselves as "Christian." It should be emphasized that this discussion does not deal with the mutual relationships of names and contents, but rather with determining and understanding the content itself. The essence of an action is not determined by the name to be given to it by the perpetrator or anyone else—it remains what it is, regardless. No one will agree that Nazism and Stalinism are essentially Christian, although both came into being in parts of the world inhabited predominantly by people who consider themselves Christians. And no one will, for example, agree that the attribute "Christian" should be attached to Auschwitz, although most of its organizers and executors considered themselves Christians.

7. Given the importance of both terms in this syntagma, additional explanations have been offered in several places in this book. A true tradition is always rooted in the sacred. Its source is religion, the renewed link between humans and heaven. The Revelation includes the principles and truths whose application is encompassed by tradition. "Tradition" may be the most appropriate translation of the Arabic word *al-din*. This notion is inseparable from the idea of a lasting and permanent wisdom, the *sophia perennis*. All traditions are earthly manifestations of the heavenly archetypes, which are, ultimately, linked to the archetype of primordial tradition, in the same way in which all revelations are linked to *Logos* or the Word. The sense of the sacred is nothing but feeling the unchangeable and the eternal, the self's nostalgia for what it really is, for sacredness is within it, primarily in its intelligence, created for knowledge of the unchangeable and contemplation of the eternal.

8. This is illustrated by Christ's reply to Satan, when Satan invites him to prostrate himself before him: "Get thee hence, Satan: for it is written, Thou shalt worship the Lord thy God, and him only shalt thou serve." (Matt., 4:10); the same meaning is conveyed by the reference to Moses as "the Lord's servant" in the Torah (Exod., 14:31), and by the same reference to Jesus in the Gospels (Matt. 12:18).

9. In the spring of 1995 Fred Cuny disappeared mysteriously in Chechenya, another country he went to with the intention of helping people who were suffering. For more on Cuny, see the book by Scott Anderson, *The Man Who Tried to Save the World: The Dangerous Life and Mysterious Disappearance of Fred Cuny* (New York, 1999).

10. Ann Norton, *Reflections on Political Identity* (Baltimore, 1988), p. 145.

11. Among many accounts of these events, including analyses of their causes, the following four books are particularly important: Roy Gutman, *A Witness to Genocide* (New York, 1993); Norman Cigar, *Genocide in Bosnia: The Policy of "Ethnic Cleansing"* (College Station, 1995); Peter Maass, *Love Thy Neighbor: A Story of War* (New York, 1996); David Rohde, *Endgame: The Betrayal and Fall of Srebrenica, Europe's Worst Massacre Since World War II* (New York, 1997).

12. On some inadequacies of the prevalent sociological interpretations of the crimes against Bosnia, see the book by Keith Doubt, *Sociology after Bosnia and Kosovo: Recovering Justice* (Lanham, MD, 2000).

13. Campbell, *National Deconstruction*, p. 110.

14. Ibid.

Chapter 6: The Extremes

1. Francis Fukuyama, *The End of History and the last Man* (New York, 1992), pp. 272–274. Although he did not properly understand the place and role of Bosnia between two hostile nationalist programs, the cited conclusion follows from his entire speculation on the "civil war in Yugoslavia."

2. This is how the crime committed against Bosnia and its context was described in the "Report of the Secretary-General Pursuant to General Assembly Resolution 53/35 (1998): Srebrenica report" (New York, 15 November 1999).

3. Transcript according to Mak Dizdar, *Stari bosanski tekstovi* (Sarajevo, 1971), p. 45. Although there is much earlier evidence of a distinct Bosnian identity, the *Charter of Ban Kulin*, the Bosnian sovereign in the late twelfth and early thirteenth century, may unquestionably be regarded as a document of Bosnian state sovereignty at the time. This document reads: "In the name of the Father and Son and Holy Spirit. I, Ban Kulin of Bosnia, swear to thee, Prince Krvaš, and to all citizens of Dubrovnik, that I shall remain your true friend forever, and that I shall nurture our friendship and true faith until the end of my days. All the citizens of Dubrovnik that dwell in my country for the purposes of trading, whether they stay there or pass through with the true faith and true heart, shall be welcomed without any obligations, except when somebody gives me a gift of his own accord, and shall not be persecuted by my officers, and shall receive advice and help within my power without a second thought. So help me God and this Holy Gospel." On the Charter see Asim Peco, ed., *Osamsto godina Povelje bosanskog bana Kulina*, 1189–1989 (Sarajevo, 1989). This period of the Bosnian state, too, is characterized by different Christologies, as the *Abjuration* at Bilino Polje in 1203 shows. On the earliest period of Bosnian history, which goes back several centuries, see Nada Klaić, *Srednjovjekovna Bosna: Politički položaj bosanskih vladara do Tvrtkove krunidbe (1377)* (Zagreb, 1994).

4. On this historical pluralism of Sarajevo, see a convincing description in Dževad Karahasan, *Dnevnik selidbe* (Zagreb, 1995).

5. This model of a concurrent inclusiveness and exclusiveness, of yes/no, was given shape in the historically important document that restored Bosnian sovereignty at the session of the Anti-Fascist Council of National Liberation of Bosnia and Herzegovina in 1943.

6. Vuk Stefanović Karadžić, "Srbi svi i svuda" (Serbs all and everywhere) in *Izvori velikosrpske agresije* [Origins of the Greater-Serbian Aggression], ed. Bože Čović (Zagreb, 1991), p. 95. Given the inadequacy of Orthodoxy, which is pervaded by Serb ethnophilia, for Macedonians, Montenegrins, Vlachs, Bosniaks, and Croats, Vuk Stefanović Karadžić, one of the most important progenitors of the Serb national ideology, introduced a linguistic criterion, declaring all South Slavs of the štokavian dialect to be genetic Serbs: "From what has been said here we can see that all South Slavs, except Bulgarians, are divided into three groups according to language: the first group includes *Serbs*, who say *što* or *šta* (what) (accordingly, we can call them *štokavci*, in contrast to *čakavci* and *kajkavci*), and who have *o* instead of *l* at the end of the syllable; the second group includes *Croats*, who say *ča* instead of *što* or *šta* (which is why they are called *čakavci*) and who do not change *l* into *o* at the end of the syllable, but who differ very little from Serbs in other respects; the third group includes *Slovenians*..."

7. See Banac, *The National Question in Yugoslavia*, p. 108. The integral ideology of Croathood was founded by Ante Starčević, whereas the most ardent advocate of its reduction to Catholicism was Josip Stadler, "who denied the primacy of national over religious sentiment and sought to build Croat nationhood on a firm Catholic basis."

8. See Qur'an 3:37–38.

9. Ibid., 4:169.

10. Ibid., 2:62.

11. For more examples of the use of this term in historical documents of the language, see in Pero Budmani, *Rječnik hrvatskoga ili srpskoga jezika III* (Zagreb, 1887–1891), p. 413. *Grehota* is the innermost nature of phenomena which can be comprehended through intellectuality. It rather belongs to metaethics and enables comprehension of *grijeh* (sin). The relationship between these two terms can be compared with the one between *goodness* and *the good*; for some remarks on this, see Bernard Williams, *Ethics and the Limits of Philosophy* (Cambridge, MA, 1985), p. 73.

12. Ivan Meštrović, *Uspomene na političke ljude i događaje* [Memories of Political Figures and Events] (Buenos Aires, 1961), p. 73. Although it is possible to adduce many incredible examples of the advocacy and perpetration of genocide against Bosnian Muslims, Stojan Protić's words uttered towards the end of World War I provide a striking illustration of the continuity of these campaigns with the eruptions in World War II and in the last war against Bosnia: "When our army has crossed the Drina, we shall give 24, or even 48, hours to the Turks [the Bosnian Muslims] to revert to their ancestral faith [which, in Protić's opinion, was Orthodoxy], and those who will not be willing to do so will be cut down, as we did in Serbia in our time."

13. On sources and advocates of these anti-Bosnian paradigms, see Rusmir Mahmutćehajić, *The Denial of Bosnia*, especially pp. 29–55.

14. A number of participants in this meeting have been charged with crimes committed in Bosnia from 1992. to 1995 by the International War Crimes Tribunal for the former Yugoslavia, established in 1993 under Resolution No. 827 of the United Nations Security Council.

15. This is an excerpt from the shorthand notes taken during the meeting between Franjo Tuđman and the leadership of the Croatian Democratic Union of Bosnia and Herzegovina, held on 27 December 1991 in Zagreb; the notes were published in the weekly *Globus* (Zagreb, 29 October 1999): 29–30 under the title "The Hague Tribunal possesses a document proving that Franjo Tuđman wanted to divide Bosnia!" Tuđman's speculations on such plans, the implementation of which resulted in widespread killings, expulsions and destruction all over Bosnia, were also reported by Warren Zimmermann, the last U.S. Ambassador to the Socialist Federal Republic of Yugoslavia, in his book *Origins of a Catastrophe: Yugoslavia and Its Destroyers* (New York, 1996). On the basis of this ideology, there emerged a number of pseudoscientific treatises, among which Petar Vučić's book *Politička sudbina Hrvatske: Geopolitičke i geostrateške karakteristike Hrvatske* (Zagreb, 1995), is very much indicative of the anti-Bosnian attitude.

16. According to Stipe Mesić's testimony in the weekly *Globus* (Zagreb, 19 November 1999): 69.

17. Ibid.

Chapter 7: In Bosnia or Against It?

1. See Ćazim Sadiković, *Ljudska prava bez zaštite* [Human Rights without Protection] (Sarajevo, 1998); On the legal manifestations of the causal dynamics of the war.

2. For a more detailed discussion on this matrix and its elements, see Rusmir Mahmutćehajić, *The Denial of Bosnia*.

3. For more on the construction of this project in a narrative which the identity needs, see Tim Judah, *The Serbs: History, Myth and the Destruction of Yugoslavia*.

4. Zimmermann, *Origins of a Catastrophe*, p. 145. The author of the book himself directly witnessed this statement. One of its versions can also be found in a public source. The Slovenian President Milan Kučan told the last American Ambassador to Yugoslavia that immediately after the pluralistic elections in Slovenia in January 1990 Milošević had said to him "several times" that "Slovenia was free to leave Yugoslavia, but he always added that Croatia, with its Serb minority, must never leave." Milošević's public statements to this effect from the first half of 1991 are also quoted by Laura Silber and Allan Little in *The Death of Yugoslavia*, p. 113.

5. Dobrica Ćosić, in a conversation with a Greek parliamentary delegation, 11 March 1993, as quoted in the 12 March 1993 issue of *Borba* (Belgrade): 3.

6. *Vjesnik* (26 March 1991). According to the official press release of the state news agency HINA, the two presidents met on 25 March 1991 in preparation of the meeting of six presidents of the Yugoslav Republics scheduled for 28 March in Split,

"in the border zone between the two Republics," and their "talks were an attempt to eliminate the options that threaten the interests of either the Croat or the Serb people as a whole, and to seek permanent solutions, with respect for the historical interests of the peoples." It was soon discovered that the meeting had been held in Karađorđevo, a government-owned estate on the Vojvodina side of the Danube. In the first Yugoslavia, the estate belonged to the Serb royal house of Karađorđević, named after Đorđe Petrović Karađorđe, the leader of the Serb anti-Ottoman uprising of 1804. and the founder of the dynasty. After 1945, it was confiscated and turned into an exclusive hunting ground for the new military political elites.

The agreement relied on the claims, almost two centuries old, of two conflicting national projects—the Serb and the Croat—to Bosnia. In 1939 these projects reached a compromise in the division and full denial of Bosnian Muslims under the Cvetković-Maček Agreement. For example, if Catholics made up 34 percent of the total population of a district, and Orthodox 33 percent, the district was then allocated to the Banovina Hrvatska. The 33 percent of Muslim population was not taken into account at all. Muhamed Hadžijahić, *Od tradicije do identiteta: Geneza nacionalnog pitanja bosanskih Muslimana* (Sarajevo, 1974), p. 237; on this Agreement, also see Ljubo Boban, *Sporazum Cvetković-Maček* (Belgrade, 1965).

7. Tim Judah, "Creation of Islamic buffer-state discussed in secret," *The London Times* (12 July 1991). As Judah testifies, "a senior adviser" of Franjo Tuđman's, that is, Mario Nobilo, confirmed to him that secret talks between Tuđman and Milošević had taken place "to resolve the Yugoslav conflict by carving up the Republic of Bosnia and Herzegovina and creating an Islamic buffer-state between them." Nobilo said that this deal, which was "maybe now the best option for a lasting solution," was discussed "in at least two meetings."

8. Peter L. Berger, *The Sacred Canopy*, p. 96. The three key political organizations in this drama—the Serbian Democratic Party, the Croatian Democratic Union and the Party of Democratic Action—had to work from the very start on finding a source of legitimacy for their struggle for power. The first two parties found it in the "pan-Serb and pan-Croat ethno-national totalitarianisms," programs whose legitimacy relied on ethno-national ideologies in which religious homogeneity, too, participated to a lesser or greater extent. The Bosniac program, too, was frantically seeking to "place" its legitimacy within the context of religious homogeneity. Under these circumstances religious organizations were directly or indirectly participating in the process of denying and destroying the Bosnian unity in diversity. Prevalent here was that understanding of religion of which Peter L. Berger says: "Thus it would be gravely misleading to regard the religious formations as being simply mechanical effects of the activity that produced them, that is, as inert 'reflections' of their societal base." This understanding of religion as a "reflection" stems directly from the Leninist, that is, "vulgarly Marxist" heritage.

9. Svetozar Pribičević, *La Dictature du Roi Alexandre* (Paris, 1933), p. 81. In the Serb national project Yugoslavia was perceived as instrumental to the expansion of the national state. This is why it was acceptable only as a centralized state. When Slovenians

and Croats asserted that they did not want such a state, they were told that they could leave it. The talks between Svetozar Pribičević and King Alexander held in July 1928 are paradigmatic in this regard. The King then sent a message to Stjepan Radić through Pribičević: "Since we cannot live together, it is better to separate in peace as Sweden and Norway. If Radić accepts my proposal, he can declare secession tomorrow." The King said on that occasion that he preferred separatism to federalism. Pribičević asked him: "If you have amputation in mind, the question remains of who will hold the knife with which this state will be cut up." The King replied: "It will not be as difficult as you think. The majority of Serbs will stay in their state, which will be small, but homogeneous and significantly stronger than now." This model—"either a centralized state or partition"—became the fundamental means of reliance on the power of the majority in relation to the Others living in the same geopolitical region. The application of this model was accompanied by the weakening and breaking up of the historical, cultural, and political entities that made up Yugoslavia. Given the nature of its complex structure, minorities or Others formed part of it in different ways as allies against the Croat project, and the Croat project was the main means of weakening and destroying the Others. This model was evident in the most recent war as well.

10. At the meeting held in Paris on 10–11 January 1992, the Badinter Commission discussed the requests for recognition submitted by Slovenia, Macedonia, Croatia and Bosnia and Herzegovina. It was established that the first three republics met the requirements, whereas in the case of the fourth republic it was held "that the will of the peoples of Bosnia and Herzegovina to constitute the SRBH as a sovereign and independent State cannot be held to have been fully established." See "Sažetak mišljenja Arbitražne komisije o Jugoslaviji (10–11. siječnja 1992.)" in *Dokumenti o državnosti Republike Hrvatske*, ed. Anđelko Milardović (Zagreb, 1992), pp. 152–153. Slovenia had held a referendum in 1990, Croatia in May 1991, and Macedonia in September 1991, all three with very positive results, whereas the Memorandum on Sovereignty accepted by the Assembly of Bosnia and Herzegovina on 15 October 1991 was not considered to be sufficient, because it was contested by the Serb Democratic Party.

11. A comprehensive analysis of the genesis and development of the Serb national ideology shows that it considered state centralism the best instrument of assimilation of people and territories. In this regard, there are no essential differences between Serb radicals' advocacy of Greater Serbia and unitarist democrats' advocacy of a centralized Yugoslavia. Since the Croatian national idea always emerged in response or opposition to the Serb one, it, too, reflected pan-Yugoslav unitarism in its pan-Croatian ethnocentrism. Both ideas denied Bosnia's unity through history as a major obstacle to the achievement of their goals. Advocating Serb and Croatian unitarism was thus expressed in Bosnia as antiunitarism. Those who were persistently and zealously breaking up Bosnia and Herzegovina's statehood, justifying it by opposition to unitarism, were actually working for a unitarism which went beyond Croatia and Serbia.

12. Two retrograde tendencies can be recognized behind this rhetoric. The first is the attempt to legitimize the ethno-national program and its elite within the corre-

sponding religious organization, and the second is the call for the desacralization and monopolization of religious tradition, which in the case of Bosnia leads to a breakup of plurality. The devastating effects of the war are manifested in the establishment of ethnic policies, ethnic territories, ethnic armies. This reflects a return to the principle *cuius regio eius religio.*

13. The breakup of Bosnia and Herzegovina's integrity had been envisaged much earlier as an alternative should it prove impossible to incorporate it into Greater Serbia. If the Bosniacs did not accept state unity under Serbia, they should be convinced, as František A. Zack and Ilija Garašanin held in the mid-nineteenth century, that "what would surely ensue is a carve-up into provincial small principalities under particular ruling families that would inevitably surrender to foreign influence, since they would be jealous and envious of each other." Dragoslav Stranjaković, "Kako je postalo Garašaninovo 'Načertanije'," *Spomenik Srpske Kraljevske Akademije* 91 (1939): 87.

14. Due to their links to decision-making centers in Belgrade and Zagreb, the "national issue" of Bosnian Serbs and Bosnian Croats conflicts with the survival of Bosnia and Herzegovina as a state. This gives rise to a paradox: Bosnian Serbs and Bosnian Croats are deconsolidated in relation to Bosnia and Herzegovina, while Bosniacs go the rest of the way to ethno-national consolidation, but remain confused with regard to the fact that these three ideologies conflict in relation to the one common state.

15. Alija Izetbegović, *Čudo bosanskog otpora* [The Miracle of Bosnian Resistance] (Sarajevo, 1995). Izetbegović himself was astonished by the thoroughness and speed with which the defense system was established and developed, since this did not match his perception of the relationship between the apparently powerful attackers and the weak defenders. He tried to incorporate this unexpected development into his ideological matrix, which resulted in reducing the Bosnian-Herzegovinian character of the defense while using the confusion and fear of the threatened people, to those aspects which eventually weakened it to a significant degree. This only helped the attackers. It is telling that Izetbegović calls this defense effort a "miracle."

16. For more details, see Tone Bringa, *Being Muslim the Bosnian Way: Identity and Community in a Central Bosnian Village* (Princeton, 1995).

Chapter 8: On the Self

1. Williams, *Ethics and the Limits of Philosophy,* p. 110. "Some versions of indirect utilitarianism," notes Bernard Williams, "fail to provide any location at all for the theory. They treat it as transcendental to life, existing in a space quite outside the practice it is supposed to regulate or justify. In the psychological version, the temptation to do this is found in a certain picture of the time of theory: it is an hour in which the agent leaves himself and sees everything, including his own dispositions, from the point of view of the universe and then, returning, takes up practical life. But any actual process of theorizing of that sort would have to be part of life, itself a particular kind of practice. One cannot separate, except by an imposed and illusory dissociation, the theorist in

oneself from the self whose dispositions are being theorized. In the case of indirect utilitarianism, this dissociation helps to disguise a particular difficulty, the conflict between the view the theorist has of these dispositions and the view of the world he has from those dispositions."

2. Arabic *nafs*, Hebrew *nepes*, Greek *psyche*, English *self* (*soul*).

3. Ibn al-'Arabi, *Al-Futuhat al-makkiyya* (Cairo, 1911), 4: 68.9.

4. See William C. Chittick, *The Self-Disclosure of God*, p. xiii.

5. Ibn al-'Arabi, *Al-Futuhat al-makkiyya*, 2: 298.29.

6. See note 5 of chapter 7 for the source of this quotation.

7. The term used here, *form*, corresponds to the Arabic *sura*, Hebrew *selem* and *demu*, Greek *eikon* and *homoioma*.

8. Stevan Moljević, "A Homogeneous Serbia," in *Genocid nad Muslimanima 1914–1945: Zbornik dokumenata i svjeodčenja* [Collected Documents and Testimonies], eds. Vladimir Dedijer and Antun Miletić (Sarajevo, 1990), pp. 8–10. The goal of establishing a "nation-state" presupposes a "homogeneous ethnic space." If there is no such space, the goal justifies its establishment, even if this necessitates genocide. In the case of the Serbian, as that of any other, national program, there are many clear proofs of such a logic. A continuous thread of such a construction ran through several centuries. "A Homogeneous Serbia" by Stevan Moljević (1941) and "The Political Ideologies of the Twentieth Century and the Serb Ethnic Being" by Veselin Đuretić (1993) are relevant recent examples. In the case of the Serbian national program, the former says: "[The Serb people] can again achieve those identical views of the state, meaning and the love of the state and its independence only if gathered within a homogeneous Serbia. . . . Therefore, what imposes itself on the Serbs as their first and basic duty is: to create and organize a homogeneous Serbia which is to comprise the entire ethnic area in which Serbs are living, and to secure for it the necessary strategic and traffic communications and junctions, as well as economic areas, in order to allow and ensure a free economic, political and cultural life and development for good. . . . Resettlement and exchange of population, especially of Croats from the Serb territory and Serbs from the Croat territory, is the only way to make the delineation and create better relations between them. . . ."

9. The place and role of poetry in the Serb national program is a telling example of such a construction.

10. Charles Taylor, *Sources of the Self: The Making of the Modern Identity* (Cambridge, 1996), p. 21.

11. The symbolism of the "house in the desert" in different forms of tradition corresponds to the "mountain-top," the "high places," the "golden fleece," the "tree with the golden apples." Their meaning, however, is always the same: a center comprising the totality of manifestations.

12. Qur'an, 41:53.

It is important to underline again that the corner and finishing stone of this paper is the premise of the original perfection of the human self and the undeniability of its equally perfect ultimate potential. Any limited knowledge is therefore conditional. The goal is the "position without a position," or "understanding without understanding." This comprises all positions and understandings. The knowledge of the messenger establishes the scope of narratives and negotiations in a community. The people within it rely on the security of different examples, sayings, and texts which seem clear and proven per se in the relevant cultures and times. In traditional cultures, this security is mainly linked to religion. Those examples, sayings, and texts are universally accepted, accessible, and powerful. They serve as instructions and confirmations of the ultimate premises. The frequent references to Qur'an and Hadiths (the entire body of accounts of the example of the messenger Muhammad) take into account the inner circle of those whom this discourse targets. But generally identical instructions can be found in any tradition in the world. Readers who are interested in this are invited to refer, for example, to the book by Whitall N. Perry already referred to, *A Treasury of Traditional Wisdom*, as an important presentation of this view.

13. *Sahih al-Bukhari*, Riqaq, 38. Conveying God's speech, the Messenger says: "And the most beloved things with which My slave comes nearer to Me, is what I have enjoined upon him; and My slave keeps on coming closer to Me through performing extra deeds till I love him, so I become his sense of hearing with which he hears, and his sense of sight with which he sees, and his hand with which he grips, and his leg with which he walks."

14. Though an aspect of every identity is discernment, through which the Good always remains the objective of the one who discerns, in tradition the path is always determined by a historical and known person. In the case of the Abrahamic circle of tradition, it is God's emissary or messenger. However, discernment leads to one and the same God. That is why one and the same essence is recognizable in the differences between emissaries and messengers. If *Christ* (Arabic *Masih*, Hebrew *Masiah*, Greek *Hristos*) and *Muhammad* (Aramaic *Mawhamana*, Greek *Periklytos*) are, for instance, messengers of one and the same God, it is then fair to say that their real selves, too, are the same. If *Hristos* is the highest human potential designated by God's anointment, then it is *Muhammad*, too, as God's praise and commendation, and vice versa.

15. See Martin Heidegger, *Sein und Zeit* (Tübingen, 1927), div I, chap. 5.

16. Qur'an 22:67.

17. Ibid., 10:47.

18. Ibid., 14:4.

19. Ibid., 30:22.

20. Ibid., 49:13.

21. Ibid., 5:2.

22. The term "tradition" (Latin *traditio*) is used to mean "transmission" or "delivery" of what was revealed "from the other side" of the phenomenal world through a chain of carriers. Discerning the non-real from the real is, therefore, shown in the language and example of the "perfect" person, the truth about whom is preserved in tradition. For more details, see Seyyed H. Nasr, *Knowledge and the Sacred*.

23. See, for example, Frithjof Schuon, *The Transcendent Unity of Religions* (Wheaton, 1984).

24. On the relationship of the recognition of an individual self and its link with the collective see Charles Taylor, "The Politics of Recognition" and Jürgen Habermas, "Struggles for Recognition in the Democratic Constitutional State," in Charles Taylor, *Multiculturalism: Examining the Politics of Recognition*, trans. Shierry Weber Nicholsen (Princeton, 1994).

25. The title "pontifex" points to the former, and "khalifatallah" to the latter. In both cases, the aim is to emphasize the link with intellect, revelation, and reality. On human viceregency or vicegerency according to the traditional view, see more in Gai Eaton, *King of the Castle: Choice and Responsibility in the Modern World* (Cambridge, 1990), in particular in the chapter "Man as Viceroy," pp. 114–141.

26. This view is the essence of the advanced reflections in *The Essence of Christianity*, New York: Prometheus Books, 1989, the best-known work of Ludwig A. Feuerbach. In the first section of the book, which had a marked influence on Karl Marx, Feuerbach reflects on the "true or anthropological essence of religion," and draws the conclusion that God is the external projection of an inner human need.

Chapter 9: Whence and Whither?

1. The meaning of the term "tradition," as adopted in these discussions, should be pointed out here once again. Human individuality, linked and determined by the totality of its relationships with itself, other individualities, and the world as a whole, has an "uncreated and undeniable" aspect, through which it maintains a link with transcendence. One can say that this is the inexhaustible creative word relative to which the individual and total existence is only a kind of extension. From this extension, which forms a harmonious set of signs that communicate the Word, one can move closer to the living and inextinguishable source of individuality. Every movement away from or closer to that "uncreated" center takes a different form, but those differences never remain without a link to one and the same essence, which is always outside time and space, though manifest within them. The root of tradition, with the totality of its many forms, is in that Word, its revelation, sacred knowledge, and the knowledge of the sacred.

2. The idea of man's link with the highest good is expressed in the institution of "covenant" in the Torah, Gospels, and Qur'an. For more details see, for example, in Robert Murray, *The Cosmic Covenant: Biblical Themes of Justice, Peace and the Integrity of Creation* (London, 1992).

3. For more details see Frithjof Schuon, *Stations of Wisdom* (Bloomington, IN, 1995), pp. 147–157.

4. See, for example, Franz Pfeiffer, *Meister Eckhart*, trans. C. de B. Evans, Vol. I, London: John M. Watkins, 1925, p. 114.

5. For Meister Eckhart, for instance, the root of intellect is in God, because intellect is *increatus et increabillis*. In man's soul there is a spark which Eckhart calls *Seelenfünklein*. This spark is the center of consciousness through which man can attain the knowledge of God. The soul has access to the planes of knowledge leading from

sensorial to "abstract" forms and, finally, to that "spark" which is both the heart or root of intelligence and the way through which God becomes known. This possibility lies in intelligence itself, though mercy is needed for this knowledge to be realized *per speculum et in lumine.* See Vladimir Lossky, *Théologie négative et connaissance de Dieu chez Maître Eckhart* (Paris, 1960), p. 180.

6. Schuon, *The Transcendent Unity of Religions,* pp. 51–52.

7. The messenger explicitly indicates those boundaries of moral space: "Both the permitted and the prohibited are clear, but between them there are doubtful things and most of the people have no knowledge about them. So whoever saves himself from these doubtful things saves his religion and his honour." (*Sahih al-Bukhari,* I, 2:40, p.44). The permitted corresponds to "yes," and the prohibited to "no."

8. On this see Heidegger, *Sein und Zeit.*

9. Qur'an 41:53.

10. Ibid., 95:4.

11. Ibid., 31:28 and 5:32.

12. Ibid., 30:30.

13. Ibn al-'Arabi, *al-Futuhat al-makkiyya,* II: 298.29.

14. Adin Steinsaltz, *The Thirteen Petalled Rose* (New York, 1980), p. 69. "Holy" is the crucial term of primordial tradition. "The root meaning of . . . 'the holy' is separation: it implies the apartness or remoteness of something. The holy is that which is out of bounds, untouchable, and altogether beyond grasp; it cannot be understood or even defined, being so totally unlike anything else. To be holy is, in essence, to be distinctly other."

15. Qur'an 70:19 and 30:54.

16. Jürgen Habermas, *Strukturwandel der Öffentlichkeit: Untersuchungen zu einer Kategorie der burgerlichen Gesellschaft* (Frankfurt, 1993), p. 153.

17. Taylor, *Sources of the Self,* p. 82.

18. Iris Murdoch, *The Sovereignty of Good* (London, 1970), p. 80.

19. Taylor, *Sources of the Self,* p. 77.

20. Seligman, *Modernity's Wager,* p. 111.

21. Taylor, *Sources of the Self,* p. 80.

22. The difference between the traditional and modern meanings of the term *tradition* which has been interpreted in several places requires distinction of the views of the term *primordiality* as well. For tradition, it is the full attunement of each individual for perfection, that is, the ability to distinguish between truth and untruth and embrace truth through the revealed path (Arabic *fitrah*). For modern sociology, it is a set of given circumstances that cannot be either acquired or lost (origin, race, etc.); they are there as given aspects of the self, unlike others that can be both acquired and lost.

23. Seligman, *Modernity's Wager,* p. 127.

24. Taylor, *Sources of the Self,* p. 15.

25. Williams, *Ethics and the Limits of Philosophy,* p. 195.

26. Jürgen Habermas, *Theorie des kommunikativen Handelns,* 2 vol. (Frankfurt, 1981), I, chap. 3.

27. Taylor, *Sources of the Self,* pp. 63–64.

28. Ibid., p. 79.

29. Ralph Dahrendorf, "Homo Sociologicus," in *Essays in the Theory of Society* (Stanford, 1968), pp. 77–78. "As long as sociologists interpret their task in moral terms," says Ralph Dahrendorf, "they must renounce the analysis of social reality; as soon as they strive for scientific insight, they must forgo their moral concern with the individual and his liberty. What makes the paradox of moral and alienated man so urgent is not that sociology has strayed from its proper task, but that it has become a true science. The former process would be reversible, but the latter leads to an inescapable question. Is man a social being whose behavior, being predetermined, is calculable and controllable? Or is he an autonomous individual, with some irreducible measure of freedom to act as he chooses?"

Chapter 10: The Decline of Modernity

1. The words of 'Ali ibn Abi-Talib to Kumayl ibn Ziyad are paradigmatic in this regard:

> *Nahjul Balagha: Sermons, Letters and Sayings of Imam Ali* (Qum, 1989), p. 522. "I wish to find someone to transmit it (knowledge). Should I seek one who is quick of understanding, but who cannot be relied upon, who would exploit the religion for worldly gains, and by virtue of Allah's favors on him seek to dominate the people and through Allah's proofs rule His devotees? Or one who is obedient to the bearers of the truth but has no capacity of understanding in his heart. At the first appearance of doubt he would entertain misgivings in his heart. So know well that neither the first nor the second will it be. Or a man who is eager for pleasures, easily led away by passions; or one who is covetous for collecting and hoarding wealth. Nor is either of these among the guardians of the faith. The most appropriate example for these is abandoned cattle. This is the way knowledge dies away with the death of its bearers. Yes, by Allah; but the earth is never devoid of those who maintain Allah's pleas and proofs, whether openly and generally known, or fearfully and covertly, so that the proofs and clear knowledge of Allah should not be rebutted. How many are they and where are they?"

2. Taylor, *Sources of the Self,* p. 27.

3. Ibid., p. 88.

4. Nasr, *Knowledge and the Sacred,* p. 4.

5. Taylor, *Sources of the Self,* p. 89.

6. Ibid., p. 91.

7. Ibid., pp. 103–104.

8. Benedict Anderson, *Imagined Communities* (London, 1983).

9. Taylor, *Sources of the Self,* p. 106.

10. For more on the construction of this project through a narrative necessary to identity, see Tim Judah, *The Serbs.*

11. See, for example, Nasr, *Knowledge and the Sacred,* pp. 233–234.

12. Tom Nairn, *The Break-up of Britain: Crisis and Neonationalism* (London, 1981).

13. On the traditional symbolism of Janus, see René Guénon, *Fundamental Symbols: The Universal Language of Sacred Science,* trans. Alvin Moore (Cambridge, 1995), pp. 89–94.

14. John Schwartzmantel, *The Age of Ideology: Political Ideologies from the American Revolution to Postmodern Times* (New York, 1998), pp. 168–169.

15. See Campbell, *National Deconstruction,* pp. 209–243. Given the misinterpretations of the "Bosnian case" based on modernistic approaches, the deconstructivist thinking on Bosnia offers some useful perspectives. The *ethos* of deconstructive thought can appreciate the contradictions, paradoxes, and silences of political problems in a complex world, and enable flexible strategies that are neither merely pragmatic nor purely ad hoc by fostering and negotiating their agonistic interdependencies.

16. Ernesto Laclau, *Reflections on the New Revolution of Our Time* (London, 1990), p. 187.

17. Huston Smith, *Beyond the Post-Modern Mind* (New York, 1989), p. 131.

18. David R. Griffin and Huston Smith, *Primordial Truth and Postmodern Theology* (New York, 1989), p. 146.

19. See Huston Smith, "The Crisis in Philosophy," *Behavior* 16, no. 1 (1988): 51–56.

Chapter 11: Changing the State of Knowledge

1. Thomas Paine, *The Rights of Man* (London, 1969), p. 104. Currently there are no efforts that would be adequate and strong enough to contribute to a major change. This situation may be defined as ignorance, which is like a veil. "When once the veil begins to rend, it admits not of repair. Ignorance is of a peculiar nature: and once dispelled, it is impossible to re-establish it. It is not originally a thing of itself, but is only the absence of knowledge; and though man may be *kept* ignorant, he cannot be *made* ignorant."

2. Banac, *The National Question in Yugoslavia,* p. 59. Though national identities were most frequently presented as complex identities, only religious differences were "fundamental." "Adherence to the three principal religious communities was of decisive importance for the cultural and political content of nationality."

3. Berger, *The Sacred Canopy,* p. 41. This includes the desire to produce different "memories" of the past, together with a general oblivion to commonalities. For society, in its essence, is a memory. It may be added that "through most of human history, this memory has been a religious one."

4. Lovrenović, *Unutarnja zemlja,* p. 33. Current use of one and the same language by different political movements that operate within single communities constitutes an attempt to negate a continuous linguistic flow through time. This attitude forces one to forget the indisputable fact that "the rich literal production over the

centuries to come (starting from the ninth century) in their own language and alphabet reflected the request for linguistic equality with the 'sacred languages'—Latin, Hebrew, and Greek—and preserved a feeling of cultural and spiritual autonomy."

5. Banac, *The National Question in Yugoslavia*, p. 221. We should note here the tendency within the Serb national program to reduce the historically different identities that entered the Kingdom of Serbs, Croats, and Slovenes in 1918 to Serb elements alone by negating and destroying their historical character. The authorities of five autocephalous Orthodox Churches—the Metropolitanate of the Kingdom of Serbia, the Metropolitanate of the Kingdom of Montenegro, the Metropolitanate of Karlovci, the Metropolitanate of Bukovina-Dalmatia, and the Ecumenical Patriarchate of Constantinople (Bosnia and Herzegovina, Sandžak, Kosovo, and Macedonia)—were merged into a single Serb Church after 1918.

6. Ibid., p. 225. This statement suggests very complex and for the most part unknown aspects of the role of the intelligentsia in the construction and promotion of ideological simplifications. Summing up his conclusions drawn in the examination of the initial phase of Yugoslav centralism, Ivo Banac notes: "Yugoslavia's intellectuals were not distinguished by a high level of democratic spirit. They were intolerant, often irascible, largely ignorant of history, narrowly rationalistic, and unduly impressed with the superiority of Western Europe. They looked upon themselves as engineers who would pull a passive backward country into modernity, if need be by force. Instead of recognizing that the separate South Slavic peoples were long formed and could not now be integrated, they tried to bring about a Great Serbia or a Great Yugoslavia, some out of sheer idealism, some for more pragmatic reasons. . . . Instead of creating a powerful modern state, the intellectual makers of Yugoslavia paved the way for instability, dictatorship, and foreign intervention."

7. For more on this relationship, see Bernard Barber, *Intellectual Pursuits: Toward an Understanding of Culture* (New York, 1998); especially the chapter "Culture and Intellectual Pursuits," pp. 23–43.

8. Qur'an, 31:29.

Chapter 12: At the Turn of the Millennium

1. Ignatij V. Jagič, *Rassuždemija južnoslavjanskoj i russkoj stariny o cerkovnoslavjanskom jazyke* (St. Petersburg, 1885), pp. 396–397. It is worth noting that as part of the preparations and conduct of the war against Bosnia and Herzegovina, there was widespread debate about language. As the differences making up the unity of this country were exposed to strong pressure from the new political identity that appealed to exclusivity, the "Serb" or "Croat" languages were emphasized as a measure of the intended homogenization. The Bosnian language is, however, merely a name for the opposition to this political violence. This highlighted the need to give different names to what is essentially one and the same language, within which there are no obstacles to full communicational openness. The view of Konstantin Filozof, a southern Slav grammarian

from the first half of the fifteenth century, points to the historical reality of this contemporary situation: ". . . some are mistaken when they say of them: one that it should be said so in the Serb language, the other in the Bulgarian, or some other. It is not so, because at the start those who wanted to issue it in the Slovenian language, clearly could not do it in the Bulgarian language, though some are saying that it was issued in that language. For, how could Hellenic, or Syriac, or Hebrew subtlety be expressed in too harsh a language; or, in the Serb high-pitched and narrow voice. Therefore, these good and wonderful men decided to choose the most delicate and beautiful Russian language, which was aided by Bulgarian, and Serb, and Bosnian, and Slovenian, and part of Czech and Croatian language, for divine documents. And it was thus issued."

These matters of language, outlined in this way so long ago, include disputes over its name, vocabulary, alphabet, grammar, and orthography but do not deny that it is a single language in the region from the Sutla in the west to the Marica in the east. Translators were never needed in that region, though this same, single language was used by people and nations of different religions, national ideologies, political organizations. Its descriptive name is the "central south Slav language." It is spoken by Bosniacs, Montenegrins, Croats, and Serbs; by Catholics, Orthodox, Muslims, and others, as well as by other peoples and groups whose direct or first language it is not, but who are culturally linked to it and to the region where it is present. Strong disputes stoked by opposing political and national ideologies can be mitigated—and, hopefully, even overcome in the future—by channeling them in accordance with the contemporary theory and practice of human rights. This might result in a number of solutions to each of the disputes, whereby the language will be enriched and enabled to contribute to the necessary understanding within the widest range of inexhaustible possibilities of the living civilizations.

2. Veselin Đuretić, "Političke ideologije XX veka i srpsko etničko biće", in *Srbi u evropskoj civilizaciji* (Belgrade, 1993), p. 65.

3. For more details on this, see Vlado Strugar, *Jugoslovenske socijaldemokratske stranke 1914–1918* (Zagreb, 1963); Enver Redžić, *Austromarksizam i jugoslavensko pitanje*, Belgrade, 1977; and Branko Petranović, *Balkanska federacija 1943–1948* (Belgrade, 1991).

4. *"The Declaration of the Sarajevo Summit on the Stability Pact in South Eastern Europe,"* 30 July 1999.

5. Ivo Banac, *The National Question in Yugoslavia.* It follows both directly and indirectly from the research of Ivo Banac that the key factors of the internal tensions and instability of the Yugoslav state project are precisely the ethno-national ideologies. From this research it also follows that the relationships between cultural or religious specificities in the region have always been mediated by ethno-national ideologies.

6. A comprehensive philosophical account of the modern question of identity is offered by Charles Taylor in *Sources of the Self: The Making of the Modern Identity* (Cambridge, 1996); on the relationship between the project of modernity and ideologies, see John Schwarzmantel, *The Age of Ideology: Political Ideologies from the American Revolution to Postmodern Times* (New York, 1998).

7. The author expresses his gratitude and respect to his friend Adam B. Seligman from the Boston University, for conversations with him that contributed to the formation of some of the views presented. In this respect particularly important were discussions of the theses from the manuscript of his book *Modernity's Wager: Authority, the Self and Transcendence* (Princeton, NJ: Princeton University Press), forthcoming.

8. For more on the meaning and more detailed interpretations of tradition referred to in this essay, see René Guénon, *Introduction générale a l'étude des doctrines hindoues* (Paris, 1997), pp. 75–94; Guénon, *Aperçus sur l'initiation,* pp. 282–288; Ananda K. Coomaraswamy, *The Bugbear of Literacy* (Middlesex, 1979), especially pp. 68–91; Frithjof Schuon, *Spiritual Perspectives and Human Facts,* trans. Peter N. Townsend (Middlesex, 1987), pp. 9–24; Schuon, *Light on the Ancient Worlds,* trans. Lord Northbourne (Bloomington, IN, 1984), pp. 7–57; Nasr, *Knowledge and the Sacred* pp. 65–86.

9. Georg Jellinek, *The Declaration of the Rights of Man and Citizens: A Contribution to Modern Constitutional History* (Westport, 1979), p. 48.

10. There have been many studies and interpretations of trust and confidence in the past decade. It is worth noting here in particular: Michael Platzkoster, *Vertrauen: Theorie und Analyse interpersoneller, politischer und betrieblicher Implikationen* (Essen, 1990); James Samuel Coleman, *Foundations of Social Theory* (Cambridge, MA, 1990); Francis Fukuyama, *Trust: The Social Virtues and the Creation of Prosperity* (New York, 1995); Barbara A. Mistzal, *Trust in Modern Societies: The Search for the Bases of Social Order* (Cambridge, MA, 1996); Seligman, *The Problem of Trust.*

11. Clifford Geertz, *The Interpretation of Cultures* (New York, 1973), p. 89.

12. See Rusmir Mahmutćehajić, "La Serbie dans le monde nouveau," *Les idées en mouvement* (Paris, June 1999), p. 12.

13. On the prevalent view and modeling of the American influence on the reshaping of the world order and its picture of the future, see Zbigniew Brzezinski, *The Grand Chessboard: American Primacy and Its Geostrategic Imperatives* (New York, 1997).

14. On this statement by Adam Smith, see Jerry Z. Muller, *Adam Smith in His Time and Ours* (New York, 1992).

15. See Fukuyama, *Trust: The Social Virtues and the Creation of Prosperity,* p. 13.

16. Michael Emerson, Daniel Gros, Wolfgang Hager, Peter Ludlow, and Nicholas Whyte, "A System for Post-War South-East Europe: Plan for Reconstruction, Openness, Development and Integration," *Working Document No. 131,* (Brussels: Centre for European Policy Studies, 3 May 1990).

Bibliography

Al-Amaali. *The Dictations of Sheikh al-Mufid.* Translated by Mulla Asgharali M. M. Jaffer. Middlesex: The World Federation of KS1 Muslim Communities, 1998.

'Ali ibn Abi-Talib. *Nahjul Balagha: Sermons, Letters and Sayings of Imam Ali.* Qum: Ansaraiyan Publications, 1989.

Anderson, Benedict. *Imagined Communities: Reflections on the Origin and Spread of Nationalism.* London: Verso, 1983.

Anderson, Scott. *The Man Who Tried to Save the World: The Dangerous Life and Mysterious Disappearance of Fred Cuny.* New York: Random House, Inc., 1999.

Anzulović, Branimir. *Heavenly Serbia: From Myth to Genocide.* New York and London: New York University Press, 1999.

Aristotle. *Nikomachean Ethics II:* 7–9; IV: 3.

Banac, Ivo. *The National Question in Yugoslavia: Origins, History, Politics.* Ithaca, New York: Cornell University Press, 1984.

Barber, Benjamin R. *Jihad vs. McWorld.* New York: Ballantine Books, 1996.

Barber, Bernard. *Intellectual Pursuits: Toward an Understanding of Culture,* Lanham, MD: Rowman & Littlefield Publishers, Inc., 1998.

Bennett, Christopher. *Yugoslavia's Bloody Collapse: Causes, Course and Consequences.* London: Hurst, 1995.

Berger, Peter L. *The Sacred Canopy: Elements of a Sociological Theory of Religion.* New York: Anchor Books, 1990.

Berger, Peter L. and Thomas Luckmann. *The Social Construction of Reality: A Treatise in the Sociology of Knowledge,* London: Penguin Books, 1991.

Boban, Ljubo. *Sporazum Cvetković-Maček.* Belgrade: Institut društvenih nauka, 1965.

Bringa, Tone. *Being Muslim the Bosnian Way: Identity and Community in a Central Bosnian Village.* Princeton, NJ: Princeton University Press, 1995.

Brzezinski, Zbigniew. *The Grand Chessboard: American Primacy and its Geostrategic Imperatives.* New York: HarperCollins Publishers, Inc., 1997.

Budmani, Pero. *Rječnik hrvatskoga ili srpskoga jezika III.* Zagreb: Jugoslavenska akademija znanosti i umjetnosti, 1887–1891.

Bukhari, Imam al-. *Sahih al-Bukhari.* Translated by Muhammad Muhsin Khan, Vols. I–IX. Beirut: Dar al Arabia, 1985.

Campbell, David. *National Deconstruction: Violence, Identity and Justice in Bosnia.* Minneapolis: University of Minnesota Press, 1998.

Carter, Stephen. *The Culture of Disbelief: How American Law and Politics Trivialize Religious Devotion.* New York: Basic Books, 1993.

Chittick, William C. *The Sufi Path of Knowledge: Ibn al-Arabi's Metaphysics of Imagination.* Albany: State University of New York Press, 1989.

———. *The Self-Disclosure of God: Principles of Ibn al-Arabi's Cosmology.* Albany: State University of New York Press, 1998.

Cigar, Norman. *Genocide in Bosnia: The Policy of "Ethnic Cleansing."* College Station: Texas A&M University Press, 1995.

Cohen, Leonard J. *Broken Bonds: Yugoslavia's Disintegration and Balkan Politics in Transition.* 2d ed. Boulder, CO: Westview Press, 1995.

Cohen, Roger. *Hearts Grown Brutal: Sagas of Sarajevo.* New York: Random House, Inc., 1998.

Coleman, James. *Foundations of Social Theory.* Cambridge, MA: Harvard University Press, 1990.

Coomaraswamy, Ananda K. *What is Civilisation?* Ipswich: Golgonooza Press, 1989.

———. *Time and Eternity.* Bangalore: Select Books Bangalore, 1989.

———. *The Bugbear of Literacy.* Middlesex: Perennial Books Ltd., 1979.

Crnobrnja, Mihailo. *The Yugoslav Drama.* Montreal: McGill-Queen's University Press, 1994.

Dahrendorf, Ralf. "Homo Sociologicus," in *Essays in the Theory of Society.* Stanford: Stanford University Press, 1968.

Dedijer, Vladimir, and Antun Miletić. *Genocid nad Muslimanima 1941–1945: Zbornik dokumenata i svjedočenja.* Sarajevo: Svjetlost, 1990.

Denitch, Bogdan. *Ethnic Nationalism: The Tragic Death of Yugoslavia.* New Haven: Yale University Press, 1994.

Dizdar, Mak. *Kameni spavač/Stone Sleeper.* Translated by Francis R. Jones. Afterword by Rusmir Mahmutćehajić. Sarajevo: DID, 1999.

———. *Stari bosanski tekstovi.* Sarajevo: Svjetlost, 1971.

Donia, Robert J., and John V. A. Fine, Jr. *Bosnia and Hercegovina: A Tradition Betrayed.* London: Hurst, 1994

Doubt, Keith. *Sociology after Bosnia and Kosovo: Recovering Justice.* Lanham, MD: Rowman & Littlefield Publishers, Inc., 2000.

Drakulić, Slavenka. *The Balkan Express: Fragments from the Other Side of the War.* New York: Norton, 1993.

Durkheim, Emile. "Individualism and the Intellectuals." In *Emile Durkheim on Morality and Society.* Edited by Robert Bellah. Chicago: University of Chicago Press, 1973.

Đuretić, Veselin. "Političke ideologije XX veka i srpsko etničko biće." In *Srbi u evropskoj civilizaciji.* Belgrade: Srpska akademija nauka i umetnosti, 1993.

Eaton, Gai. *King of the Castle: Choice and Responsibility in the Modern World.* Cambridge: The Islamic Texts Society, 1990.

Eisenstadt, Shmuel N. "Heterodoxies and Dynamics of Civilizations," *Proceedings of the American Philosophical Society*, 128, No. 2 (1984).

Ekmečić, Milorad. *Ratni ciljevi Srbije 1914.* Belgrade: Srpska književna zadruga, 1973.

Emerson, Michael, Daniel Gros, Wolfgang Hager, Peter Ludlow, and Nicholas Whyte. "A System for Post-War South-East Europe: Plan for Reconstuction, Openness, Development and Integration." *Working Document No. 131*, Brussels: Centre for European Policy Studies, 3 May 1990.

Evans, Arthur J. *Through Bosnia and the Herzegovina on Foot during the Insurrection, August and September 1875.* London: Longmans, Green, 1877.

Feuerbach, Ludwig A. *The Essence of Christianity.* Translated by George Eliot. New York: Prometheus Books, 1989.

Fukuyama, Francis. *Trust : The Social Virtues and the Creation of Prosperity.* New York, London: Hamish Hamilton Ltd., 1995.

————. *The End of History and the last Man.* New York and London: New York Free Press, 1992.

Geertz, Clifford. *The Interpretation of Cultures.* New York: Basic Books, 1973.

Griffin, David Ray and Huston Smith. *Primordial Truth and Postmodern Theology.* Albany: State University of New York Press, 1989.

Guénon, René. *Introduction générale à l'étude des doctrines hindoues.* Paris: Guy Trédaniel Editeur, 1997.

————. *Fundamental Symbols: The Universal Language of Sacred Science.* Translated by Alvin Moore. Cambridge: Quinta Essentia, 1995.

————. *Man and his becoming according to the Vedanta.* Translated by Richard C. Nicholson. New Delhi: Oriental Books Reprint Corporation, 1981.

————. *The Crisis of the Modern World.* Translated by Marco Pallis and Richard Nicholson. London: Luzac and Company Ltd., 1975.

————. *Aperçus sur l'ésotérisme islamique et le Taoisme.* Paris: Gallimard, 1973.

————. *Le Regne de la Quantité et les Signes des Temps.* Paris: Editions Gallimard, 1972.

————. *Aperçus sur l'initiation.* Paris: Editions Traditionnelles, 1946.

Gutman, Roy. *A Witness to Genocide.* New York: Element, 1993.

Habermas, Jürgen. "Struggles for Recognition in the Democratic Constitutional State." Translated by Shierry Weber Nicholsen. *Multiculturalism: Examining the Politics of Recognition,* by Charles Taylor. Princeton: Princeton University Press, 1994.

————. *Strukturwandel der Öffentlichkeit: Untersuchungen zu einer Kategorie der burgerlichen Gesellschaft.* Frankfurt: Suhrkamp, 1993.

————. *Theorie des kommunikativen Handelns,* 2 vols. Frankfurt: Suhrkamp, 1981.

Hadžijahić, Muhamed. *Od tradicije do identiteta: Geneza nacionalnog pitanja bosanskih Muslimana.* Sarajevo: Svjetlost, 1974.

Hegel, G.W.F. *Philosophy of Right.* Translated by Samuel W. Dyde. New York: Prometheus Books, 1996.

————. *Fenomenologija duha.* Translated by Nikola M. Popović. Belgrade: Grafički Zavod, 1986.

Heidegger, Martin. *Sein und Zeit.* Tübingen: Niemeyer, 1927.

Huntington, Samuel P. *The Clash of Civilizations and the Remaking of World Order.* New York: Simon & Schuster, 1996.

Ibn al-Arabi. *Al-Futuhat al-makkiyya.* Cairo: Al-Hay'at al-Misriyyat al-Amma li'l-Kitab, 1972.

Imamović, Mustafa. *Historija Bošnjaka.* Sarajevo: Preporod, 1998.

Isaković, Alija. *Bosnia and the Bosnian Muslims: the Bosnian Language.* Sarajevo: Did, 1991.

Izetbegović, Alija. *čudo bosanskog otpora.* Sarajevo: BiH Press, 1995.

Jagič, Ignatij V. *Rassuždemija južnoslavjanskoj i russkoj stariny o cerkovnoslavjanskom jezyke.* Sanktpeterburg: Tipografija imperatorskoj akademii nauk, 1885.

Jellinek, Georg. *The Declaration of the Rights of Man and of Citizens: A Contribution to Modern Constitutional History.* Westport: Hyperion Press, 1979.

Judah, Tim. *The Serbs: History, Myth and the Destruction of Yugoslavia.* New Haven: Yale University Press, 2000.

————. "Creation of Islamic buffer state discussed in secret." *The London Times* (12 July 1991).

Kaplan, Robert D. *Balkan Ghosts: A Journey Through History.* New York: St. Martin's Press, 1993.

Karadžić, Vuk Stefanović. 'Srbi svi i svuda'. In *Izvori velikosrpske agresije.* Edited by Bože Čović. Zagreb: August Cesarec, 1991.

Karahasan, Dževad. *Dnevnik selidbe.* Zagreb: Durieux, 1995.

Klaić, Nada. *Srednjovjekovna Bosna: Politički položaj bosanskih vladara do Tvrtkove krunidbe (1377. g).* Zagreb: Grafički zavod Hrvatske, 1994.

Kovač, Nikola. *Bosnie: le prix de la paix.* Paris: Editions Michalon, 1995.

Krasner, Stephen. "The Accomplishments of International Political Economy." In *International Theory: Positivism and Beyond.* Edited by Steve Smith, Ken Booth, and Maryisa Zalewski. Cambridge: Cambridge University Press, 1996.

Laclau, Ernesto. *Reflections on the New Revolution of Our Time.* London: Verso, 1990.

Lanzmann, Claude. *Shoah.* Translated by Almasa Defterdarević-Muradbegović. Sarajevo: Mes & Saint, 1996.

Lings, Martin. *Muhammed: His Life Based Upon the Earliest Sources.* London: George Allen & Unwin, 1988

————. *Muhammed: život njegov osnovan na vrelima najstarijim.* Translated by Rusmir Mahmutćehajić. Ljubljana: Oslobođenje International, 1996.

Locke, John. *Two Treatises on Government.* Edited by Peter Laslett. Cambridge: Cambridge University Press, 1960.

Lossky, Vladimir. *Théologie négative et connaissance de Dieu chez Maître Eckhart.* Paris: Libraire Philosophique J. Vrin,1998.

Lovrenović, Ivan. *Bosnien und Herzegowina: Eine Kulturgeschichte.* Translated by Klaus Detlef Olof. Wien: Folio Verlag, 1998.

————. *Unutarnja zemlja: Kratki pregled kulturne povijesti Bosne i Hercegovine.* Zagreb: Durieux, 1998.

Luhmann, Niklas. *Risk: A Sociological Theory.* New York: W. de Gruyter, 1993.

————. "Familiarity, Confidence, Trust: Problems and Perspectives." In *Trust: Making and Breaking of Cooperative Relations.* Oxford: Basic Blackwell, 1988.

Maass, Peter. *Love Thy Neighbor: A Story of War.* New York: Alfred A. Knopf, 1997.

Maclean, Fitzroy. *Eastern Approaches.* London: Penguin, 1991.

Mahmutćehajić, Rusmir. *Bosnia the Good: Tolerance and Tradition.* Budapest: Central European University Press, 2000.

————. *The Denial of Bosnia.* University Park, PA: Pennsylvania State University Press, 2000.

————. "La Serbie dans le monde nouveau." *Les idées en mouvement.* Paris, June 1999.

Malcolm, Noel. *Bosnia: A Short History.* London: Macmillan, 1996.

Meštrović, Ivan. *Uspomene na političke ljude i događaje.* Buenos Aires: Knjižnica Hrvatske revije, 1961.

Milardović, Anđelko. (editor): *Dokumenti o državnosti Republike Hrvatske.* Zagreb: Alinea, 1992.

Misztal, Barbara A. *Trust in Modern Societies: The Search for the Bases of Social Order.* Cambridge: Polity Press, 1996.

Mojzes, Paul. *Yugoslavian Inferno.* New York: Continuum, 1994.

Moljević, Stevan. "A Homogeneous Serbia." In *Genocid nad Muslimana 1941–1945: Zbornik dokumenata i svjedočenja.* Edited by Vladimir Dedijer and Antun Miletić, 8–10. 1941, Reprint. Sarajevo: Svjetlost, 1990.

Muller, Jerry Z. *Adam Smith in His Time and Ours: Designing the Decent Society.* New York: Free Press, 1992.

Murdoch, Iris. *The Sovereignty of Good.* London: Routledge, 1970.

Murray, John Courtney. "Arguments for the Human Right to Religious Freedom." In *Religious Liberty: Catholic Struggles with Pluralism.* Edited by Leon J. Hooper. Westminster: John Knox Press, 1993.

Murray, Robert. *The Cosmic Covenant: Biblical Themes of Justice, Peace and the Integrity of Creation.* London: Sheed and Ward, 1992.

Muslim, Ibn Hajjaj. *Al Jâmi' us Salih, (Sahih Muslim).* Translated by 'Abdul Hamid Siddiqi, I–IV. Riyadh: International Islamic Publishing House, s.a.

Nairn, Tom. *The Break-up of Britain: Crisis and Neonationalism.* London: Verso, 1981.

Nasr, Seyyed Hossein. *Knowledge and the Sacred.* Albany: State University of New York Press, 1989.

Norton, Ann. *Reflections on Political Identity.* Baltimore: Johns Hopkins University Press, 1988.

O'Ballance, Edgar. *Civil War in Bosnia.* London: Macmillan, 1995.

Paine, Thomas. *The Rights of Man.* London: J.M. Dent & Sons Ltd., 1969.

Pallis, Marko. *The Way and the Mountain.* London: Peter Owen Publishers, 1991.

Peco, Asim. *Osamsto godina Povelje bosanskog bana Kulina, 1189–1989.* Sarajevo: Akademija nauka i umjetnosti Bosne i Hercegovine, 1989.

Pennington, Anne, and Peter Levi. *Marko the Prince: Serbo-Croat Heroic Songs.* London: Duckworth, 1984.

Perry, Whitall N. *A Treasury of Traditional Wisdom.* Cambridge: Quinta Essentia, 1991.

Petranović, Branko. *Balkanska federacija 1943–1948.* Šabac: Zaslon, 1991.

Pfeifer, Franz. *Meister Eckhart.* Translated by C. de B. Evans, vol. I. London: John M. Watkins, 1924.

Platzkoster, Michael. *Vertrauen: Theorie und Analyse interpersoneller, politischer und betrieblicher Implikationen.* Essen: Beleke, 1990.

Popper, Karl R. *Otvoreno društvo i njegovi neprijatelji: Čar Platona.* Translated by Branimir Gligorić. Sarajevo: Open Society Institute, 1998.

———.*Otvoreno društvo i njegovi neprijatelji: Plima proročanstva, Hegel, Marx i posljedice.* Translated by Branimir Gligorić. Sarajevo: Open Society Institute, 1998.

Pribičević, Svetozar. *La dictature du roi Alexandre.* Paris: Bossuet, 1933.

Primorac, Igor, ed. *O toleranciji.* Translation entitled "Pismo o trpeljivosti" by Vladimir Gligorov. Belgrade: Filip Višnjić, 1989.

Ramet, Sabrina Petra. *Balkan Babel: The Disintegration of Yugoslavia from the Death of Tito to the War for Kosovo,* 2d ed. Boulder, CO: Westview Press, 1999.

Redžić, Enver. *Austromarksizam i jugoslavensko pitanje.* Belgrade: Prosveta, 1977.

"Report of the Secretary-General Pursuant to General Assembly Resolution 53/35 (1998): Srebrenica report." New York, 15 November 1999.

Rohde, David. *Endgame: The Betrayal and Fall of Srebrenica, Europe's Worst Massacre Since World War II.* New York: Farrar, Straus and Giroux, 1997.

Sadiković, Ćazim. *Ljudska prava bez zaštite.* Sarajevo: Bosanska knjiga, 1998.

Schluchter, Wolfgang. *The Rise of Western Rationalism.* Berkeley: University of California Press, 1981.

Schuon, Frithjof. *Stations of Wisdom.* Bloomington: World Wisdom Books Ltd., 1995.

———. *Logic and Transcendence.* Translated by Peter N. Townsend. London: Perennial Books Ltd., 1984.

———. *Light on the Ancient Worlds.* Translated by Lord Northbourne. Bloomington: World Wisdom Books, 1984.

———. *The Transcendent Unity of Religions.* Wheaton: Quest Books, 1984.

———. *De l'unité transcendante des religions.* Paris: Editions du Seuil, 1979.

———. *In the tracks of Buddhism.* Translated by Marco Pallis. London: George Allen & Unwin Ltd., 1968.

———. *Language of the Self.* Translated by Marco Pallis and Macleod Matheson. Madras: Ganesh & Co, 1959.

Schwarzmantel, John. *The Age of Ideology: Political Ideologies from the American Revolution to Postmodern Times.* New York: New York University Press, 1998.

Seligman, Adam B. *Modernity's Wager: Authority, the Self and Transcendence.* Princeton, NJ: Princeton University Press, 2000.

———. *The Problem of Trust.* Princeton, NJ: Princeton University Press, 1997.

Silber, Laura, and Allan Little. *The Death of Yugoslavia,* 2d rev. ed. London: Penguin Books/BBC Books, 1996.

Smith, Huston. "The Crisis in Philosophy." *Behavior,* 16, No. 1 (1998): 51–56.

———. *Forgotten Truth: The Common Vision of the World's Religions.* San Francisco: HarperCollins, 1992.

———. *Beyond the Post-Modern Mind.* New York: Quest Books, 1989.

Steinsaltz, Adin. *The Thirteen Petalled Rose.* Translated by Yehuda Hanegbi. New York: Basic Books, 1985.

Strugar, Vlado. *Jugoslavenske socijaldemokratske stranke 1914–1918.* Zagreb: Jugoslavenska akademija znanosti i umjetnosti, 1963.

Stranjaković, Dragoslav. "Kako je postalo Garašaninovo 'Načertanije'." *Spomenik Srpske Kraljevske Akademije, XCI.* Belgrade, 1939.

Šabanović, Hazim. "Turski dokumenti u Bosni i Hercegovini iz druge polovine XV stoljeća." *Istorisko-pravni zbornik,* vol. 2. Sarajevo, 1949.

Šanjek, Franjo. *Bosansko-humski krstjani i katarsko-dualistički pokret u Srednjem vijeku.* Zagreb: Kršćanska sadašnjost, 1975.

Taylor, Charles. *Sources of the Self: The Making of the Modern Identity.* Cambridge: Harvard University Press, 1996.

———. *Multiculturalism, Examining the Politics of Recognition.* Princeton: Princeton University Press, 1994.

The Declaration of the Sarajevo Summit on the Stability Pact in South Eastern Europe. Sarajevo, 30 July 1999.

Tocqueville, Alexis de. *The Old Regime and the Revolution.* Garden City: Doubleday, 1955.

Vučić, Petar. *Politička sudbina Hrvatske: Geopolitičke i geostrateške karakteristike Hrvatske.* Zagreb: Mladost, 1995.

Wensinck, Arend. J. *Concordance et indices de la tradition musulmane.* Leiden: Brill, 1936–71.

West, Rebecca. *Black Lamb and Grey Falcon: A Journey through Yugoslavia.* New York: Penguin Books, 1982.

Wiesel, Elie. "The Question of Genocide." *Newsweek,* 12 April 1999.

Williams, Bernard. *Ethics and the Limits of Philosophy.* Cambridge: Harvard University Press, 1985.

Woodward, Susan L. *Balkan Tragedy: Chaos and Dissolution after the Cold War.* Washington D.C.: Brookings Institution, 1995.

Zametica, John. *The Yugoslav Conflict.* London: Brassey's, Adelphi Paper no. 270, 1992.

Zimmermann, Warren. *Origins of a Catastrophe: Yugoslavia and Its Destroyers.* New York: Times Books, 1996.

Index of Names and Terms

Abraham, prophet, 63, 64, 176
Absolute, 8, 16, 18, 21, 34, 40, 51, 60, 74,
    84–86, 89, 90, 100, 112, 115, 131, 138,
    140–41, 144, 149, 151–54, 156, 165–66,
    169–71, 174, 182–84, 212–13, 217, 223,
    233, 247n1
absoluteness, 101, 149, 151–52, 156–57,
    165–66, 212, 240n2
Abu Bakr Siraj ad-Din. See Lings, Martin.
Adam, prophet, 246n13
Adriatic Sea, 206
Alexander, king, 255n9, 256n9
'Ali ibn Abi-Talib, 262n1
'Ali son of Husain, 246n13
Allah. See God.
ancestors, 19, 108, 140, 214
Anderson, Benedict, 178, 262n8
Anderson, Scott, 251n9
Anointed. See Christ.
anti-Bosnianism, 96, 105, 113, 128, 197,
    200, 253n13, 254n15
anti-Muslim, 91
Anzulović, Branimir, 249n1
Arabs, 63
Aristotle, 158, 241n6
arrogance, 43, 59, 60, 72, 218
art, 143, 191, 243n12
ascent, 221
Asgharali M. M. Jaffer, Mulla, 246n13
Assisi, Francis of, 67
associating, 166
Austria-Hungary, 205, 244n8
authority, 10, 32, 36, 54, 56, 70, 93, 94,
    100, 131, 135, 137–38, 141, 144, 146,

153, 155–67, 169–70, 184, 190, 202,
    213, 215, 219, 221–23, 233–35, 266n7
awareness, 2, 6, 7, 10, 15, 16, 20, 21, 53,
    60, 64, 66, 69, 72, 75, 80, 85, 86, 101,
    113, 129, 136, 139–42, 153, 173, 185,
    191, 196, 198, 220, 222

Badinter, Robert, 122, 126, 256n10
Balkans, 41, 86, 206, 214–15, 217, 221,
    224–28
Banac, Ivo, 245n11, 248n5, 248n7, 248n9,
    249n9, 249n13, 253n7, 263n2, 264n5,
    264n6, 265n5
Barber, Benjamin R., 20, 23, 237n2,
    239n30, 239n32, 240n36, 240n41
Barber, Bernard, 264n7
beauty, 109, 143, 146, 150
belief, 11, 15, 16, 37, 39, 40, 46, 53, 57, 64,
    71, 95, 130, 138, 145, 153, 160, 164,
    176, 187, 238n17
Bellah, Robert, 238n14
Bennett, Christopher, 243n26
Berger, Peter L., 244n1, 249n10, 249n12,
    250n4, 255n8, 263n3
Boban, Ljubo, 255n6
Bosnia: Austria-Hungary, 10; Bosnian Army,
    73, 128–29; and Europe, 5, 10, 40, 41,
    47, 52, 70, 85, 106, 227, 248n6;
    medieval state, 5, 247n1; multiethnic
    community, 1, 8, 114; Ottoman Empire,
    6, 103; partition of, 33, 57, 77, 111,
    122–23, 254n15, 255n8, 256n11,
    257n13; reconstruction of, 7, 41, 44, 57,
    73, 77, 80, 81; social transition, 43, 55;

By the Same Author

Original works

Krhkost. Sarajevo, 1977.
Krv i tinta. Sarajevo, 1983.
Zemlja i more. Sarajevo, 1986.
Živa Bosna. Ljubljana, 1994 and 1995.
Living Bosnia. London, 1996.
O Nauku znaka. Sarajevo, 1996.
Dobra Bosna. Zagreb, 1997.
Kaligrafski listovi Ćazima Hadžimejlića. Sarajevo, 1997.
Kriva politika: Čitanje historije i povjerenje u Bosni. Tuzla, 1998.
Riječi kao boje zdjela: Odrazi vječne mudrosti u sonetima Skendera Kulenovića. Sarajevo, 2000.
Bosnia the Good. Budapest, 2000.
The Denial of Bosnia. Pennsylvania, 2000.
Prozori: Riječi i slike. Sarajevo, 2000.
Sarajevski eseji: Politika, ideologija i tradicija. Zagreb, 2000.
Subotnji zapisi: S političkih razmeđa. Sarajevo, 2002.
Bosanski odgovor: O modernosti i tradiciji. Zagreb, 2002.

Translations With

Martin Lings. *Šta je sufizam?.* Zagreb, 1994.
Titus Burckhardt. *Uputa prema unutarnjem učenju islama.* Zagreb, 1994.
'Ali ibn Ebi Talib. *Nehdžu-l-belaga.* R. Mahmutćehajić and M. Hadžić. Zagreb, 1994.
Martin Lings. *Muhamed.* Ljubljana, 1995.
Imam 'Ali ibn el-Husejn. *Sahifa.* R. Mahmutćehajić and M. Hadžić. Sarajevo, 1997.
René Guénon. *Osvrti na tesavuf i tao.* Sarajevo, 1998.